What Ot

"This is the most encompass. ___ __ ___ career/life paths you will ever read. Carolee and Marie have provided an amazing action guide to assist in making this "Shift" an exciting and well thought through process. A must-have!"

Dr. Ed Bice, III. Peak Performance Consultant.
Author of: "Journey to Peak Experience" & "The Wisdom."

"Drs. Duckworth and Langworthy have written a tour de force that is a "must read" for members of the Boomer generation who face a myriad of issues that transcend all previous generations in the United States. "Shifting Gears" is a gold mine of hard data, anecdotal stories, and invaluable sources of information for those of us who must make critical decisions in the immediate future regarding how we will spend this last phase of our lives."

Dr. Alan Hadad, Physics Professor, Associate Vice President, Dean
of University Magnet Schools, University of Hartford

"The road to retirement is filled with high hopes and good intentions, but all too often, those on that highway find only potholes and detours. For many, that important life decision triggers anxiety, self-doubt and indecision. In "Shifting Gears," Langworthy and Duckworth provide a common-sense pathway to a confident retirement decision."

George M. Reilly, Ed.D.

A great book and a new way of framing retirement, especially for those, who have never given thought to what they would best be suited for. A great "get off the couch and get moving" incentive. Fantastic!"

Marion DiGiammo, Retired Math Teacher & Guidance Counselor

A must read. An extraordinary, mind-opening story of life and work after retirement. Possibilities are unlimited.

Jeanne Hawver, Retired Teacher & Business Owner

Shifting Gears to Your Life & Work after Retirement

Dr. Carolee Duckworth &
Dr. Marie Langworthy

Sign up for Book Downloads, Updates, Videos, and Blog at:

https://LifeandWorkAfterRetirement.com/GearShifters/

ISBN-10: 0-9845136-9-8
ISBN-13: 978-0-9845136-9-7

Library of Congress Cataloging-in-Publication Data

Duckworth, Carolee, & Langworthy, Marie
    Shifting gears to your life and work after retirement /Carolee Duckworth
and Marie Langworthy. New Cabady Press.
Includes index, URL table, references.
ISBN-978-0-9845136-9-7 (pbk) 2018
1. Retirement 1.a) Retirement—Planning   332.024
2. Career Change   650.14
3. Personal Living 3.a) Self-Actualization 3.b) Finance--Personal   646.79
HQ1062
I. Duckworth, Carolee & Langworthy, Marie
II. Title

Table of Contents

ABOUT THE AUTHORS

Dr. Carolee Duckworth spent her long career creating programs to empower people to become their own more complete and fulfilled selves. To this end, she co-created the *Center for Adult Re-employment* (winner of the *Common Cause Award*), serving displaced workers, displaced homemakers, and 55+ career changers, stimulating their mental capabilities to prepare them to select and enter new careers. She designed courses and programs for technical colleges and industries to increase critical thinking and technology skills and launched *College-Online.com* (as part of Greenville Technical College in SC to increase access for students of all ages and life situations, enabling them to enhance their skills and advance their careers "any time, any place, any person, any pace."

Since she retired and "shifted gears" herself, Carolee has focused on writing books, articles, and courses to empower individuals of all ages to reach for their dreams. In addition to *Shifting Gears to Your Life & Work After Retirement*, she has co-authored, with Brian Lane, the *Your Great Trip* series, starting with *Your Great Trip to France*.

Dr. Marie Langworthy, after retiring from 25 years as an educator and administrator, spent a few years supervising student teachers and teaching basic technology skills to the adult community. She continues to enjoy her retirement career as author and editor, and has co-authored two titles (with Carolee Duckworth), *Shifting Gears to Your Life & Work After Retirement*, and *Shifting Gears to Your Career Working Online*. She is currently working on a series (with Carolee Duckworth): *Changing Careers at 40, Changing Careers at 50* and *Changing Careers at 60*. She specializes in writing copy for website designer/developers and owners.

Marie is active with *Soroptimists International*, a volunteer organization whose mission is to improve the lives of women and girls in local communities and throughout the world. Her leisure pursuits are travel, the theatre, fishing, binging on movies and tv series, and attempting to improve her skill at solving crossword puzzles!

DEDICATION

To Carolee's dad, Dr. Wes, who was always a true believer, and a major contributor well into his 90s. He showed the way, through his own life choices. And to Minnie ("Sittoo"), Marie's mom, for her unconditional and unrelenting belief that her children could become and accomplish anything they set their minds to. She remains "the spur to prick the side of our intent."

A Note from the Authors

We based our book on experience as well as research and expertise, in the hope that by sharing actual personal experiences and challenges, we will have made you, our fellow Boomers, feel very much "at home."

The "I" in this book is a dual one. Dr. Carolee Duckworth has children and grandchildren of her own. Her pre-retirement work was with community and technical colleges, where career "transformation" was a shared goal of students of all ages. When she retired, she used on herself the process she had developed for her former students in order to shift gears to her own retirement life and work.

Dr. Marie Langworthy has step-children and step-grands. She worked at the district level in the public-school system, influencing and guiding the careers of many individuals, and leading the adoption of technology in the schools.

Rather than to identify ourselves separately with each example or story, we decided to speak from a single voice to keep the focus of the book on *you* and *your* own best life and work after retirement. We jointly envision all the best for you in this, your magnum opus.

All our best wishes,

Carolee Duckworth & Marie Langworthy

CHAPTER 1:
Introduction to the New World of Retirement

Behold the tsunami of data sweeping across America as the 77 million members of the "Baby Boomer" generation— born any time between 1946 and 1964—reach retirement age. All of the "Early Boomers," born 1946 to 1955, now have crossed the threshold to age 62, and the first of the "Late Boomers" are now beginning to do so. Even the youngest of the Boomers will have turned 55 by 2019.

Although much of the attention is focused on the millions of Baby Boomers retiring, there remain many members of the generation that preceded Boomers, The *Silent Generation*, who are still in their vibrant 70s or 80s, and eager to participate and contribute. Also, the generation following Boomers, *Gen X*, are themselves beginning to cross the retirement threshold.

The Census Bureau estimated that 15% of Americans — nearly one in six —were aged 65 or older in 2016, up from 12% in 2000. Demographers anticipate that by 2060 almost one in four will be in that age group. That means there will be some 48 million more seniors in the US than there are now.

Just log onto amazon.com, where you'll find literally hundreds of "how to retire," "where to retire," "when to retire," "why to retire," and "whether to retire" titles! The big question ahead, for employers, service providers, businesses and government agencies alike, is: "What are the wave of retirees going to do, when and where?"

Whether we are talking about financial resources, projecting health conditions and needs, discussing personal relationships, planning career options, or anticipating the lasting impact on the culture, the data is conclusive and compelling. The Boomer group of 77 million senior citizens is a force to be reckoned with.

As a group, retiring Boomers will require and provide significant quantities of products and services. And, as we always have, we will contribute to and change the American landscape as no other generation has before. Constituting about 30% of the population, we will continue to exert substantive political, social, cultural, and economic clout. Simultaneously, we retirees will find that, voluntarily or otherwise, we are being buffeted about by these same political, social, cultural and economic forces that we ourselves have contributed to.

WOW FACTOR
Beginning in 2011, and continuing for 19 years, about 10,000 Baby Boomers will turn 65 every day.

Unprecedented Demands on Retirees

As the first generation to fully experience many profound changes, Boomers have arrived at life situations that would have been unusual, even highly unlikely, in the past, including:

- Dual professional marriages
- Globalization of work, home and family
- Serial marriages and singlehood
- Late life and prolonged parenthood
- Parenting the parents
- Parenting the grandchildren

Dual Occupational or Professional Marriages

Retiring Boomers have pioneered a new territory of dual occupational or professional marriages, where both husband and wife obtain educations and go on to pursue long-term careers. In these marriages, both partners were accustomed to a work life of challenges, engagement, and high demands that paid them handsomely, both financially and in terms of recognition and respect.

In some cases, both parties had the support of "staff" who carried out their wishes and to whom they could delegate tasks. Theirs were the households of "all chiefs and no Indians," possibly complete with business-related travel, regular professional development or training, and the excitement associated with addressing and meeting challenges with skill and even brilliance. In many cases, both partners were used to experiencing the power and privileges that accompany professional success.

Globalization of Work, Home & Family

Another highly significant phenomenon that Boomers have been the first to experience fully is the globalization of work, as well as home and family. This is the generation that not only left the farm, but, in all probability, left the city, the state, and possibly, left the country!

Even if they continued to live close to their childhood roots, many Boomers have had opportunities to work and travel internationally. Some have lived abroad in one or multiple countries. Some have family members living abroad—children, siblings, parents.

Late Life and Prolonged Parenthood

Many younger Baby Boomers, who started their families later in life, now find themselves approaching their 60's with children still in college. Given that college costs are soaring to as much as $50K annually, these parents are facing a unique "sticker shock." Because they bore their children in their early forties, these 55-and-overs now find themselves in the unlikely position of educating their offspring as they themselves approach, or even enter, retirement.

Education-related financial constraints on parents due to prolonged dependencies of their children, because they are straddled with high college loans or a tight job market, prevail not only through the college years, but afterwards as well. Even after college is behind them, many of our children are being forced to remain home longer than expected—sometimes much longer.

Serial Marriages & Singlehood

Also, let's not underestimate the effect that divorce has had on "young" grandparents. Arrangements and rearrangements of marriages have resulted in family responsibilities that extend backwards and forwards, with blended families that include his children, her children and their children, as well as the offspring of all these children, not to mention an assortment of in-laws. The complexities compound exponentially with each new round of merged families, yielding an assortment of children and stepchildren, grandchildren and step-grandchildren, in-laws and ex in-laws.

Parenting the Parents

Boomers have been called the "sandwich" generation for good reason. While our children now remain at home longer, our aging parents are living longer, eventually needing more from us in terms of financial support, and sometimes personal care. Many of us have barely seen our children through college and out of the house on their own, before our parents have moved in to take their place.

These factors have caused changes in household demographics and priorities, with increased pressure on Boomers to meet our parents' needs as well as those of our children, in what can come to seem an almost perpetual generational cycle of needs and demands.

Parenting Grandchildren

Through an assortment of life's curve balls, some Boomers have found themselves, officially or unofficially, back in the child-rearing business—this time raising their grandchildren! Thus, some Boomers are entering their retirement years with responsibilities for teenagers, young children, or even babes in arms. Their futures have come full circle, back to the perpetual demands to provide hearth and home, food and nurture, as well as the ever more expensive college education.

SNAPSHOT: Mary Lou & Don

Mary Lou and her husband Don worked hard, she as a college researcher, he as a carpenter. Don's passion was deep sea fishing, and after several trips to Costa Rica, Mary Lou and Don began to seriously look for retirement property there. Their plan was to move to Costa Rica, where Don would establish a small commercial charter fishing business.

But shortly before they were ready to retire, one of their sons went through a bitter divorce, then soon thereafter died, leaving behind his young daughter. So Mary Lou and Don suddenly found them-selves back in the parenting business, as they assumed the guardian-ship of their granddaughter.

This placed their retirement plans on hold indefinitely. Once again, they had a child to raise and a college account to fund. Mary Lou has continued working, now as a tutor of high school students, while Don has become a prolific writer, sharing his experiences as a world-class deep-sea fisherman.

Unprecedented Possibilities for Retirees

Just as Boomers are the first generation to experience unprecedented *demands*, they also are presented with *possibilities* that would have been less likely in the past, including:

- Longevity: longer lifetimes
- Prolonged health and vitality
- 20-year to 30-year retirement timespans
- Early retirement—expected or unexpected
- Discretionary spending power
- Technology mindfulness and capability
- Entrepreneurial capacity
- Global experience and awareness

Longevity: Longer lifetimes

So ... the good news is that, through a combination of nature and nur-ture, many Boomers will be blessed with good health, the harbinger of a long, productive, active life. It's true. Because of all the progress and research in preventive medicine, as well as current and emerging advances in medical technology and diagnostics, a healthy 65-year-old male can expect to live 22 more years, while the average female can expect to live 25 more years (*demographicsnow.com*). The Na-tional Center for Health Statistics predictions are slightly lower, but still anticipate an additional 17 or more years for a 65-year old male and 20 or more years for a female.

In fact, in part because of continuing exponential advances in sci-entific and medical research, but also because of other changes such as our increased involvement in lively pursuits, our expected lifespans continuously increase with every additional year we live. Also, as female and male partners continue to live, the celebrated gap between their expected lifespans, women versus men, begins to close.

According to the National Center for Health Statistics, for those who live to age 50:

- A female can expect to live at least 32 more years, to age 82½.
- A male can expect to live at least 28 more years, to age 78½.
- The gap between male and female lifespans is four years.

For those who live to 65, these life expectancies increase by 2.5 years for females and 3.7 years for males.

- A 65-year-old female can expect to live at least 20 more years, to age 85.
- A 65-year-old male can expect to live at least 17 more years, beyond age 82.
- The sex gap narrows from four years to three years.

Those who live to 75 see yet another increase in life expectancy.

- A 75-year-old female can expect to live at least 13 more years, to age 88.
- A 75-year-old male can expect to live at least 11 more years, to age 86.
- The sex gap narrows further to two years.

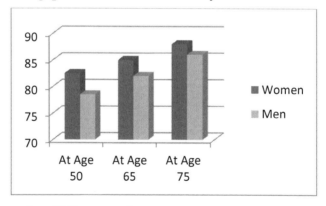

Many people will live even longer.

- A man who lives to age 65 has a 30% probability of living an additional 25 years, to age 90.
- A woman who lives to age 65 has a 40% chance of living an additional 25 years, to age 90.
- The possibility that at least one member of a 65-year-old couple will live past 90 is even higher—60%.

Beyond the 90-somethings emerge the centenarians, whose numbers are growing at a stunning rate, and will continue to do so.

WOW FACTOR

Numbering an estimated few thousand in 1950, the 100+ population escalated to over a third of a million worldwide by 2010, with highest concentrations in the U.S. and Japan. The centenarian population continues to increase at more than *20 times the growth rate* of the total population and is projected to number nearly 6 million by 2050 (*Aging*, 2009).

Prolonged health & vitality

In the past, our ancestors were easy prey to the debilitating results of diabetes, hypertension, cancer, Alzheimer's and a whole array of related ailments and chronic illnesses. But with each passing day, through a combination of education, lifestyle change, preventive care, and advances in science and medicine, we are gaining more control over these and other diseases.

Advances in disease control

Even the heinous disease of diabetes is being controlled to degrees unheard of in the past. Progress in hypertension, and its villainous results in heart failure and stroke, is also making great strides. Research provided by several studies under the sponsorship of the American Heart Association concludes that, because the medical community is experiencing increased success in treating hypertension, strokes have become less lethal and disabling over time. And let us not forget that weight, diet, activity level, and lifestyle habits all play an important part in keeping hypertension at bay. Cardiovascular disease mortality also is in decline, as attested to consistently by study results (*AHAJournals.org*, 2011).

Regarding the dreaded disease of cancer, types of therapy and treatment, the emphasis on prevention as well as cure, and millions of dollars being poured into research for both the causes and the cures for all types of cancer—these factors give us hope that this killer will continue to lose its momentum. In fact, we now seem to have turned a corner where most of us have more personal experience with family, friends, and acquaintances who have beat this dreaded disease than have succumbed to it.

The Baby Boomer generation's addiction to sun worshipping and smoking has unfortunately resulted in epidemic occurrences of skin and lung cancer. Additionally, our ignorance of the dangers of certain types of chemicals in the workplace also has left many of us victims. But organizations such as the American Cancer Society have made major contributions in educating the public and creating changes in behavior and lifestyles that have decreased our exposure to elements that are dangerous to us.

Another dreaded condition is dementia (loss of brain function that occurs with certain diseases), and the particular form of dementia called Alzheimer's (affecting memory, thinking, and behavior, and worsening over time). But with every passing day, medical science is achieving more successful results, both in determining the causes of Alzheimer's and in warding off its consequences.

WOW FACTOR

A vaccine against Alzheimer's disease is in early testing. The mechanism for this vaccine is to block the buildup of the toxic amyloid proteins responsible for destroying the brain. Early findings indicate that the vaccine is safest and most effective when administered before the protein buildup has begun.

Advances in disease prevention

Our advances in disease control are paralleling our increased understandings of factors that underlie the development of diseases, the better to head them off. These advances include emerging knowledge of the role played by dietary and other lifestyle factors, such as regular physical and mental exercise, and the relief of stress.

We have made other significant health and wellness advances that enable the prevention of age-associated decline. One such development that promises major improvements, is our increased understanding of the role of age-related decreases in essential hormones and the health problems that stem from these developing deficiencies. This understanding has clarified the need to replace deficient hormones using bio-identical hormone supplementation (not synthetic!) in order to maintain health and vigor, and even to reverse health patterns that otherwise could lead to disability or disease.

Other advances that impact our anticipated lifespans involve various environmental hazards. Here again, increased knowledge of consequences, combined with remedial action, has had the effect of protecting us from these risks. These advances, collectively, are having a significant impact on our likelihood of living longer and healthier lives.

20-year to 30-year retirement timespan

As Baby Boomers enter their mid-60's and retire from their occupations, with life expectancies up into their late eighties or nineties, or even past 100, they face the opportunity—or the challenge—of a retirement timespan that will range from 20 to 30 years. Because retiring Boomers are energetic and vital, we are far from the point of being ready to step aside. We may be ready to "retire" a job, but most of us are not yet ready to retire ourselves.

There has been much discussion about how the financial crisis would affect the retirement of Baby Boomers. It seemed that certainly most of us would need or want to wait to retire late because of the impact of the difficult economy on our savings.

Early retirement—expected or unexpected

However, while many may wish to wait past the standard retirement age to leave employment, whether for financial or psychological reasons, some of us have not been given the opportunity to do so. Mass layoffs and budget cutbacks have led to an increase in early retirement numbers. In fact, the pattern of planned versus actual retirement from long-term careers is strikingly in reverse of our intentions and preferences.

According to surveys carried out by the Associated Press, 42% of Boomers plan to delay retirement, and 25% claim they will never retire. Findings from the 2010 *MetLife Retirement Readiness Index Study* show an even higher proportion who desire to retire late:

- *46%* plan to retire *late;* only *3%* of us do so.
- 47% plan to work until the standard retirement age; *33%* do so.
- *6%* plan to retire *early; 64%* end up retiring early.

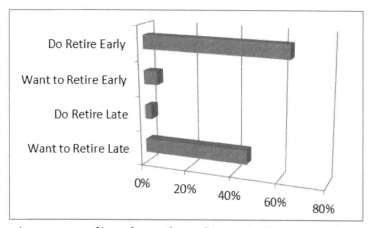

What is most startling about these figures is the reversed pattern between retiring late and retiring early. While many of us hope to retire late (46%), only a few are able to (3%). And while very few of us expect to be ready to retire early (6%), a solid majority of 64% end up doing just that, for whatever reason. *Put another way, although the vast majority of us (94%) intend to retire either on time or late, just over 1/3 of us (36%) are able to do so. And of the almost 2/3 of us*

(64%) who find ourselves retiring early, very few of us (6%) had planned or wanted to.

Although these discrepancies between when we wish to retire and when we actually do so may seem out of place on the list of possibilities for retirees, that depends on one's perspective. With early retirement providing a baseline income as well as freedom, and with continued health and vitality, the potential for launching a compelling and engaging post retirement career is significantly increased.

Discretionary spending power

Also, on the list of positives, is the discretionary spending power of retiring Boomers. As a group, Boomers in the U.S. alone control over 50% of *discretionary spending power*. And, according to research by the Center for Retirement Research at Boston College, this group is expected to inherit $8.4 trillion by 2030. This means their spending power is likely to escalate, and possibly in windfall ways.

Although the healthcare sector is one area where Boomers dominate spending, purchasing 61% of the over-the-counter medications sold and 77% of all prescription drugs, we also are major spenders in other categories. According to *Bloomberg Business Week*, Boomers purchase half of the computers and two-thirds of the new cars sold annually. They also spend a lot of money on their pets, as well as an astonishing 80% of all money spent on leisure travel.

Technology mindfulness and capability

Nearly half (49%) of those aged 52 to 70 spend at least 11 hours a week online, according to the *2015 State of the User Experience* report from Limelight Networks, a content delivery specialist. Wayne Best, chief economist at Visa, adds: "This older generation, those over 50, 60 and 70, they have computers, they have smartphones, and they're using them...to order things online."

WOW FACTOR

Builders of 50+ housing complexes may incorrectly assume that their buyers do not use the Web or e-mail. In fact, this group is very Internet-savvy. Increasingly, seniors expect and require that wi-fi hot spots be readily available, both in their community centers and clubhouses, as well as in the high-tech home offices in their new homes (from *Nation's Building News)*.

Because we are *techno-savvy*, we can and will remain connected and engaged for many years to come. The Internet has changed how people work, connect, communicate, and create. It provides many venues for work and creativity that are unaffected by age. We can and will avail ourselves of these barrier-reducing advances. In fact, throughout this book, our frequent specific technology references, descriptions, and applications bear witness to how current and emerging technologies can, do, and will continue to impact every aspect of retirees' current and future lives and activities.

Entrepreneurial capacity

Entrepreneurial capacity is another positive of retiring Boomers. Over the past decade, the highest rate of entrepreneurial activity belongs to the 55 to 64 group. Even more noteworthy is that startups with older business owners are more successful as measured by their survival rates (from the *Ewing Marion Kauffman Foundation Study of Entrepreneurship*).

Because we are *entrepreneurial*, we have the potential to remain employed long into the future with or without a traditional job—by working for others or working for ourselves or working for each other. For many of us, our so-called retirement years will constitute our most creative and purposeful time of life. And we have the resources needed, either individually, or by joining forces, to conceptualize and start potentially lucrative enterprises of our own.

Global experience & awareness

Global experience and awareness create retirement work and life potential too. Because we are *globally aware*—through our work lives, our experiences, our travels, and our involvements—the scope of our retirement work can and will extend beyond our local neighborhood, and even beyond our state or nation, to include international venues.

Again, Internet technology, and the interconnectedness that it supports, makes all manner of retirement pursuits possible.

The global market for products and services makes it possible for us to work abroad while continuing to live at home, or to live abroad and work back home. We can live in Jacksonville and work in Paris or live in Paris and work in Jacksonville. The world, quite literally, is our domain, with all the many opportunities this entails.

Retirement Paradigm Shifts

It has become eminently clear that the paradigm of retirement has shifted and will continue to shift. The old retirement pattern—a long career of hard work, followed by no work, and utter freedom to pursue leisure activities—is no longer typical, or even all that attractive. A point made repeatedly by many retirement authors, agencies, and researchers is that Baby Boomers are "reinventing retirement."

According to the old paradigm of retirement, work ended at or around age 65. At that point we were expected to withdraw from the world of work and "enjoy" a life of leisure. Retired people were mainly defined by what they would *not* be doing, rather than by what they *would*. This perception was consistent with the industrial model of standardized life and work patterns.

Old paradigm "retirees" were relegated to a life of reduced expectations in terms of social, professional, and vocational contribution, as well as of physical abilities and mental agility. Once they retired, seniors were defined by what they *had been* in the past. "I *was* a teacher." "I *was* a doctor." "I *was* the CEO of a company." They were referred to, and referred to themselves, in the past tense.

The retirement paradigm has shifted, and is continuing to shift, in major ways. As we leave jobs that we once performed well and energetically and enter a new life stage of 30 years or so, we discover that we are *not done yet*. The "encore" career is on the minds of many, if not most, retiring Boomers.

As we stand before our about-to-be-former colleagues, receiving our proverbial golden watch, our minds are racing with ideas about what we plan to do next. Arriving at what once would have been an endpoint, our eyes remain focused on the horizon, looking ahead.

Boomers are "the most educated, most techno-savvy generation in our country's history," says William Frey, a demographer and visiting fellow at the Brookings Institution. "They will want to stay engaged in their work and be physically social." Ken Dychtwald, author of *Going from Success to Significance in Work and Life*, concurs, adding: "I think we are going to see adult education, re-careering and personal reinvention become a standard part of the later years."

Plans to Continue Working After Retirement

The combination of longer anticipated lifespans, entrenched patterns of consumption, and other factors, such as losses in retirement account funding due to the economy, has led many Boomers and other new retirees to consider post retirement as a time of transition to a "next phase" of their work life.

A recent Merrill Lynch survey of Boomers found that more than 80% plan to continue to work even after they retire from their long-time careers. *This means that over 61 million of the 77 million Boomers are in the "new" retirement position of seeking their next work after they are "set free" from their former work* (Dream, 2011). Fewer than 20% see themselves as stopping work altogether.

For the majority of these retiring Boomers who plan to continue to work after retirement, financial readiness is only part of the picture. Over 2/3 of them (67%) say they will continue to work to stay mentally active; 57% in order to stay physically active. Additional reasons to continue to work include rewards essential to a sense of well-being, social engagement and meaning. Some plan a return to work in search of adventure or challenge. Others seek to continue enjoying the respect of colleagues and clients. Some still hope to have an influence... Or a way to be creative... Or a chance to use their expertise... Or an opportunity to help others.

Confirming this trend in retirement planning, a study by the Pew Research Center, based on 2,003 telephone interviews of adults 18 years and older, reported that more than three quarters (77%) of adults expect to work for pay even after they retire. Most of these say they will continue working because they want to (60%) versus because they have to (30%).

Life & Lifestyle Plans After Retirement

The post-retirement paradigm has also shifted in terms of life and lifestyle plans. According to the MetLife Mature Marketing Institute, 91% of pre-retirees ages 50-65 responded that they want to live in their own homes after retirement. Where traditional retirement may have led to major uprooting—moving closer to, or even in with, grown children, or making major migrations to the south—current relocation patterns have shifted dramatically.

Most current retirees who move, stay close to their previous homes, opting to save money and reduce property upkeep, while also remaining within reach of their friends and engagements. Only a small proportion of retirees move very far from home. In 2010, just 1.6 percent of retirees between age 55 and 65 moved across state lines, according to an analysis of U.S. Census Bureau data by Richard Johnson, director of retirement policy research at The Urban Institute. Of this small proportion who did move across state lines between 2005 and 2010, only one out of seven moved to Florida, in contrast to one out of four in 1990.

Of those Boomers who do plan to move, many are motivated to relocate not in order to decrease stimulation and involvement, but to increase it. One such migration pattern is the shift to urban living, with its cultural offerings and efficient public transportation systems. Johnson reports that among the most popular cities for retiree relocation are: Atlanta, Las Vegas, Dallas, Phoenix, New York, Washington DC and Chicago.

WOW FACTOR

15% to 20% of older people living in the suburbs would like to relocate to urban areas. These moves are motivated by a lifestyle change. [Jane M. O'Connor, chairwoman of the *National Association of Home Builders*.]

Other appealing living options for Boomers are college towns, because of the vitality and intellectual stimulation that these communities offer. Also, job opportunities in college towns are likely to be recession-resistant and age-blind—adjunct teaching, event coordination, cultural institution work, museums, bookshops, writing/editing of publicity material, research, career coaching.

Another emerging trend—more retiring Boomers are pursuing the ultimate travel experience of living abroad, full-time or part-time. The number of retirees living abroad, based on the number of benefit checks Social Security mails overseas, has skyrocketed from 396,000 in the year 2000 to 529,311 by 2012, and 613,650 by 2014.

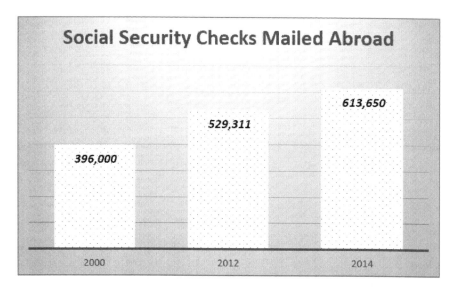

Many retire to Mexico, Central America, or the Caribbean. Growing numbers retire to Italy (19,600), Greece (13,882), Portugal (8,590), France (7,975), Spain (6,232), Croatia (948) and Malta (334) (from Retiring Outside the United States). Japan has seen the biggest uptick in US retirees moving in, with a 42% increase.

Other retirees design lives based around outdoor living, migrating back and forth between warmer climates in the winter and cooler climates in the summer. They do this not just for greater comfort, but also to be able to enjoy expanded access to outdoor activities—hiking or golfing, boating, or swimming, fishing or biking.

Alternative housing models are gaining in popularity with Boomers who are in transition. One such model, inspired by projects in Denmark and other European countries, is termed "co-housing." These complexes are mostly *mixed-age* by design and foster the sense of community by clustering homes around large pedestrian-only areas, with a shared "common house" where many of the social activities take place. These co-housing developments become deliberately tight-knit, with residents agreeing in advance to socialize "more than is usual" with their neighbors.

And So...

There you have it. Boomers are reaching retirement age in torrents, and then are living longer. And, although many Boomers find themselves nudged (or propelled) into retirement from lifelong careers earlier than they expected, wanted, or could afford, their health is so good, and their drive to remain engaged is so strong, that the sum effect will be for 80% of them to return to work, and then continue to work at least part time well beyond the once traditional retirement age of 65.

If and when they relocate, they will live in more stimulating environments, not less—urban, international, with expanded access to outdoor activities and community engagement. Their intent will be to continue to enjoy engaged, connected, active lifestyles.

If you include yourself among the 80% who want and expect another round of life and work after retirement, and you have not yet arrived at the particulars of your re-involved or newly involved post-retirement life and work, now is the time to "rethink" your own remaining years, workwise and otherwise.

As you head into the unknown of this next life phase, this new frontier of retirement, you will need to arm yourself with tools and a process to discover your way before you become entrenched. And that, my Boomer friends, is what this book is all about—figuring out what you plan to do with the rest of your life—a life that all signs indicate will be longer, more energetic, and more engaging than you ever imagined...one that you will find challenging and rewarding.

CHAPTER 2:
Retirement is a Process, Not an Event

Given that Boomers are "the most educated, most techno-savvy generation in our country's history, and will want to [continue to] stay engaged in their work and be physically social," the idea of doing nothing for the next 30 years or so of our lives is not an attractive option for many of us. We need to remain intellectually stimulated, to continue to grow as professionals, albeit, perhaps, in a direction different from the one we pursued in our former work lives.

In contrast to previous generations, many, if not most, Boomers do not see a future where their work stops abruptly when they reach age 65. Instead, many of us see on-again, off-again, work mixed with periods of leisure. Some of us will continue to work because we need to financially; many others will continue to work because we want to.

The Retirement to Re-launch Timeline

Transitions from "retirement to re-launch" take time and creativity, particularly when that retirement comes upon us suddenly. Even for those of us who are fortunate enough to have been given the time and opportunity to plan ahead, once retirement is upon us, many of us find ourselves unready after all.

Retirement, even when it is long-anticipated, and certainly when it occurs earlier than expected, creates a void. The life we once led is done. The world as we know it ceases. Change of the most profound nature snatches us up like a great wave and tumbles us into unfamiliar territory–dazed and confused, and perhaps even angry and a bit frightened. When our retirement date is upon us, many of us find that we have major creative work to do in the form of reframing our lives, focusing on the personal life and work we envision doing next.

Although many of us have determined that we want and/or need to find our next work after retirement, only 54% of us have completed the steps to identify what we specifically want to do, and what options we have available (MetLife Retirement Readiness Index Study). Even fewer of us have gone beyond identifying what we want to do next to take action.

STOP, Do NOT Pass Go

When we face the void, our inclination may be to move ahead with whatever comes to mind first. A sense of urgency drives us forward, even though we don't know *yet* where or how we want to spend our remaining years and energies. The urge for resolution and direction exerts powerful pressures on us to just do something.

But even as we feel impelled to thrust our way forward, this is not the time to race ahead. It is critical to give ourselves the gift of time. Ironically, we allow more time to the process of selecting our next refrigerator than we do to designing the rest of our lives.

Halt forward motion until you have found your compass. For the next three to six months, or even more, refuse to agree to *any* long-term commitments. Instead, sit down with this book, your own self-knowledge, and your life partner if you have one.

If this sounds extreme, remember that we are talking about the rest of your life here. Demand to take as much time as you need to design your own best after retirement life and work. Then, and only then, will it be time for you to make your move.

Include What You Don't Know YET

As you consider what you want to do next, and where you want to do it, recognize that there is no reason to limit your scope to what you already know and can do. Also central to these questions about where you are heading next is the potential, and even the excitement, of additional education and training.

Whatever we learned during our first round of education is certainly an asset. But it may not represent all that we would like to accomplish academically. Some of us already have degrees in something we love. For others, our degrees represent something we enjoyed once, but do not want to do anymore. Still others of us have yet to earn our first degree but have always wanted to achieve this milestone.

Whatever we have earned and learned to date, many of us find ourselves once more in search mode, exploring our best next alternatives for intellectual growth, either inside or outside the confines of a formal academic program. Degrees or not, certifications or not, credentials or not, most of us find ourselves at a juncture where our immediate questions are: "What do I know so far?" and "What do I want to learn next?"

As we shift gears into retirement, we can safely expect that whatever pursuits we choose, they likely will come with a study list–books, classes, workshops, seminars, websites, webinars, research, even apprenticeships or mentorships. Become fluent in French? Learn to build stone walls? Master Internet Marketing? Study Brain Research? Become a bee keeper?

Education is lifelong pursuit, not a terminal event. The continuum of what we know and what we need to know next can be broad and wide. This is good news. There is nothing more revitalizing than to set off on a new learning task, a "learning adventure," if you will, at any age—new laptop in your backpack—equipped with new notebooks and pens—with new questions in mind and new quests and challenges ahead.

Plan the "Whole Enchilada" at the Same Time

During this temporary pause in your life, your primary questions are necessarily about you and what you want to do with the next 20-30 years of your life. But there also are other complexities to be considered. Factor these into your pondering.

For starters, take time to think through these five:

1. *Life situations*
2. *Lifestyle choices*
3. *Your retirement work redefined & redesigned*
4. *Retiring with your partner*
5. *Serial retirement*

Life Situations

Again, many variations exist, especially by this point in life. We now may be single, married, divorced or widowed. We may be remarried, perhaps more than once. We may be parents or not, with an empty nest or with children living at home, either young or grown. Our parents may or may not still be living, either with us or elsewhere, nearby or at a distance. We even may have our grandchildren living with us, with or without having full-time responsibility for them.

If we live alone now, some of us may be considering a long-term extended family living relationship–sharing a household with a sibling, a parent, or a grown child. Or we may be thinking of moving in together with a close friend or a romantic partner.

All of these variations impact our retirement. But they do not preclude our taking charge and following through on what we want to do with the rest of our lives. Our families are significant factors in our lives, but so are we.

Not only does our diversity stem from our past, it also informs and defines us in terms of where we are now, and where we are heading next. What are the realities of our current and our future retirement situation: financially, physically, personally, and educationally?

Lifestyle Choices

Throughout this process, we need to assume that we are governed in many aspects by real life limitations that either we have created throughout our lives or that life circumstances have imposed upon us. Let's start with money—a major consideration that will inform all other decisions. Then we need to add family ties as a lifestyle determinate. And now, more than ever before, retirees are not willing to put up with undesirable climate conditions. They also have strong opinions as to residence preferences, which are closely allied to their personalities and definitions of autonomy. Lastly, and probably the number one consideration that underlies the whole theme of this book, retirees are highly motivated to determine what, how, when, and where their professional capabilities, considerations and limitations will direct their decision-making process.

Now let's talk more about each of these factors that determine our retirement lifestyle choice.

- *Finances*
- *Family considerations*
- *Location choices: warm, cool, city, suburb?*
- *Residence picks: condo, house, separate, communal?*
- *Personality considerations: introverts vs extroverts*
- *Professional considerations*

Finances

Money may make the world go around, but, according to Maurie Backman, in *10 Retirement Stats Every Baby Boomer Should Know*: "The average baby boomer has $163,577 saved for retirement" (TMF-BookNerd, March 2017). This amount will not buy you that idyllic private Caribbean island! Although many retirees can boast that they are financially well-healed as they embark on a new lifestyle, others must first deal with their very real financial limitations. In fact, this book will prove to be especially helpful to this group, because its whole premise is based on helping you find your professional retirement niche.

On the other hand, if you are fortunate enough to have healthy streams of ongoing income, or at least a comfortable nest egg, your options grow exponentially. As we consider all the aspects below (family, climate, personality, job opportunities), you are not constrained by financial limitations.

Family Considerations

For better or worse, life has taught us that we do not bond with, partner with, or marry a person only; we inevitably inherit our partner's family as well. This is an inescapable, and, hopefully, a happy truth. The result—the draw of family ties often becomes the bond that keeps us close. In particular, grandchildren become our "raison d'etre", either out of our desire to remain near, or out of our need to assist in their rearing. In either case, retirees often find their role as grandparents the major decision maker in where they live, work, and play.

And this is a good thing. It cannot be overstated to remark that, especially during the last and current centuries, the society of the family has undergone radical change. Our entire concept of what constitutes a traditional family has been altered. Children now have multiple parents, grandparents, half and step siblings, same sex parents, interracial parents, and single parents.

One might argue that now, more than ever, the society of the family needs and yearns for coherence, stability, and roots. How else can we account for the continued increase in travel, by any means, during holiday seasons so that families can be together.

Location Choices: Warm, Cool, City, Suburb?

It's somewhat fascinating and telling to study the various articles regularly published describing prime retirement communities, both in the US and abroad. Conventional wisdom would seem to dictate that the list would consist solely of sunbelt destinations. On the contrary, depending upon the criteria used, most often we find a healthy mix of north, south, east, and west destinations.

For example, in a recent *USA Today* article, "Five Places Where You May Want to Retire," (Tamara Holmes, November 2017), the five places listed were Asheville, NC, Central Florida, Pittsburgh, PA, Evanston, Illinois, and El Paso, TX. While Florida and North Carolina are often at or near the top of many retirement destinations, the other three represent a departure from the traditional locales that conventional wisdom might consider to be highly desirable.

Why so? Because the choice of a retirement community is as varied as the priorities and personalities of those seeking a particular life style. Some prefer the stark beauty of the hot, dry desert environment. Others could never see themselves living far from the ocean. Some look forward to the refreshing change of seasons, others to a consistently warm (or cool) climate. Some are most interested in communities offering cultural, intellectual, and social opportunities.

Residence Pick: Condo, House, Separate, Communal?

As more than 11,000 members are joining the ranks of the retired every year for the foreseeable future, it is not surprising to see the growth of diverse types of residences ranging from traditional independent one-family estates to total assisted community living situations that provide for every type of physical and social need. This variety of living arrangements is meant to accommodate the various categories of retirees we referred to earlier—young-old, middle-old, and older-old. For the most part, depending upon your personality type, the "young-old" still prefer either single family property ownership, with all the trappings, or upscale independent condo living within the city or suburbs.

The "middle old" are finding a surge in "over 55" condo complexes, where they can enjoy independent living without all the responsibilities of property maintenance, within a community of like-minded adults. The "older-old" have an even greater variety of living options as more and more senior living communities crop up offering a menu of living configurations, all the way from the option of renting your own apartment, owning your own vehicle, and experiencing full independence to opting to have all your physical, medical, social and mobility needs provided for in a community living environment.

In "Americans of All Ages are Coming Together in Intentional Communities," in the November/December 2017 issue of Time, Jeffrey Kluger points out that having a supportive multi-age community as one grows older is a wonderful alternative to assisted care living.

Personality Considerations: Introverts vs Extroverts

Do not underestimate your needs as a social animal. In the movie, "Cast Away," Tom Hanks, desperate for human interaction after being marooned on an island for four years, converts a soccer ball into a human-looking head in order to simulate the presence of a "pretend friend." Even those of us who are most introverted need to recognize our need to interact with others on a somewhat regular basis.

Whether in the supermarket, the factory, the office, the park—whether we are consciously aware of it or not—the research tells us that "socialization spreads positivity, can reduce stress, can boost self-worth" (ChartWell Retirement Centers Website).

Although, as the song says, "people who need people are the luckiest (and happiest!) people in the world," each of us individually must ask: "To what degree does that premise refer to me?" Some of us need a "family-friend-fix" daily. Others of us feel the need to be detoxed if we are forced to interact with others too much and too often. Some of us never turn on the TV but prefer to listen to music or bury ourselves in a good book. Others of us keep the TV on 24/7, simply because we have the constant need to hear a human voice.

The point is...each of us must determine our sociability needs index in order to choose the living situation and life style that best fulfills our level of need to interact with others.

Professional Considerations

Especially if you are among the group who plan to continue to work after retirement, whether full or part time, your professional work considerations are undoubtedly of paramount importance in where you choose to live.

Those of us who are retired and plan to work, fall into one of two groups. Financially, you are "well-heeled" and don't need to supplement your already robust retirement income and fund. But you are still so young-at-heart and filled with creative energy that you have no intention of slowing down. You intend to continue to work at your life's chosen profession, or you are chaffing at the bit to branch out into a new, very different career path. The other possibility is that you find you need to work to supplement an inadequate retirement income or to help family members or to earn extra money for travel or to pursue a hobby. In either scenario, if you decide to remain employed after retirement, this decision, in large measure, will help to determine where you land geographically.

Retirement Work Redefined & Redesigned

As we find ourselves entering the post-retirement stage of work, we need to step back and redefine ourselves as professionals—who we are, who we want to become, where we want to go, how we plan to get there.

For many of us, this point of redefining finds us more in control of our future than we were during earlier stages in our lives. We bring forward all the talent, skill and experience that have come before, to recombine them into our "what happens next." We are ready to ask ourselves, "What captures my mind, attention and efforts most fully, resulting in my total sense of losing track of time?"

We differ not only in terms of what skills we have developed, but which of these skills we did or did not ultimately use during our work lives, and whether the skills we did use were the ones that we most enjoyed. Did our work take us in the direction of our interests? Was the work meaningful to us, reflecting the underlying values that make us who we are? Did our work suit our personality and temperament?

We will return to these questions about our own uniqueness, and how we have or have not been able to express it so far, as part of the *5-Step Process* in the chapters ahead. Here you will have the opportunity to clarify your own essence, and thus to ensure that your "you-ness" is incorporated into your own "new" retirement plan.

Retiring Jointly

Retiring jointly with your partner can prove to be a double-edged sword. Many young couples, frazzled and frenzied by the pace of mutual careers, fantasize about the day when they can retire to be together, to play golf in unison, to travel as a couple, to leisurely read the daily paper and do the crossword puzzle, to savor that second cup of coffee, indifferent to the weather, flight schedules, and project deadlines. But, alas, when that day arrives, couples often find themselves beset with a whole array of unexpected dilemmas. They never expected to have different interests, goals, and priorities.

He wants to travel the world; she plans to spend time and money at home with and near the grandchildren. He likes to sleep late; she is an early bird who recently joined the local gym in the hopes that they both would spend the early morning working out together. He intends to devote much of his free time volunteering at the local veteran's hospital; she has decided to establish a small facility in their home to shelter stray animals.

Now comes the balancing act, perhaps the need to compromise, or to scale back, what each expects of the other. Retiring with your partner can and should be a time of deep satisfaction for both parties. If the stars align for you and your partner, in that you are in sync in terms of interests, goals, and lifestyles, then your journey promises smooth sailing under sunny skies. If, on the other hand, you find that your partner's retirement aspirations are radically different from yours, the challenge will be to find common ground while simultaneously providing for the pursuit of individual interests and goals.

We Need a Process to Shift Gears

Before you embark on this terrific life-invigorating experience that will be your last, and hopefully, your most enriching passage, you first need to re-learn, or re-remember a few basic caveats about embracing any new adventure. First, recall the adage, "Know thyself." Next, measure twice, cut once. In a word, do your homework *before* the exam!

The retirement story that follows shows what level of disaster can lie ahead if you skip the process and just take a leap. It serves as a negative roadmap, indicating what to avoid in order not to wake up in the wrong life as Alan did.

SNAPSHOT: Alan

Alan had a very successful career as a prominent CEO of a large corporation. When retirement came, he was too young and too active to even consider a traditional life of retirement, such as hitting the golf course with his colleagues each morning. Instead, he wanted to try an entirely different type of career.

Surfing the Internet on Realtor.com and Zillow, he spotted for-sale a large, old, ocean-front inn on the coast of Maine. Hmmm ... wouldn't it be fun for our family to leave our city life behind and to start a whole new family adventure as innkeepers! With support from his two teenage children and an eager wife, he prematurely withdrew a substantial piece of his retirement nest egg and plunged into what they all were sure would be a most satisfying adventure. And initially, it appeared to be so. They moved into the annex of a stately white inn atop a hill, featuring a wraparound porch with inviting rocking chairs, overlooking a bay darted with just a few fishing boats. And as an unexpected bonus, at the base of the hill stood a weathered lobster house, where the lobstermen docked at the end of their day to weigh and bargain for their catch. Just think, all the inexpensive, fresh lobster available for the family and the guests at the inn!

The inn itself was a charming throwback to our early 20th century life, with antiques, nautical artifacts, and at least a dozen rooms, each with its unique charm, all with a view of the bay. Alan determined that he would be its financial/business operator, while his wife would take care of all domestic matters, including providing inviting, scrumptious meals, with the help of their two young kids.

By the end of their first financially disappointing season in business, Alan had serious misgivings about this hasty decision. First, he realized that he had not done any research on the practical aspects of operating a large, old property. Certainly, as a CEO, he had no responsibility for or interest in maintaining a building's infrastructure. Plumbing and carpentry and electricity and heat had been non-issues for him—all taken care of by company outsources. Now, since he was totally unqualified to solve even the smallest of household problems and had no interest in learning the how-to of maintenance, he had to seek out and deal with a myriad of local tradesmen who, as natives, seemed to enjoy reminding him of how expensive it was to maintain such an old homestead!

Second, as innkeeper, Alan quickly realized that the task of "greeter" fell to him each time a new group of travelers arrived. And furthermore, these guests presumed they could turn to him for all sorts of advice on where to eat, to shop, to sail, to fish, to hike. My goodness, he and his family were themselves new to the area. How could these strangers expect him to accommodate them with information on "places to go and things to do?" He began to realize something else about himself—he really did not enjoy meeting and greeting and making himself accessible to the myriad of guests coming and going. In fact, he began to resent them as intruders into his privacy and his would-be independence. He had not realized that the life of an innkeeper demanded 24-7 attention to his guests. And he was not the gregarious, social type who relished pleasing others or showing interest and curiosity about their lives. He would much rather retreat to his ESPN programs, alone in his man cave!

Third, there was another reality check to deal with. In their former life, Alan's wife enjoyed, in fact, prided herself on her culinary skills. She enjoyed nothing more than preparing special meals for her family, and often impressed their wide circle of friends with her latest Martha Stewart dinner feasts! However, the simultaneous cooking demands imposed by any number of different groups proved too challenging for one person, even with two assistants. Early on she learned that it was costly to inventory a variety of perishable foods to be prepared to provide even limited options. And she had to deal with the challenge of preparing and serving several different dishes simultaneously, in consideration of varied culinary limitations and tastes. After their first season, the family decided that henceforth they would provide only breakfast.

Lastly, as their children entered their teens, they began to realize that this bucolic environment wasn't much to their liking. They longed to return to the vibrant urban life they had left behind.

And So... A 5 Step Process to YOUR New Life & Work

So many questions! So many options! So many configurations! Hopefully, as we move through the 5-Step Process in this book, you will begin to sort out some of these options and make them more concrete, less nebulous, more attainable. The benefit of taking the time you need to complete this process is nothing less than the rest of your life well spent—with vitality, engagement, purpose, and enjoyment. The penalty for skipping the process, and just taking a leap, can be finding yourself living the wrong life, doing the wrong work.

CHAPTER 3:
Step #1: Count Down & Break Free

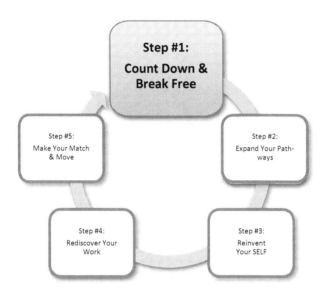

Retirement sometimes happens more suddenly than we expected—before we think we are ready for it. We still have so much to offer, yet suddenly we find ourselves shifted to the sidelines. The retirement countdown that we thought was far in the future is suddenly upon us. For those among the 64% who have had retirement thrust upon us earlier than we had anticipated, there is no time to complete the countdown before arriving at that last and final day. Others of us, who can dictate our own retirement date, or for whom retirement still lies ahead, have the luxury of completing the countdown in advance, so that we are prepared for that final day of work.

Whether or not you have already retired, or your retirement date still lies (or looms) ahead, the temptation may be to fill the vacuum immediately–with *something*. But therein lies a problem. If you skip *Step #1: Countdown* (of the 5-step process), and move ahead too quickly, you may find yourself trapped on a path or paths that are not your best or most resonant choices. You may even find yourself piggy-backing on someone else's life, while putting your own retirement life and aspirations on permanent hold.

To find *your* own next best work requires a letting go and a rediscovery process. Navigating through the full retirement countdown is necessary to bring your past work life to a close before attempting your next beginning. The momentum and focus of your earlier pursuits propelled you along a path. You have gone one way, and not the other, at each juncture. Your work life has entrenched itself in your every day and thought. This has been the life you have lived, mastered, and grown familiar with, possibly for many decades. In order to change directions, it is necessary first to *stop* moving in the direction you were formerly headed.

If you are one of those who did jump ahead to fill the void before you had your own next direction clearly in mind, return to accomplish those missed countdown tasks now. By doing so, you will release yourself from the past and be freed to rediscover yourself completely. As with most life changes of real importance, there are no shortcuts...and the outcome *does* matter.

The "what happens next" is all important, particularly when it is *your* life we are talking about. Give yourself the time and space that is essential for you to regroup and find your own best next direction.

Retiring Together

Of course, this countdown eventually becomes a joint activity for couples, but not before it is accomplished individually. This may be the time to get a second copy of this book so that each of you can complete your own process, beginning with your own countdown.

Later, once you have moved through your own sequence of counting down, followed by the other four steps of the *5-Step Process*, it will be time to design your combined future. But starting off at this point with joint planning risks one partner overpowering, or subordinating themselves to, the other.

Your Retirement Countdown

So, let your countdown begin... As a start, consider the full countdown sequence to see where it leads. Then progress through each count separately, all the way through to final BLASTOFF.

Honor the Endings

Before the *"next"* can begin, the *"last"* needs to end. This is not an automatic, or a simple process. Begin your countdown by *ending* fully what has come before. *End your story well.* Leave graciously, and, of course, burn no bridges. You may want to use some of your past contacts either as future clients or as links to future connections.

Be kind to yourself. Acknowledge that what you are going through is difficult and probably emotionally jolting. Spend time talking with friends and family. Take long walks. Plan a trip that will facilitate your exit from the entrenched habits and practices of your past life.

Take time to grieve and let go. Learn from the grieving process as it applies to other losses. Based on the work of Kubler Ross, this process has five distinct stages, leading up to acceptance. We may experience some stages of the process more intensely than others, depending upon the circumstances surrounding our retirement.

All five stages of the grieving process, leading up to acceptance, can apply to retirement. They include:

1. Shock and denial

2. Anger

3. Pain and guilt

4. Bargaining

5. Depression and loss

These five stages do not necessarily occur in order. We often move back and forth between stages simultaneously, one stage gradually diminishing as another seems to consume us. And as in dealing with the death of a loved one, when we experience the "death"—or end—of our career as we have known it, we spend varying lengths of time working through each step of a grieving process.

Depending on how wedded you were (or are) to your work, you, too, will identify with this comparison. You'll be nodding your head in agreement, saying, "Yeah, that's me, alright! How did you know?!"

Let's look at these stages and observe how they mirror where you are on the continuum of "retirement grief." These stages are based on Julie Axelrod's article, *5 Stages of Loss and Grief,* that "paints a typical portrait of the emotional roller coaster we ride to arrive at this passage called retirement" (Axelrod, 2011).

Stage 1—Shock & Denial

The beginning of the process, the stage of *shock and denial,* will involve more passive inaction than positive action. This is to be expected, and it cannot be circumvented. We need this time of muddled inactivity. Denial is a defense mechanism that buffers an immediate shock of some kind. Our instinct is to hide from the facts, to attempt to dismiss them from our minds.

In the context of retirement from work, we can end up feeling numb with disbelief. "My work defines me as a person–it is an integral part of who I am. It provides meaning and purpose to my life. This can't be happening to me. Where did this come from?" And, for those who retired voluntarily, "What have I done? What was I thinking?"

Stage 2—Anger

Anger is particularly powerful if our retirement has been unexpectedly forced upon us, either by internal political or economic forces, or by external health, family, personal causes. The pain of loss is very real. "How dare you suggest that I retire? After all that I've done for this company? How much of myself I've invested into this organization? How necessary I am to the successful functioning of this company? With any early retirement, whatever the reason, we probably did not have the luxury of having the time we needed to take charge of our own destiny. As a result, we may not feel prepared–financially, personally, psychologically. We are angry because we have lost our sense of being in control of the process. And let us not forget that anger is generally a function of fear.

Depending on the catalyst that is forcing us to shift gears, we may direct our anger, justifiably or not, at ourselves, or at persons, places and entities outside ourselves. The organization, our boss, the current political/economic climate, our own confusion, perceived or real shortcomings, family, friends. All of these can become potential targets of our anger. We are filled with a sense of helplessness, injustice, unfairness. How dare this happen to me?

Stage 3—Pain & Guilt

Even for those of us who were not "forced" to retire, we still may experience pain and guilt after it happens...a sense of work left undone. "How can they possibly manage without me there doing what I've always done? I am the one who developed these courses, this program, this product. I am the manager who knows best how to gain optimum performance from this team I brought together. Certainly, I am indispensable. And if I am not, what does that mean about my value, not only now but in the past? I have always felt needed. How is it possible I am no longer essential to the vitality of the organization?"

Stage 4—Bargaining

Depending upon the circumstances of our leaving, bargaining can take several forms to "make it go away." If we were forced out of a position, or, as they call retirement in England, if we are "made redundant" (Imagine! What an insensitive, culturally offensive term—*redundant*!), we may attempt to negotiate an interim type of position, where we can remain with the organization on a part-time, consulting, work-from-home type arrangement. Months later, when we look back on our attempts to survive the trauma of full retirement, we may come to realize that in most cases such a proposed solution was either not in our best interest, or even impractical. But, at the time of our impending separation, we were desperate. Any solution seemed preferable to "leaving forever."

Stage 5—Depression, Fear, Loneliness

In this stage, we finally realize the true magnitude of our loss, and it depresses us. Denial has given way to reality, and anger, pain, and bargaining are abating, making room for depression and fear of the unknown future ahead. David Harris, in an article entitled, "Psychological Aspects of Retirement," says that, "Retirement is a normal phenomenon [where] ...some will experience mild symptoms of anxiety, as part of an adjustment reaction to late life. A minority will suffer a significant depressive reaction" (Harris, 1983).

Then Comes Acceptance

At the end of the five stages of this grieving process, this honoring of the ending and loss, comes *acceptance*. When this is achieved, it is time to move to the next step in the countdown...

Recover & Renew

As we emerge from this time of grieving and separating, after we process and move through all the emotions that accompany any profound loss, we reach a point where we do begin to cope—to "accept" this change in our lives. With this acceptance, comes a return of vitality and forward thinking, preparing us to move on through the recovery process. Eventually, a sense of quiet calm permeates our psyche. We gradually make peace with our status. At this point, we at last are ready and able to get down to the business of moving forward to reimagine life as it will become, free from the shadows of our past life.

SNAPSHOT: Dr. Murphy

Dr. Lynch Murphy was a Marcus Welby kind of doctor in the small town where he grew up, where he returned after completing his education and serving in World War II. He was beloved by his patients and deeply involved in the community, with a large and thriving practice where he cared for the health and well-being of multiple generations of families.

Dr. Murphy's work day followed a pattern that had become ingrained over 40 years of practice. He was up before dawn, followed by coffee and breakfast and a brisk half mile walk over to his medical offices. On Mondays through Wednesdays... see patients in the morning, make rounds in the afternoon. Thursdays and Fridays, early morning surgeries, then see patients and make rounds. When Dr. Murphy sold his practice and retired, he still lived within walking distance of his office. And many of his patients understandably preferred to talk with him instead of the new "young" doctor who had purchased his practice.

Fortunately, Dr. Murphy's wife, Lou, anticipated that he was going to have difficulty breaking free from his lifelong career as a physician. So, she planned for the two of them to set off on a 3-month driving trip in France to break the pattern of Dr. Murphy's long entrenched lifestyle.

Since he did not speak French, and so certainly could not do the driving, Lynch had a very peaceful time of it. Lou, whose mother was from France, did speak fluent French and understood the French road system. So, she handled all the arranging, communicating and driving, leaving Lynch free to observe, learn, enjoy, and otherwise decompress.

> *When they returned home from their trip, Dr. Murphy was refreshed and ready for his new life. As his retirement pursuits emerged, they took a much different direction from his lifelong career path. He became an avid reader and a student of emerging science, history, woodworking, and photography. In the shop he set up in his garage, he spent countless hours designing and building one-of-a-kind cabinets and chests for his own home and as gifts for his children and grandchildren.*

Reorder...Make Room for What's Next

 Even after you have honored the ending, recovered, and renewed, your physical world still may remain much as it always was. It is now time to:

- Remove the old,

- Reorder what remains,

- Welcome what is new, and

- Make room to focus on what is next.

You have your own personal legacy of priorities, people, time use and "stuff." There are the textbooks loading down your shelves from the courses that you taught over the past 30 years. Or the computer manuals. Or the medical journals. Or the building codes notebooks. Or the parts manuals. Or whatever made up the basis of your past career and expertise. Your file drawers are still filled with the grade sheets for all your past students, or the minutes from the committees you served on, or the building specs from every project. Box these up and store them for now.

In your closet are the black, gray, and navy business suits, and your lineup of white and blue shirts or blouses. These stand as a constant reminder that you no longer wear them, and that you may never need or want to wear them again, except for an occasional wedding or funeral. Out with them. Free up the hangers. Make Goodwill happy.

So, too, with your personal and professional people connections. Your LinkedIn, and perhaps even your Facebook, account may still be loaded with people you may or may not even like, but with whom you once needed to maintain strategic relationships as part of your former work. Trim these lists down to the people you choose to keep.

As you begin to reorder your world—priorities, people, activities, time and stuff—there will be something almost cathartic about removing the old in order to make room for the new. And as empty shelves appear... that's where you will put the books about France or writing or woodcarving or fishing or astronomy. And in your now uncluttered closet, you will hang the clothes that you love and that express the you who is about to break free.

You will know what needs to go, and you may be surprised by what you decide to keep. Some of the oldest items on your shelves actually may make the cut of what you decide to keep. You may find that your next path loops you back to an earlier time in your career when you were more essentially engaged, and where you now are being drawn to return. Some past pursuits, even passions, may have been set aside when your previous life and work intervened. These unexpected "keepers" may provide powerful clues to your "what comes next." Like a diamond cutter chipping away the stone, you may uncover a gem.

The physical evidence of what you choose to reject and dispose of, and what you retain, or even promote into a prominent place on your shelves and in your file drawers, is a map, of sorts, plotting the trajectory from your past career and life to your next one.

Now What About You?

Your personal reordering will take its own shape and reveal its own map. Its purpose is both symbolic and practical—to remove what binds you to past pursuits and free up the mental, as well as the physical space you will need for what will emerge next. This reordering task will require *action*. Remove from your shelves and files, your closets and address books, anything that you clearly know you will no longer need. As space empties, think ahead to what you will want to put there next. What will need to be brought down from the attic, up from the basement, in from the garage, retrieved from past thumb drives, repurchased, or added new?

This winnowing process will feel freeing—even uplifting. Observing your ultimate choices may be highly illuminating in terms of clarifying what your future holds.

Expand Your Pathways

 With your new order established, your next pathway (or pathways) for retirement may begin to take shape in your mind. Perhaps these ideas have been on your mind for some time. The three classic pathways for retirement have been:

1. **Life of Leisure:** Entertainment or hobby. Physical or mental. Skilled or unskilled. Engaging or merely amusing.
2. **Life of a Volunteer:** Artistic or political. Community or individual. Involved with people, data, or things.
3. **Life of a Traveler**: Traveling as a visitor, as a "temporary local," or even as a part-time or full-time resident.

Now four additional pathways are also open to you. Expand your thinking to include them for a total of seven potential pathways, as well as various combinations thereof.

4. **Life of Engaging New Work**: Self-employed or for hire, online or in person, part or full-time.
5. **Life as an Entrepreneur**: Finding needs and meeting them, for profit or otherwise.
6. **Life in the Creative Class**: Creating for a living, or for pleasure, or both.
7. **Life of a Student**: Ongoing or periodic study, classroom or workshop, academic or artistic, online or in person.

You may end up pursuing a single primary path, or you may combine two or more paths. *Creative* combined with *Student*. *Entrepreneur* joined with *Traveler*. *Work* merged with *Leisure*. We will discuss and consider these seven pathways further in Chapter 4. For now, just take a moment to review the list and note your initial thoughts about what paths you may consider for your future life, and in what proportions.

Rediscover Your SELF

 Next in the countdown, take the time you need to reinvent your SELF. With your pathway (or pathways) in mind, you may have a strong urge to jump ahead and begin your next life. This is entirely understandable. But forging ahead at this point can also be a mistake. This is the rest of your valuable, and highly significant life you are considering here. Allot the time and attention you need to get it right!

Soon after you retire, you will be presented with any number of pressures to choose a direction—any direction—and get on with it. These forces will emerge from various directions, appearing to be the single, simple solution to your retirement situation.

Yes, I know... Your grandchildren need to be picked up from school and watched until your son or daughter-in-law comes home from work. Your husband, who has not retired yet, needs someone to do the bookkeeping for his business. Your local library needs a volunteer to shelve books three days a week. Your former employer wants to hire you back part-time at reduced pay and without benefits, to continue doing what you already were mortally tired of doing.

Wait! Step back from all these demands and possibilities until you first have arrived at your own version of what *you* want to do with the rest of your life. In the meantime, protect your "space" and time. Nature may "abhor a vacuum," but you need to preserve yours for now.

To retire well, and in your own unique way, give yourself this gift of time to know your SELF. Then, and only then, will you succeed in making the shift *from* your past work that was dictated by others *to* your future lifework that optimizes your personal gifts, hopes, values and purpose. Take the time to ponder and to decide: "Where do *I* want to focus *my* time, talents and energy now? What more do *I* want to accomplish, for whom and how?"

Now What About You?

Who are you and who are you *really*? To a degree, your past work life may have come to define you instead of the other way around. Return now to the question you struggled with 40 or more years ago: "*Who* do I want to be, and *what* do I want to do when I grow up?" The task of rediscovering yourself begins with finding or re-finding your *voice*.

What do you have to say with your life? Have you had the opportunity to say it yet?

We will return in Chapter 5 to complete the complex, and possibly surprising, process of rediscovering your unique and capable SELF. For now, just take a moment to think about yourself in all your complexity, talents, natural gifts, values, and passions. Note any hidden aspects of yourself. Postpone being selective or practical. Narrowing down to an actual plan will come later.

Reenvision Your Purpose—Your WHY

 As you envision what comes next, avoid being bound by images from your past. Maybe the *earlier you* was a doctor, but the *future you* will be a woodcarver. Why? Because you want to create and see the tangible results of your work. The *past you* may have been a woodcarver, but the *future you* may be a history tutor or a "bird guide." Why? Because your life purpose is shifting away from working with objects towards working with people.

This is a time to cast your nets far and near—a time to arrive at your own "short list" of the goals and visions you want to realize. Resist any inclination you may have to limit your thoughts and goals based on so-called reality. Many things that may once have been impossible could be completely possible now. Control the urge to be overly "realistic" and self-censoring, or any other negative mental thoughts or habits that lurk just below the surface of your thinking, ready to insert barriers, and otherwise to ambush your goals before these positive possibilities even make their way onto your list.

More is possible than may be immediately apparent. If a goal is sufficiently important to be included on your short list, you will find ways to accomplish it. See beyond whatever boundaries, either real or imagined, may have stood in your way so far—those voices, external and internal, saying "yes but." Your firm response could be: "If not me, *who*? If not now, *when*?" "And *why not*?"

Now What About You?

At this point the goal is to envision your future life and work purpose, however fuzzy the vision. Later there will be time to consider the specifics of the "how" and to adjust your plans to make all this happen.

For now, the task is to begin to figure out the "what" and its underlying "why."

Reconsider Your WHO

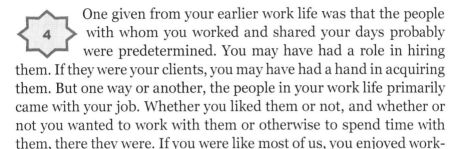 One given from your earlier work life was that the people with whom you worked and shared your days probably were predetermined. You may have had a role in hiring them. If they were your clients, you may have had a hand in acquiring them. But one way or another, the people in your work life primarily came with your job. Whether you liked them or not, and whether or not you wanted to work with them or otherwise to spend time with them, there they were. If you were like most of us, you enjoyed working with some of your colleagues, and others...not so much.

As you enter your retirement career, the colleagues you choose to work with, and the friends or family members with whom you elect to enjoy leisure pursuits, will be a deliberate choice on your part. Where once the people who surrounded may not have been ones you selected yourself, now *you* are the chooser. When you say goodbye to all of those people who once formed your daily circle, you will enter a life populated mainly by the people you elect to be with, to work with, to spend time with, to travel with.

This fact can be freeing and gratifying. If you choose well, you will be rewarded with more companionable, and even more productive, alliances and associations. But now that you will be populating your own world, the other side of this coin is "no action, no people." As you listen to the silence, and eat lunch alone for the third consecutive week, you may look up one day and wonder "where is everybody?"

Take time now, at this point in your retirement countdown, to put some deliberate thought into your WHO. From among your past colleagues, are there some with whom you wish to stay in contact, or even possibly to collaborate? Some of your *"keepers"*–your intentional colleagues and associates—may be from your recent work. Others may be from your deeper past. You may need to track down and reconnect with this group. Or there may be new colleagues you will want to find, nearby or out in the world, face-to-face or online.

If your next direction of choice is to be a writer, you may want to find a writers' group, and possibly a writing mentor or teacher. Depending on your writing genre choice, you may want to consider partnering with a co-author. Or perhaps you know someone who has an important message to offer, but who needs a ghostwriter to transform it into print. And you certainly will want to add an editor to your "intentional colleagues" base.

If you decide to take up painting again, you may need to locate a workshop and a life studies teacher or join a "plein air" group and "paint under the sky" in the great outdoors. Or maybe you will want to team up with an enamel craftsman who can convert your work into "painted glass" to sell as decorative objects.

If the path you choose is a life of travel, who will be your travel partner? If you intend to get serious about improving your chess game, who do you know who plays well enough to challenge you? If you plan to do more fishing, who will be your fishing partner—or mentor? What about your tennis partner, or golf group, or book club, or hiking club?

If you are married, or have a life partner, that person will undoubtedly be one of the major people in your retirement life. But there could be changes even here. Possibly your partner could assume an additional and different role in your mutual relationship. You may be surprised to discover activities and interests that you want to share, workwise and otherwise.

Although now it will take effort and initiative to identify and engage the people who will be your associates in your new life—the people with whom you will spend time and communicate on a regular basis—the good news is that you will find yourself associating more with people you genuinely enjoy, value, and admire. You may even discover on your WHO list someone with whom there may be exciting potential for an intentional partnership. We will be discussing this "partnering up" option more fully in Chapter 10.

Now What About You?

Think of the most exciting, energizing, enjoyable group of people you know. Be creative in your listings. Include people even if you have not been in touch with them for many years. Thanks to the Internet, you will be able to find them again. Also, consider what your commonalities are. As you think this through, remove any preconceived boxes. Concentrate on their gifts and strengths beyond the bounds of the work roles and positions they held when you knew them.

You may have known Bill as an engineering instructor, but he could be more interesting and have more in common with you as an artist, playwright, and poet. And, yes, Stuart may have been a computer scientist in his career, but he also created cellos by hand as a hobby. Chris may have been a beautician, but she also lived abroad for a number of years earlier in her life and thus would be an excellent resource for you as you plan to travel, or even to move overseas, and then write a book about it.

Think of your potential people in the broadest terms, selecting the facets that reverberate with you as you transform into your retirement persona and take up your retirement work. Take a few minutes now to make some notes for yourself about your "intentional colleagues"–your WHO. Include both their names and the reasons you want to keep them in your life.

Rethink Your WHERE

Again, the WHERE of your life was likely determined *for you* by your job and employer. Whether you found work close to home, or moved away from your hometown to meet the demands of your work… Whether you then remained in one location throughout your career, or were required by your employer to relocate, once or repeatedly… In all these cases, you were planted in a place by your work. Probably you never questioned this or tried to change it, settling, and compromising for a variety of reasons.

Now, at this point in your countdown, it is time for you to explore new horizons, and reconsider where *you* want to live. It may seem easier just to stay where you are. Moving is such a hassle. But don't sidestep this piece of your retirement puzzle. As with reconsidering your WHO, rethinking your WHERE may take effort and initiative. Giving this the thought it requires will yield gratifying results.

The place where you are living now may be your favorite location thus far—your own version of Utopia. Or possibly one of the past places you lived suited you better. You may have always wished you lived in a larger city–downtown where you could take in all its cultural and entertainment possibilities and walk everywhere instead of always driving. Perhaps you have dreamed of living abroad. You may wish for a more temperate climate, so that you can spend more of the year outdoors. You may even envision living in two locations, migrating back and forth according to season, following the sun (or snow).

If you have a partner, the two of you will have areas of joint decision-making that will require serious discussion and thought. At this point in the retirement countdown, let those discussions begin, if they haven't started already. Jointly, you may arrive at even more exciting possibilities than you ever could have imagined on your own.

The idea is to explore the full range of dreams and possibilities. Think beyond the "what is" to the "what could be." Then imagine yourself there and assess how you feel.

Now What About You?

Take a minute now to consider your own WHERE. If your own best WHERE is the place you live now, why is this exactly? If you are drawn to live elsewhere, what drives this yearning? For each WHERE, write a brief comment that expands your thinking. Ask your partner to make notes too, preferably without seeing yours, so that he or she feels free to think independently. Once you have envisioned your WHEREs independently, compare notes and begin to envision your next WHERE together.

Refocus Your Learning

 We have all heard the term "lifelong learning." This concept of continuing to learn throughout life is a powerful one, but one that requires thought and preplanning at this point in the countdown. When you were in the *pre-career* phase of your life, the task of learning what you needed came with considerable pressure. Your education years were primarily geared to gain you entry into a career. For many of us, these education choices were made on the fly or under duress. For some of us, our career path, and its educational requirements, was clear from the outset, and we followed a direct path from studies to work. Our parents may have influenced us to pursue a particular profession or trade. And we had to declare a major when our college required it.

As you "refocus your learning" now, note how your situation has changed. This time you will not hurl through a single-path education in order to emerge at the other end as quickly as possible so that you can check school off the list. This time your learning can be varied and self-directed. It can be exploratory, starting off in one direction, or three, then changing direction later, or adding directions, or combining several directions into an intriguing whole.

This time you do not need to choose among doctor, lawyer, and Indian chief. You can begin by studying history, then add art and dance, then read about cultural differences, and learn a new language, then set off as a world traveler. You may opt to master wood crafting, and study the physics of sound, then learn to play the cello and make your own cello by hand.

Learning, as always, is an invigorating, empowering, and challenging enterprise. It will introduce you to interesting people, including some who may turn out to be key additions to the gathering WHO list in your retirement life and work.

As you contemplate what you want to learn next, follow these five key guidelines...

- *First*, be wide open to ideas about what you want to learn.

- *Second*, become your own teacher, or find one, so as to have regular assignments and an expectation of effort, persistence and active participation.

- *Third*, adopt a "yes I can" approach to learning. If there is something you think you cannot learn, reconsider this! Whatever you may have struggled to learn in school, you can learn now, if you so determine. Any notion that there is a subject you are unable to learn is incorrect. You may not have had the right teacher or been mentally receptive or developmentally ready to absorb the subject matter at that time. You now are in an entirely different place, with a mature mind and life experience to make your new learning more meaningful and thereby more attainable.

- *Fourth*, branch out to broaden, to synthesize. Combine what you already know with what you are studying next.

- *Fifth*, remember that, with learning, the journey itself is part of the pleasure. Experience the exhilaration and the "hard fun" of stimulating your mind and honing your talents.

Now take a moment to create your own list of "*What Have You Got to Learn?*" The sky is the limit... Logistics and follow-through will come later. Note why you want to learn these subjects or skills... Pleasure? Curiosity? Future work?

Break Free, then Blastoff!

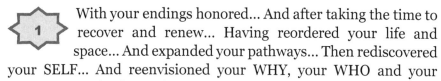 With your endings honored... And after taking the time to recover and renew... Having reordered your life and space... And expanded your pathways... Then rediscovered your SELF... And reenvisioned your WHY, your WHO and your WHERE... And refocused your learning... What comes next?

As many times as we have watched rocket launches, we know the answer to this question. The culmination of a countdown, including your new retirement countdown, is to *Break Free*, and BLASTOFF.

This breaking free and relaunch is the focus of the rest of this book. Exciting times lie ahead... Your times.

And So...

The retirement countdown does take time, but what comes next is fully worth this investment of time and energy. With your countdown completed, you will find yourself ready for, even excited about, breaking free from what came before to discover and relaunch into what comes next.

So, what does come next? Read on to work through *Step #2* of the *5-Step New Retirement Process*. As part of this next action task, you will have the opportunity to complete the task that you began to think about in this chapter—to *Expand Your Pathways*. Whereas your past life's work may have followed a single pathway, your new retirement career can, and probably will, be a combination of pathways. Contrary to what your mother always told you, you are entering a time when you may be able "to have your cake and eat it, too."

CHAPTER 4:
Step #2: Expand Your Pathways

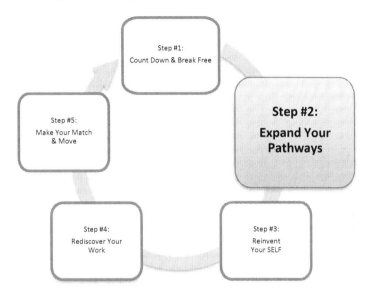

How many pathways do you have ahead? This may seem to be an moot question, since, at the point of our retirement, most of us are exiting work that was primarily devoted to a single pathway. Even for those of us who made significant career changes one or more times, we still are accustomed to lives where doing one thing, for the most part, meant *not* doing another.

From this point on, this is no longer so. Whereas your primary career may have followed a single pathway, your retirement career can and probably will follow a combination of pathways. As you design your own new retirement, it is time to exit the world of either/or and enter the world of "not one or the other, but both, or even several."

The groove of your old life may be a deep one, even entrapping. The challenge is to pull free of your past, and consider, then reconsider, the direction, or directions of your new life. This process is worthy of time and effort because it is so very important to get it right. As an essential part of the process of retiring well while remaining fully engaged and productive, take the time you need to look creatively at the pathways and combinations of directions that lie ahead for you. This is a new time for you, and new things are possible. Even after you have arrived at an initial plan, you later may return to these pathways to do some rethinking, the better to expand your choices and recombine them in even more fulfilling ways.

Seven Pathways for What Comes Next

There are at least seven retirement pathways, as well as their many combinations. Three of these are traditional. The other four are not so conventional. And you can combine two or more pathways.

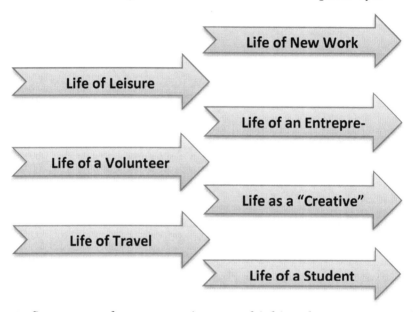

At first, some of us enter retirement thinking that we want to do *nothing*, at least for now. We may still feel the after-effects of being on the work treadmill. So now we are eager to escape from the 9 to 5 or 8 to 6 or even 7 to 7 regimens. That's OK. If you identify with this scenario, you should, for the time being, do just that—*nothing*. BUT, in the event that you someday do tire of that activity, and you probably will (perhaps sooner than you expect to), you might want to give some thought to what you really want to do with the rest of your life.

Perhaps you want to pursue a hobby full time. Maybe you've given some thought to volunteering. Travelling to places near and far has always been your dream. Or there's the possibility that you might want to combine leisure and some type of work. Let's explore each of these scenarios a little more in depth.

Retiring Together

For couples, expanding your pathways will again become a joint activity. But first this needs to be accomplished individually. Later, once you have moved through your own tasks of expanding your pathways, it will be time to discuss how your pathways will combine, or possibly diverge. Each partner needs to consider these possibilities on his/her own before looking at how such pursuits can be combined and shared.

Three Traditional Retirement Pathways

Pathway 1: Life of Leisure

The life of leisure still appeals to many retiring Boomers. As a retirement pathway, leisure activities place higher in the priority list of daily living and take on new focus and importance. Some of us choose to enjoy a hobby we have pursued before, or one that we have wished to pursue. These hobbies and other leisure pursuits can be combined with work, or even turned into work. A one-time interest in fishing can turn into a passion for it, with an almost hunter/gatherer zeal to keep the freezer, and possibly all the neighbors', stocked with fresh fish. An interest in quilting can turn into a production line, sewing security blankets for the Linus Project so that each child who enters a homeless shelter will have a blankie to snuggle. The boundary between work and play can and does become blurred as we follow our passions with renewed energy and zeal.

Our performance during our primary work life is not necessarily an accurate predictor of how we will spend the last third of our lives. In fact, the theory of "for every action there is an equal and opposite reaction" holds true here, too. It is common to find that those who leave the workforce after holding high-profile, high-powered jobs sometimes "drop out" totally from their demanding professional lives in favor of more mellow pursuits. No, I do not want to "stop by the office... have lunch with former colleagues... be invited to parties... keep current on office gossip... Rather, I want to fade into oblivion from a work standpoint, never to be heard from again! In our family, we had a standing joke about an aunt who described her main retirement activities to be "shopping and LUNCH."

Will one of your retirement pathways be a life of leisure? Could you find contentment forevermore enjoying a hobby that you have always wanted to pursue? Is there a sport that you particularly enjoy, or a skill that you developed part time when time was at a premium, and now would like to develop more fully? Perhaps you feel renewed being outdoors. Or seeing the products of your own hands. Or performing in community theater. You may not have had the time until now to even scratch the surface or plunge the depths of your passion. Now is the time. It's your turn. Go for it, even if this is only one of several pathways you will ultimately select.

It would not be an exaggeration to say that every one of us should cultivate at least a partial life of leisure into our "new" retirement. Train for that triathlon you've always felt you could complete. Get that aviator's license you've hankered to earn. Plant that English garden that you visited and admired on your last trip to England!

Any of these pursuits, plus a myriad more, can and will easily bring you days and years of satisfaction, fun, and fulfillment! You've always wanted to learn to sail, to own a loom and weave exotic patterns, to write that memoire within you, to raise goats! Do it! Give yourself permission to follow your passion!

Pathway 2: Life of the Volunteer

Volunteerism has long been a possibility for retired people. And now, as Baby Boomers retire in numbers, volunteer work has generally come to assume more meaningful forms. Beyond the envelope licking and phone answering stereotypes, meaningful volunteering options, and the capacity to match people to these options according to their own unique capabilities and interests, are plentiful and widespread.

To the degree that volunteering options are more optimally aligned with the individuals offering their time and services, volunteering takes on more of the engaging nature of employment. The new paradigm of volunteering requires a level of energy, deliberation and matchmaking formerly reserved for job hunting. Increasingly volunteers do not want to do "just anything," and agencies that enlist volunteers do not want "just anyone" to do it. We may be willing to work for free, but we are not willing to do work that is unfulfilling.

Will volunteer work be one of your pathways in retirement? Volunteerism isn't for everyone, but neither is travelling, or hobbying, or working. For those who are inclined to give of their time, their skills, their talent, their caring, volunteerism can be extremely rewarding.

WOW FACTOR

A University of Michigan study of adult males found those who volunteered their time, skills, and money to be happier and more positive about their lives, and to outlive their peers (*https://EzineArticles.com).*

Volunteering has some great residual rewards too, as it:

- Provides structure, meaning and purpose to your life;
- Affords opportunity to use your unique capabilities;
- Offers the chance to establish social contacts;
- Sets an example for others; and
- Sometimes can lead to fulfilling paid employment.

If your choice is to follow a volunteering pathway, then Chapter 12 will be for you. There we will focus the process of designing and seeking meaningful volunteer work that is uniquely fulfilling to you—work that aligns with your life purpose—your legacy—and to which you will bring your gifts and capacities.

Pathway 3: Life of a Traveler

Many Boomers are globally aware and world-connected. Many of us have traveled, and even lived, abroad. When we enter retirement, we may have a bucket list of places we want to visit, experiences we want to have, and even locations abroad where we may consider relocating permanently.

WOW FACTOR

Nearly one in five of all Americans have thought about moving abroad. Among the college-educated, this proportion is even greater—about one in four. In 2016, the US

State Department estimated that around 9 million Americans lived abroad, a 125% increase from an estimated 4 million in 1999.

Travel can be expensive. But moving abroad can be economical, and an excellent way to experience a different lifestyle. Some retirees are choosing destinations like South or Central America, where they can live more successfully, and receive more affordable healthcare, on limited incomes. Others are choosing countries they are drawn to for a variety of other reasons—a sense of adventure, an interest in learning, a desire for a temperate year-round climate, access to culture and art, the appeal of an outdoor lifestyle.

Will You Want the Life of a Traveler?

Wait until you begin to explore the world of travel, if you have not already done so. So many options, so many places, so many adventures! Because many Baby Boomers now have the time and the financial resources to travel, the entire travel industry has exploded with options of all types.

If you are a groupie who is more comfortable travelling with fellow Americans and wants someone to do all the "leg work" for you, there are many companies that cater to your taste. The only physical exertion required on your part is to "show up" at the departure point! The rest is taken care of for you.

If you are the independent, adventurous, do-it-yourself type, who likes surprises, and doesn't get rattled by setbacks or unexpected glitches, you might want to research, plan, and take trips totally on your own. Although this option requires a substantial investment of time and energy, it is by far the most satisfying way to experience your chosen destination's culture.

If you are somewhere in between these two extremes, there are excellent books and guides available (the *Your Great Trip Series*, Karon Brown, Rick Steves) that enable you to take an independent trip "as though you were traveling to your destination for the second time." These resources provide you all the guidance you need, but without the tour bus, giving you the best of both worlds—expert assistance and freedom, too. Self-managed exploration has its own rewards. Negotiating train schedules, reading a menu written in a foreign language, shopping at the local street market, finding treasures in specialty shops away from tourist traps—all these experiences can be challenging, but such fun! And what a feeling of accomplishment, what a sense of self-empowerment and independence!

And then there is cruising. If you want to travel in a laid-back, serene, "far-from-the-madding-crowd" mode, there are all manner of cruises available, offering you comfort, relaxation, good food, entertainment, and fresh sea air—all without repacking your luggage constantly.

It's like being at home—only at sea! In a lounge chair! With your own personal chef... and nightly entertainment. And each day you will wake up in a new exotic port beckoning to you to be explored. Cruises can explore the world one sea at a time—Atlantic, Pacific, Baltic, Mediterranean, Caribbean. They can be transatlantic or transpacific, with days upon days out of sight of land. They can meander along the great rivers of the world... The Rhine. The Danube. The Yangtze. The Nile. The Mississippi!

Perhaps you are an adventurer—a person who likes to travel off the beaten path, where no man or woman has set foot before. An entire industry now caters to those of us who want to travel to exotic destinations that can be reached only by two-seater plane, by local elephant, by zip line or on foot. A word of caution... These trips are not for the faint of heart, the naturally clumsy, or the couch potato. Be sure to read the fine print! If you read, "Physically Challenging; Requires Medical Immunization," you might want to reconsider, or, at the very least, be sure to purchase that optional trip insurance.

For those who love to learn while traveling, the offerings of *Road Scholar* (*https://roadscholar.org*, formerly *Elderhostel*) are a gold mine, offering approximately 5,500 educational tours and programs in 150 countries and all fifty states. These programs combine the best of both worlds, bringing learning together with direct experience of the culture, art, music, and history you are learning about. Experience Christmas in Provence, or even in Finland, traveling north to the Arctic Circle to visit Santa's workshop or to ride a sleigh pulled by reindeer.

On a trip to France: "Walk in the footsteps of Impressionists along the Seine, through Paris, Normandy, Provence, and the beautiful Côte d'Azur...study masterpieces in museums and explore the places, gardens and streetscapes that inspired them." On a trip in Italy: "Experience the best of Tuscan culinary traditions during intimate cooking classes at the International Academy of Italian Cuisine.

Smithsonian Journeys (*https://www.smithsonianjourneys.org*) is another educational travel resource, offering hundreds of fascinating tours, from "France Through the Ages" to "African Safari" to Mystical India" to "Costa Rica's Natural Treasures" to "Legendary Peru." National Graphic Expeditions are yet another excellent option: *https://www.nationalgeographicexpeditions.com*.

By joining one of their many expeditions, you can circumnavigate Iceland on a small ship, or take a photography expedition to Alaska and British Columbia. You can traverse Russia on the Trans-Siberian Railroad, or step aboard the newly renovated *Palace on Wheels* in India, traveling to the fabled cities of Rajasthan, with their majestic forts and palaces, including the rose-colored city of Jaipur, and the Taj Mahal of Agra, sparkling by day and aglow at night.

Four Additional Pathways for a New Retirement

Beyond the standard retirement pathways of leisure, volunteering and travel, four additional pathways offer even greater diversity in the paths Boomers pursue or combine in retirement. These are:

- life of engaging new work
- life as an entrepreneur
- life as a "creative"
- life of a student

Pathway 4: Life of Engaging New Work

Many of us retiring Boomers will continue to work well past our expected retirement ages, for a variety of reasons. Likely, our work will shift somewhat, or even in the extreme, from what we have engaged in throughout our careers. Whether we labor for ourselves or for others... Use our same skills or new ones or even old skills long set aside that we now find ourselves eager to return to... Work full-time or part-time, year-round or "gig by gig"... Many of us will assume the path of work as all or part of what we will do next. We may not necessarily know *yet* what work we will do, or for whom. We may still need to determine how long we will work each day, for how much money, when and when not, and for how many years. If we do want to work, we will need to chart a course to make this new work *WORK* for us, given our emerging retirement lifestyle and vision.

Are You Seeking a Life of Engaging New Work?

If one of your retirement pathways will be finding engaging new work, pause now to consider how many subpathways within this broader one will be available to you now that you have retired. The specific pathway you might think of first may be standard employment, working either part-time or full-time, for a small business or larger company. But there are other subpathways that could lead you in even more exciting and productive directions.

If you plan to continue to live where you live now, your concepts of what types of work will be available to you as a retired person may seem somewhat limited. But you need to think beyond your local area, where indeed your job options now may have narrowed, in order to explore the larger world of employment. Much has changed regarding employment. You can use this to your own personal advantage now if you decide to follow this pathway of engaging work.

First, even in the realm of traditional jobs "out there" in the workplace, labor shortages are predicted as 77 million Boomers retire with only 48 million Gen X employees available to replace them. If you aspire to a job, there will be many options, including some you may not have considered yet. Chapter 9 will explore jobs "out there," including some that are particularly likely to be filled by senior workers. Some employment opportunities can be pursued in nontraditional ways such as part-time or seasonal, or even structured as job shares.

Second, many traditional employers have shifted to outsourcing, in part as a response to a difficult economy. Outsourcing allows organizations to increase their innovation and productivity, while reducing their time-to-market. The contract talent that companies engage on a project-by-project basis, exactly when they need it, enables them to run leaner enterprises, yet ramp up when necessary to accomplish specific, potentially profitable goals. By outsourcing, employers are able to gain access to skills, knowledge and expertise that would be difficult or time consuming for them to develop in-house.

WOW FACTOR

Non-traditional contract workers make up more than one third of the US workforce. This segment is growing at twice the rate of the standard workforce.

The outsourcing movement is creating a flood of new contract-based work opportunities that may ideally match your skills, talents and interests. According to a report by ODesk (now *UpWork*), more than 90% of US firms now use contract talent on a regular basis and spend upwards of $120 billion annually on this type of expertise.

Third, telework is fast becoming a mainstream alternative to employment in the brick-and-mortar workplace. By online work we mean work that is performed online for clients with whom communication and work exchanges take place without meeting "face to face." According to a recent Gallup poll, 37% of American workers have worked virtually, four times the numbers in 1995.

In Chapter 8 we will explore the new retirement option of working online. If you are considering the pathway of engaging new work, read Chapter 8 before you decide on your own specific employment plan, and certainly before you take a position locally, to consider the larger picture of potential employers, nationwide, or even worldwide.

WOW FACTOR

Your ideal work environment may not have even existed at the time of your last job search. And your ideal job may be in a field you haven't even heard of—yet.

If you have rejected the idea that work will be a pathway you will pursue, consider the "why" of your decision. You may be thinking in terms of an either/or lifestyle—either work OR travel, either work OR leisure activities. But the Web has transformed and translated work to be "anytime, anyplace, any person, any pace."

Whereas you may be finished with work that ties you down, dominates your days, and otherwise consumes you, you may find work where you control the *where* and the *when* to be exhilarating and engaging. Today, the Internet grants you the ability to work and have your freedom, too.

Pathway 5: Life as an Entrepreneur

Entrepreneurialism is a process of finding needs and meeting them, for profit. There are plenty of needs, both existing and emerging, that can become the backbone of a successful business. Such a business can contribute significantly in meaningful ways to the health, happiness, and well-being of others—human, animal, plant, or environment. So, we can balance our desire to earn money with our values and our goal to contribute something worthwhile to individuals in particular, as well as to society as a whole. Retiring Boomers are primed and ready to create such businesses and to make such differences. We bring considerable assets, know-how and energy, as well as a capacity to interact and communicate, to any enterprise we set out to create or co-create.

As part of our world view, coming of age as we did in the 60's and early 70's, we bring to the present a history of idealism that has long been our trademark as a generation. Back then we thought we knew what needed to be changed. We may still know, perhaps better than those who have come after us, how to make the world a better place.

WOW FACTOR

"Older entrepreneurs now lead the way in new business formation. The trend has continued during the past three years and spans even high-tech businesses once thought [to be] the sole turf of 20-somethings. What's even more noteworthy is that start-ups with older owners are more successful, at least as measured by their survival rates." *Phillip Moeller in US News & World Report, October 2010*

Boomer know-how and vision translate globally as well, providing us competitive advantages when we carry our expertise and perspectives abroad. According to Kathleen Peddicord, in her article *How to Retire at Any Age:* "As a citizen of the US, you have a big advantage in the global arena. You've grown up in the world's most competitive marketplace. You have watched niches filled and businesses launched, and you have seen innumerable examples of entrepreneurial success and failure... Being an industrious American, you can't help but look around and notice all kinds of market voids. And you may find yourself coming up with ideas to address them" (*money.usnews.com*).

SNAPSHOT: Ann & Mike

Ann and Mike entered an early retirement with savings and retirement funds, expecting to have decades of healthy living ahead of them. They moved to Ambergris Caye, Belize, and built a house. But they wanted and needed to continue earning an income. So, they looked for opportunities to fill a need and earn a living, but with time left to enjoy their island paradise.

The better they got to know the island, the more niches they saw needing to be filled. Among the ideas they considered were starting a restaurant, building a small hotel, opening a wine specialty store, running eco-tours, and finally, launching a fitness club. Their final decision, to go with the health club idea, was based on two main reasons. First, they found that there were no fitness centers on the island. Secondly, and possibly even more important, they found the idea of starting a fitness center to be particularly exciting.

Cashing in their savings, they made the leap and launched the San Pedro Family Fitness Club, with tennis courts, a 250,000-gallon pool, and a workout facility. Their enterprise has been a great success—and it still leaves them free time to enjoy and explore their idyllic island.

Will Yours Be the Life of An Entrepreneur?

Will the entrepreneurial pathway be one that you pursue during your retirement? If your immediate answer is "no," pause and rethink this, based on a broader definition of "entrepreneur." Many people think that entrepreneurship is defined as "starting a business." By this definition, a relatively small population of people are entrepreneurs. The United States Global Entrepreneurship Monitor (GEM) shows that less than 8% of the US population is actively engaged in starting a business.

Candida Brush, contributor to the *Forbes.com Entrepreneurs' Blog*, takes a broader view: "Entrepreneurship is a set of actions—it is identifying or creating an opportunity, marshaling the resources and providing the leadership and building a team to create something of value, either social or economic."

Have you identified a possibility, an opportunity you might create or explore? Before you answer this question, stimulate your thinking, by considering some of the examples from the popular television program Shark Tank (*abc.go.com/shows/shark-tank*). Even better, record and watch this program yourself to get a sense of what kinds of ideas solve problems and make a difference, while also generating income. Some entrepreneurial ventures include:

- **CHORD BUDDY**—A guitar learning system created by Travis Perry to encourage his 10-year old daughter to learn guitar, ChordBuddy allows you to start playing the guitar instantly. Buttons over the chord strings guide you, simplifying the learning process and giving you encouragement to keep going. As you gain skill, Chord Buddy can be adjusted so you progressively do more for yourself until you are entirely on your own (*ChordBuddy.com*).

- **RENT-A-GRANDMA**—Rent-A-Grandma childcare givers are carefully selected mature women who are knowledgeable nannies, housekeepers, chefs, caregivers and personal assistants. Rent-A-Grandma has gained national attention through NPR and many news stories (*https://RentaGrandma.com*)

- *THE SWILT*—The Swilt is the sweater reinvented—blending the wearability of a sweater with the comfort of a quilt. With a few snaps, it transforms from a sweater to a full body cover, complete with pockets and a hood. The creators of Swilt are a husband and wife duo who launched the product in 2010, and soon had sold over a hundred units to people in their community, with no marketing *https://SharkTankSuccess.blogspot.com.*

- **READEREST**—Rick Hopper kept losing his glasses, and he knew he wasn't alone. So he took to his garage and created the Readerest, a magnetic and practically invisible patented clip that secures your glasses to your shirt wherever you go! This tiny product has already seen big results and is now offered at Ace Hardware and Walgreens (*ReadeRest.com*).
  DANCE WITH ME—Billy Blanks Jr. has trademarked "Dance with Me" as a new take on "Zumba," taking fitness to a new level by incorporating dance and targeting all age groups. " It is currently being sold at Walmart, Target, amazon.com, and Best Buy (*BlanksStudios.com*).

What ingenious ways have you designed to solve a problem? Would you enjoy moving your ideas forward to the next level? There is more to it than having a great idea. But having a great idea is a start.

WOW FACTOR
Of those involved in early stage entrepreneurial activities, 18% are over age 55 and 9% are over 65."
(*US Global Entrepreneurship Monitor Report*)

Pathway 6: Life as a "Creative"

In the work life we are leaving, we may or may not have been part of what is now being termed the "Creative Class." But that may change as part of our "new" retirement plan. According to research on the nature of work, nearly 38 million Americans, 30% of all employed people, working in many diverse fields, now *create* for a living.

Richard Florida, in his book "*The Rise of the Creative Class and How It's Transforming Work, Leisure, Community and Everyday Life*," describes what he terms an ongoing "sea change" that has had a huge economic impact on how the workplace is organized and what is valued.

Whereas feudal aristocracy derived power from the hereditary control of land and people, and the bourgeoisie from its members' roles as merchants and factory owners, the creative class derives its identity through their "ability to invent meaningful new forms."

Florida's claim is that the Creative Class now has become the dominant class in society--a key factor in our economy and culture. "We value creativity more highly than ever and cultivate it more intensely." "Core creatives" (as termed by Florida) are those who create art, design, or music as their life work.

Now added to these are the broader group of creative professionals in business, finance, law, health care and other fields, who create new ideas, technology, content, services, and solutions to complex problems. All of these, whether artist or engineer, musician or computer scientist, "share a common creative ethos that values creativity, individuality, difference and merit" (Florida, 2002).

WOW FACTOR

Over the 20th century, the *Creative Class* grew from roughly 3 million workers to its current size of 38 million. It has more than doubled since 1980 alone and is now larger than the traditional Working Class (from Richard Florida's *Rise of the Creative Class*).

The key difference between the Creative Class and other classes lies in what they are primarily paid to do. Those in the Working Class and the Service Class are primarily paid to fit in and carry out established plans. Those in the Creative Class are primarily paid to create new plans, ideas, objects and solutions.

Norms are different for those in the Creative Class—individuality, self-expression, openness, celebration of difference. Creatives are less likely to base their identities or self-worth on who they work for. They value being themselves, setting their own agendas, and doing challenging work that reflects their values and priorities. Although it is difficult to force Creatives to work, they are never truly not working. "Creativity cannot be switched on and off at predetermined times and is itself an odd mixture of work and play" (Florida, 2002).

Creatives use time differently, tending towards long periods of intense concentration, punctuated by complete breaks in productivity when they need to relax and recharge, or to incubate ideas. They are self-managed and set their own hours, want the ability to learn and grow, shape the content of their own work, and express their identities through their work. And they are drawn to live in stimulating, creative environments where they feel free to express themselves.

Will You Want a Life in the Creative Class?

Whether or not you already have been part of what is now being termed the "Creative Class," this pathway may become an essential component of your "new" retirement plan.

Do you have a gift for creativity–whether through art or through problem solving? Are you among the "core creatives" who can paint, write, design, or compose music? Or are you a person who can create new ideas, new technology, new content, new services, and new solutions to complex problems? In so, you may consider the Creative Class pathway, on its own or in combination with other options. Even if you have always considered the creative life to be impractical, rethink the possibilities now that your life realities have changed. What may once have seemed too impractical may be just the pathway that will suit and stretch you and allow your singular gifts to flourish.

Pathway 7: Life of a Student

Studies can be a means to an end, or they can be a pathway in themselves. Some of us will choose the path of study, either alone or in combination with other pursuits. We will make diverse choices of what to study, and to what degree. We may also differ in our reason for studying–for the pleasure of it, to write a book, to shift to a new area of work, to become skilled at an art or knowledgeable in an area of interest. But all of us who choose this pathway will experience the benefits of studying and learning something new.

Clearly, study is good for the mind. It is stimulating and can be exciting. And as our knowledge and skill increase, we relish the rewards of advancing accomplishment. Learning something new, or even learning something old in a new or better way, is "hard fun." And hard fun is, well, hard. But it is also FUN.

Will You Want the Life of a Student?

Your learning quests can be driven by topics of interest or skills to be mastered. It can be a quest to learn *about* art as a subject, or about how to *create* it. You may want to learn how to *identify* birds or how to *heal* them when they have been injured. How to *train* dogs or horses, or how to *breed* them. How to understand human behavior or research it or write fiction about it or provide guidance.

Some of your current learning options are in fields of study and work that have changed dramatically, or that didn't even exist when you went to school. You may have been a Psychology major, but how much do you know about the emerging area called "Positive Psychology"– the psychology of happiness and health? Other sciences–Biology, Physics, Astronomy–have undergone fascinating developments within the past few decades, and even within the past few years. A lot has changed since you studied them in high school or college.

You may have been a machinist or a drafter—expert at operating a lathe, a Bridgeport, or a slide rule. But now you are fascinated and ready to immerse yourself in learning all about CNC, EDM, and CAD/CAM technology.

You may set out to become an expert genealogist, or study for your boat captain's license. Or you may, like one retired college professor, rent space in an expert potter's studio, to work side-by-side with him as your guide and mentor as you learn to throw a pot, glaze it, and fire it in a kiln.

Your new studies may involve attending classes, either locally or online, or possibly attending workshops in interesting locations. What about a writer's workshop in Grass Valley, California? Or maybe a Brain Research Seminar in Jacksonville, Florida, providing you an excuse to escape the January cold at home.

Your own pathway of study may initially be reading-based. If so, a good place to start is on amazon.com, where it is possible to choose any subject or skill you want to add to your repertoire and do a search on it, yielding a wealth of results. Then select the top five books on your topic of choice and read them, taking notes and forming questions as you go. When you have read and absorbed five books on a subject, you already will be more knowledgeable about that subject than the vast majority of people.

The next five books you read, and digest will draw you even closer to becoming expert, giving you a sense of scope on the subject, and enabling you to formulate your own viable synthesis and command of your chosen topic.

Pathways Combined...

Many of us will choose some combination of these seven pathways, and perhaps others, creating balances among them. We may choose a life of work combined with travel. Or travel combined with volunteering. Or creativity combined with leisure. We may even select a pathway of extended travel, deciding to live abroad and do our paid or volunteer work from there.

Which pathways among the seven we have discussed give you a feeling of excitement about what lies ahead? Would you want to combine more than one? If you picked two pathways to combine, what would they be? Would you add a third? Feel free to write down whatever comes to mind, along with three or four ideas and why each idea appeals to you. If, at this point, you have ideas for only one or two of the pathways, that's okay, too. Later, after further thought, you may find yourself returning to expand your ideas.

What Are Your Pathways EXPANDED?

Did you skip any of these pathways? Perhaps some courses of action are just not for you. But possibly a pathway that initially seems not to be your cup of tea, may look different to you after you break free and reinvent yourself. Even if you think an idea for a path may be only a remote possibility, take a moment to note it down.

Surprisingly, you may find that some of the thoughts you added last are the most exciting to you. Yes, they may be outside your comfort zone at the moment. Yes, it may take some creative maneuvering to make them happen. But when you begin to talk *visions* and *short lists*, these pathways could be the very ones that rise to the top.

What Are Your JOINT Pathways?

For couples, look now at how your pathways and those of your partner will come together. There may be some give and take for both of you to enter a fulfilling retirement life. And there may be some exciting synergy as learning plans... or travel plans... or creative plans... or entrepreneurial plans... mutually enhance and stimulate each other.

SNAPSHOT: Judith and Roy

Judith and Roy led a busy, traditional life in Charlotte, NC, with Roy running his own insurance business, and Judith staying at home to raise their children. Then the time came when both began to think of retirement.

Roy was on a relaxed timeline, but Judith had her own plans and was ready to look at expanding her pathways sooner, rather than later. In Judith's design for retirement, she would leave their home in Charlotte behind and move full-time to their lake house. Then she would enroll in Divinity School and study to become a minister.

Soon after Judith moved to the lake, Roy expedited his own retirement timeline, quickly turning over his business in the city and moving to the lake to join his wife. For him, this new life would open up time for him to work on his sports cars.

After Judith graduated with her divinity degree and received an appointment as minister of a small church near the lake, Roy proudly became a "minister's husband," reading and commenting on her sermons in advance, and otherwise supporting her retirement career.

And So...

You have begun to think now at a mega level—the big picture—about what pathways may form your engaging and fulfilling new retirement. Although you may have some initial ideas about what pathways appeal to you, maybe even excite you, you may have no specific plans in mind at this point. Specifics will emerge later.

Where do we go from here? With your countdown completed, and your pathways identified, "all" you need to do at this point is to rediscover and reinvent your SELF. The next essential step of the process of seeking and finding your own best new retirement is knowing your SELF well, then reinventing your life and work to be the fullest expression of that SELF.

To the degree that you give yourself the time and the open mindedness you need to accomplish this rediscovery of your SELF, you could be entering one of the best, most focused, productive, exciting, significant periods of your life.

CHAPTER 5:
Step #3: Reinvent Your SELF

To arrive at your own renaissance and best next life—to determine what is (and is not) right as your unique sense of contribution and meaning—you first need to know your SELF. *"He who knows others is learned. He who knows himself is wise."* So said Lao-Tzu. *"But the most difficult of all is to know yourself."*

As Step #3 in the *5-Step Process*, it is now time for you to focus on and complete the complex, and possibly surprising, task of rediscovering your unique and capable SELF—your essence and value.

Whatever pathways you follow in this next phase of your life, knowing yourself is essential. If you follow the pathway of leisure, what is it that you love that will provide you a sense of engagement and completion? If you follow the path of volunteering, what will you volunteer to do and how will this reflect the essential YOU? If you follow the path of travel, where will you go, and how will you act when you get there? What YOU will you carry with you into other cultures through which you will connect and communicate in meaningful ways?

If you follow the path of new work, what will that work be, and how will it differ from what you have done until now? What is the essential work that is uniquely yours to do—your legacy work? If you follow the path of entrepreneurialism, what problems will you want to solve and how will you be uniquely able to solve them? If you follow the pathway of a perpetual student, what is it that you want to learn? And how does this fit with what and who you are?

Whatever you choose as your next pathway, knowing yourself is crucial to your setting off in this direction in a way that fulfills you rather than drains you. Knowing yourself allows you to determine not just the best way to fill time during your retirement, but the optimum way for you to express and engage your own unique self. To accomplish this, you will need to know your SELF extremely well.

Dr. Cecil Smith, a developmental psychologist at Northern Illinois University, in a talk entitled *The Long Weekend: Transition and Growth in Retirement*, described retirement as a long, gradual process—a beginning rather than an end—that is "a series of developmental tasks that must be recognized, negotiated, and resolved in order for the individual to find personal fulfillment."

In Chapter 3, as part of your retirement countdown, you made some initial notes about hidden aspects of your SELF. Review these notes now as we resume this exploration to identify the *fully defined you*. In the next chapter (Chapter 6) you will be asked to think about what you can *do*—your interests, values, skills, and traits—as part of redefining your work. But for now, the focus is on YOU, not on what you can *do*. To know clearly what you *want* to do next, you first need to explore your own personhood—your uniqueness—what makes the all-essential *you* thrive and flourish?

For you to be happy and fulfilled in the years ahead, you will need *enjoyment* and *engagement* and *meaning* in your life. All three of these factors are necessary, and all three are distinctive to you, based on your own unique self. Through the interactions and self-reflections of this chapter, you will have the time and opportunity to explore inward—to "mine for the gold." So now it is time to answer the question for yourself: "What has been simmering on the back burner of my heart and soul throughout my life so far?"

Who or What Is Defining Whom?

Retirement requires an identity shift. As such, it is a process, not an event. Although retirement promises to reap rewards, it also harbors challenges, and even hazards. In her article *"Emotional Aspects of Retirement,"* Elizabeth Holtzman says: "In our society, work remains a defining feature of our daily lives and our identity." She adds that because of the sheer numbers of Boomers retiring, "it is more important than ever that they retire successfully" (Holtzman, 2002).

To the degree that our past world of work defined us, keeping us certain and secure, our current (or future) status as retirees can be fraught with all kinds of uncertainties. Yet it is these very uncertainties that open potential windows—opportunities limited only by our level of risk tolerance and our self-allowance to dream and to explore. The transition that must occur at this point is a shift from *having our work define us*, to *having our SELF define our work*.

To discover what the most essential *you* wants to do—what is uniquely meaningful and compelling to you—*you* will need to be the definer. You truly are now in a position to become the "master of your fate," the determiner of your destiny. You will be the one to craft your own happiness, one day at a time.

Journal Entry

I've been thinking about the question "What is my calling?" I read that a calling is "that which we bend to easily—that which comes naturally to us. All we have to do is pay attention."

I found myself writing in response: "I want to empower people to make their lives better, fuller, and more meaningful. I have a special talent and passion for being a bridge. Anything I fully learn myself, I am then to translate and open up to others." This is a deeper vision of my calling than I had been aware of before."

Your SELF in All its Uniqueness

Another year older? You ought to be proud! You want to get boisterous, noistrous, and loud!

Just think of the things that you know how to do, the sorts of things no one can do except you.

Your brain's full of wherefores and who's whos and whys. You think someone else could be nearly as wise?

You're one-of-a-kind, you're uncommonly rare. You can't be replaced 'cause there isn't a spare.

You're another year older, I know that is true. But how many people can say they are you?!   (Dr. Seuss)

Yes, you are one-of-a-kind, and uncommonly rare. But what are the particulars of your uniqueness? And how do those particulars come together into a full picture? The four elements of your SELF to focus on here, and then to collect into a single profile are:

- What are you *like*? (your type and temperament)
- What *engages* you? (your interests)
- What has *meaning* for you? (your values)
- What can you *do*? (your skills and productive traits)

You may have ready answers to most, or even all, of these questions. But the goal here is to go beyond the obvious to a deeper level of self-renewal and personal reawakening. In this chapter the focus will be on the first of these four elements, "What are you like?" The other three questions will be addressed in Chapter 6.

As you re-examine your essential elements, your goal is to arrive at a clearer understanding of your SELF, then expand your mindset and to *expect more* from your life ahead in terms of expressing and fulfilling the true you.

What Are You Like? Your Personality Type

By now, you already know what your personality type is ... or *do* you?! Throughout your life, you may or may not have taken one of the many available personality assessments. Are you an *extrovert*, who is energized by talking and interacting with people, or an *introvert*, happiest when working on projects alone or with a few close associates? Do you tend to be a leader, organizer, or manager—a take-charge kind of person? Or do you prefer to follow directions and complete specific tasks that are assigned to you by someone else?

Do you take pride in being *rational*, and able to find logical solutions to problems? Or do you see your strength in being *caring*, compassionate, and nourishing, a good listener and encourager, aware of how people will feel as a result of a decision? Do you tend to be *spontaneous*, preferring to keep your options open? Or do you prefer *having a plan*, and reaching closure as soon as possible?

One key to career satisfaction is the degree to which there is a match between your personality type and the work that you do. Whatever your type, you can find satisfaction and meaning in many fields. And even within a given profession or pursuit, there may be a aspect of that work that best suits you. Now, as you enter your third phase, what matters most is that whatever you do next is based on a solid understanding of yourself.

A particularly illuminating assessment of personality types is the Myers Briggs, based on Carl Jung's typology. To determine your own personality type, you will be asked to complete a self-assessment based on the Myers Briggs. This will yield a *4-Letter Type Code* that encapsulates your personality type—your foundational SELF. Knowing this code will illuminate your ability to move forward with your own best renewal and reinvention process. Later, you will have an opportunity to go online and take a short version of the test to confirm your self-assessment results.

"Wait a minute!" you say. "I've been there, done that. In my college psych courses, as prerequisites for specific jobs, for my own curiosity, I've taken either this or other similar types of personality profile tests. I already know what my personality type is." Initially I thought so, too. But in the process of writing this book, I decided to re-take the test, to determine if I had changed in the 15 years since I had last taken the assessment. And, in one area, I had! According to Jung, changes like this are not unusual as we mature and develop what he called our "shadow side."

You, too, may be surprised by your new results. Even if your current results prove to be identical to your previous profile, what is most important is that you learn something new about yourself, or perhaps that you come to see the significance of one or more aspects of yourself in a new way. Besides–taking the test is fun!

Determine Your Type through Self-Assessment

In order to assess your own type, you will be asked to select one of two preferences on each of four scales, using a self-assessment that is credited to Ross Reinhold of *Personality Pathways*:

www.PersonalityPathways.com/Type_Inventory.html

For each of the four scales, ask yourself the question provided. Then read the descriptions and make your best judgment based on what you are *really* like, *not* what you think you *should* be like. There are no "right" answers. You may return later to change your choices. And you later will have an opportunity to confirm your selections by taking an online assessment.

The four scales are: Introvert versus Extrovert, Sensing versus iNtuitive, Thinking versus Feeling, and Judging versus Perceiving.

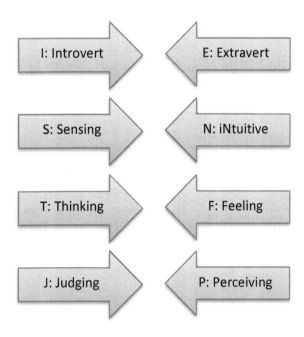

Extravert (E) or Introvert (I)

Question #1:
Which is your *most natural energy orientation,* Extraverted (E) or Introverted (I)?

Every person has two faces. One is directed towards the OUTER world of activities, excitements, people, and things. The other is directed towards the INNER world of thoughts, ideas, and imagination. While these are two different, but complementary, sides of every person's nature, most people express their innate preference for one over the other, particularly when they are tired.

Those who prefer *Extraversion* (E) are drawn to the outer world as their elemental source of energy. Rarely, if ever, do they feel "drained" by extensive amounts of interaction. To recharge their life force, they need to engage with people and activities in the outside world.

Those who prefer *Introversion* (I) gain their primary energy from the inner world of thoughts, ideas, and reflection. When circumstances require them to engage extensively with the outside world, they begin to feel drained, and need to retreat to a more private setting to recharge their batteries.

Extraverted Characteristics
- Act first, think/reflect later
- Feel deprived when cut off from interaction with the outside world
- Are motivated by the outside world of people and things
- Enjoy a wide variety of relationships with people

Introverted Characteristics
- Think/reflect first, act later
- Require "private time" to recharge their batteries
- Are motivated internally
- Demonstrate a mind that can sometimes be so active that it is "closed off" to the outside world
- Prefer one-on-one communication and relationships

87

Sensing (S) or iNtuitive (N)

Question #2:
Which way of *taking in information* is most automatic to you: Sensing (S) or iNtuitive (N)?

The *Sensing* (S) side of our brain notices the sights, sounds, smells and all the sensory details of the *present*. It categorizes, organizes, records, and stores the specifics from the here and now. It is reality-based, dealing with "what IS." It also provides the specific details of memory and recollections from *past* events.

The *INtuitive* (N) side of our brain seeks to form, understand and interpret overall patterns from all the information that is collected, and records these patterns and relationships. It is imaginative and conceptual and speculates on future possibilities.

While both kinds of perceiving are necessary, and we all do use both sensing and intuiting, we each instinctively tend to favor one over the other as seemingly more automatic or natural to us. Those of us who prefer *Sensing* (S) as our means for taking in information, favor clear, tangible data and information that fits in well with our direct here-and-now experience. Our perceptions are focused on what we observe directly through our senses—what we can see, hear, feel, smell, or taste—to determine what is going on at the moment. We trust what can be measured or documented and focus on what is real and concrete.

In contrast, those of us who prefer *iNtuition* (N) are drawn to information that is more abstract, conceptual, big-picture, and that represents imaginative possibilities for the future. We look for meaning in all things, trusting our inspirations and hunches. When we look at a situation, we want to know what it means, what its consequences might be, and how we might make it different or better.

Sensing Characteristics
- Mentally live in the now; attend to present opportunities
- Use common sense; create practical solutions
- Recall facts and past events in rich detail
- Do well when improvising from past experience

- Like clear, concrete information; dislike guessing from "fuzzy" facts

Intuitive Characteristics
- Mentally live in the future; anticipate possibilities
- Use imagination to invent new possibilities instinctively
- Recall facts and past events with an emphasis on patterns, contexts, and connections
- Do well when improvising from theoretical understanding
- Are comfortable with ambiguous data; guess at meanings

Thinking (T) or Feeling (F)

Question #3:
Which way of *making choices* is most natural to you: Thinking (T) or Feeling (F)?

The *Thinking* (T) side of our brain analyzes information in a *detached*, objective fashion, operating from factual principles to deduce and form conclusions systematically. It is our logical nature. The *Feeling* (F) side of our brain forms conclusions in an *attached* and somewhat global manner, based on likes/dislikes, impact on others, and human and aesthetic values. It is our subjective nature.

While everyone uses both means of forming conclusions, each has a natural bias towards one over the other so that when we are given conflicting directions, one side is the natural trump card or tiebreaker. Those who prefer *Thinking* (T) naturally prefer to make decisions in an objective, logical, and analytical manner, with an emphasis on tasks and results to be accomplished.

Those whose preference is for *Feeling* (F) make their decisions in a somewhat global, visceral, harmony and value-oriented way, paying attention to the impact of decisions and actions on themselves and other people.

Thinking Characteristics
- Instinctively search for facts and logic in a decision situation

- Naturally notice the tasks and work to be accomplished
- Are easily able to provide an objective and critical analysis
- Accept conflict as a natural, normal part of relationships
- Make decisions logically, through analysis

Feeling Characteristics
- Instinctively employ personal feelings and impact on people in decision situations
- Innately sensitive to peoples' needs and reactions
- Naturally seek consensus and popular opinions
- Are unsettled by conflict or disharmony
- Make decisions globally, based on values

Perceiving (P) or Judging (J)

Question #4:
What is your preferred way to *take action*: through Perceiving (P) or Judging (J)?

All people use both *Judging* (*Thinking* or *Feeling*) and *Perceiving* (*Sensing* or *INtuition*) processes to store information, organize their thoughts, make decisions, take actions and manage their lives. Yet one of these processes (*Judging* or *Perceiving*) tends to take the lead to determine the way we take action in relationship to the outside world. Those who take action using a *Judging* (J) style, approach the outside world *with a plan*. They feel compelled to organize their surroundings, be prepared, make decisions, and reach closure and completion. They need to know in advance what will happen and how.

Those who take action using a *Perceiving* (P) style take a wait-and-see approach, accepting the outside world *as it comes.* They adopt and adapt, and are flexible, open-ended, and receptive to new opportunities and changing game plans.

Judging Characteristics
- Plan many of the details in advance before moving into action
- Focus on task-related action

- Complete each meaningful segment before moving on
- Work best when able to keep ahead of deadlines
- Naturally use target dates and standard routines to manage life

Perceiving Characteristics
- Are comfortable moving into action without a plan
- Plan on-the-go
- Like to multitask, have variety, mix work and play
- Are naturally tolerant of time pressure
- Work best close to deadlines
- Instinctively avoid commitments that interfere with variety, flexibility, and freedom

Your 4-Letter Personality Type Code

Circle your *4-Letter Type Code* here, according to your self-assessment. Then read on to learn more about what this means about you and what suits you best, workwise and otherwise.

ESTJ	ESTP	ENFP	ENTP
ISTJ	ISTP	INFP	INTP
ESFJ	ESFP	ENFJ	ENTJ
ISFJ	ISFP	INFJ	INTJ

Determine Your Type Online

To confirm your self-assessment, go to the *16Personalities.com* website and complete the online version of the *Myers/Briggs Personality Profile*. Print out your type description and read it closely, highlighting important points and insights. Note that there are multiple tabs for your results, including:

- Personality

- Strengths & Weaknesses

- Emotions

- Relationships

- Friends

- As a Parent

- Careers

- Workplace

- Conclusion

Consider the *Careers* and the *Workplace* analyses most carefully. Once you have highlighted the key points, compose and write down several "I Statement" about what is essential to you, given your inherent personality. Keep these close at hand as you proceed through the remainder of the shifting gears process.

The goal is to increase your level of awareness of who you are, including your prevailing strengths and imperatives, particularly as these relate to your options for life and work after retirement. Ask yourself whether this description, based on your 4-letter code, resonates with you.

Your Temperament

The *4-Letter Code* divides up into 16 possible personality *types*. These 16 can be meaningfully grouped into four *temperaments*:

- SJ (Sensing/Judging)—Guardians

- SP (Sensing/Perceiving)—Experiencers

- NF (iNtuitive/Feeling)—Givers

- NT (iNtuitive/Thinking)—Thinkers

Based on your own *4-Letter Personality Type Code*, determine which of the four temperaments represents you best. Also note the main descriptor for your temperament: *Guardian, Experiencer, Giver,* or *Thinker*. Then read about your own temperament, as well as the other three. The benefits of reading about all four temperaments are:

1) To determine if another temperament may better describe you than the one indicated by your results;

2) To understand others whose temperaments differ from yours.

SJ	SP	NF	NT
Guardian	Experiencer	Giver	Thinker
ESTJ	ESTP	ENFP	ENTP
ISTJ	ISTP	INFP	INTP
ESFJ	ESFP	ENFJ	ENTJ
ISFJ	ISFP	INFJ	INTJ

Guardian (SJ): Service & Duty Keeper

All four types that contain S and J (Sensing and Judging) are known as "guardians" or "traditionalists" (ESTJ, ISTJ, ESFJ and ISFJ). This group comprises 46% of the American population. Their compulsion is *TO BE USEFUL*.

If you are a *Guardian*, you are drawn to base your perceptions on what your five senses tell you–facts, data, and previous experience. You value law and order, security, rules, and conformity, and are driven by a strong motivation to serve society's needs.

As a *Guardian* you have a need to belong, to serve, and to do the right thing, seeking stability, orderliness, cooperation, consistency, and reliability. You are practical, organized, thorough, and systematic, and take great pride in doing something right the first time and every time. You can be counted on to get the job done.

The four types who share the *Guardian* (SJ) temperament are:

- **Inspector** (ISTJ): Has an abiding sense of responsibility for doing what needs to be done in the here-and-now. Exhibits excellent organizing abilities and command of the facts.
- **Protector** (ISFJ): Takes practical action to help others. Brings an aura of quiet warmth, caring, and dependability to all they do.
- **Supervisor** (ESTJ): Needs to analyze and bring into logical order the outer world of events, people, and things.
- **Provider** (ESFJ): Expresses active and intense caring about people. Takes action naturally to help others, to organize the world around them, and to get things done.

If you are a *Guardian*, which specific type descriptor is yours according to your 4-Letter Personality Type Code: *Inspector, Protector, Supervisor*, or *Provider*?

MY DESCRIPTOR: _____

Artisan/Experiencer (SP): Teacher of Freedom & Joy

All four of the types that contain S and P (Sensing and Perceiving) share the "artisan" or "experiencer" temperament (ISTP, ISFP, ESTP or ESFP). This group comprises about 27% of the American population. Their compulsion is *TO ACT FREELY*.

If you are an *Artisan/Experiencer*, you are among the most adventurous of the four temperaments, living for action, impulse, and the present moment. Your focus is on the immediate situation, and you have the ability to assess what needs to be done and move into action.

You value freedom and spontaneity, and are risk-taking, adaptable, easy going, and practical. You like moving from one challenge to the next. Because you can see clearly what is happening, you are agile at seizing opportunities. You are excellent at recognizing practical problems and approaching them with flexibility, courage, and resourcefulness, and are not afraid to take risks or improvise as needed.

Four types share the *Artisan/Experiencer* (SP) temperament:

- **Crafter** (ISTP): Driven to understand how things and phenomena work in the real world in order to make the best and most effective use of these realities. Logical, realistic, and a natural troubleshooter.
- **Composer** (ISFP): Exhibits a deep-felt caring for living things, combined with a quietly playful, sometimes adventurous, approach to life. Expresses warmth and concern in very practical ways, preferring action to words.
- **Promoter** (ESTP): Has an acute sense of how objects, events, and people in the world work. Excited by continuous involvement in new hands-on activities and the pursuit of real-life challenges.
- **Performer** (ESFP): Seeks excitement through continuous involvement in new activities and relationships. Has

deep concern for people, showing this caring through warm and pragmatic gestures of helping. Prefers to experience and accept life rather than to judge or organize it.

> If you are an *Artisan/Experiencer*, what is your specific descriptor according to your 4-Letter Personality Type Code: *Crafter, Composer, Promoter,* or *Performer?*
>
> MY DESCRIPTOR: _____

Giver (NF): Bearer of Truth & Meaning

All four of the types that contain N and F (iNtuitive and Feeling) are known as "givers" or "idealists" (INFJ, INFP, ENFP, ENFJ). This group comprises about 16% of the American population. Their compulsion is *to "BE."*

If you are a *Giver*, you are highly concerned about personal growth and understanding, both for yourself and for others. You are on a perpetual search for the meaning of life, placing a very high value on authenticity and integrity in people and relationships, and focusing on human potential.

You are an excellent communicator and can be an effective catalyst for positive change. Knowing instinctively how to bring out the best in others, you understand how to motivate others to do their highest level of work. You are excellent at resolving conflicts and helping people work together more effectively.

The four types who share the *Giver* (NF) temperament are:

- **Counselor** (INFJ): Dominated by the inner world of possibilities, ideas, and symbols. Has a deep interest in creative expression as well as issues of spirituality and human development.
- **Healer**: (INFP): Captured by a deep-felt caring and idealism about people. A skilled communicator who is naturally drawn to ideas that embody a concern for human potential.
- **Champion** (ENFP): Thrives on what is possible and new— ideas, people, activities. Deeply concerned about people.

- **Teacher** (ENFJ): Takes action naturally and conscientiously to care for others, organize the world around them, and get things done. Enjoys helping others develop their potential.

If you are a *Giver*, what specific descriptor is yours according to your 4-Letter Personality Type Code: *Counselor, Healer, Champion,* or *Teacher?*

MY DESCRIPTOR: _____

Thinker (NT): Provider of Logic & Understanding

All four of the types that contain N and T (INtuitive and Thinking) are known as "thinkers" or "conceptualizers" (INTJ, INTP, ENTP, ENTJ). This group comprises approximately 10% of the American population. Their compulsion is *TO IMPROVE.*

If you are a Thinker, you are among the most independent of the four temperaments, driven by an urge to acquire knowledge and to set very high standards for yourself and others. You are naturally curious, and usually see many sides of an argument or issue. As a Thinker, you are excellent at seeing possibilities, understanding complexities, and designing solutions to real or hypothetical problems. You enjoy logically analyzing possibilities to solve problems. With your vision, you can be a great innovator. You like to be challenged, and excel at strategizing, planning, and building systems to accomplish your goals.

The four types who share the *Thinker* (NT) temperament are:
- **Mastermind** (INTJ): Attends to the inner world of possibilities and thoughts—ideas are the substance of life. Driven to understand and to know. Works intensely to transform visions into realities.
- **Architect** (INTP): Needs to make sense of the world, naturally questioning and critiquing ideas and events in a quest for understanding. Logical and analytical. Enjoys opportunities to be creative.
- **Inventor** (ENTP): Compelled by the outer world of possibilities. Energetic and enthusiastic. Seeks patterns and meaning in the world, having a deep need to analyze, to understand, and to know the nature of things.

- **Field Marshal** (ENTJ): Driven to analyze and bring into logical order the outer world of events, people, and things. Prefers a world that is structured and organized. A natural leader who builds conceptual models as plans for strategic action.

If you are a *Thinker*, what specific descriptor is yours according to your 4-Letter Personality Type Code: *Mastermind, Architect, Inventor, or Field Marshal*?

MY DESCRIPTOR: _____

Why Do Type and Temperament Matter?

In your career life, when it is probable that much was defined by your career, your employer, your clients, your family demands, you, like many others, may have set your essential self aside as you progressed and advanced, adapting to the requirements and needs that drove your work and life.

You now are entering a time when, as we have discussed, external definitions drop away and YOU become the definer. To the degree that you know yourself at a deeper level and give yourself full permission to BE yourself as a condition of your retirement work and career, your work and life ahead will be highly fulfilling, even remarkable.

Now that you know yourself, your type and temperament, your needs and compulsions, your natural abilities and instinctive ways of operating, you have achieved the all-essential first step. But *knowing* is not all that is important now. The other part of the equation is *acting*. Now that *you* are the definer, it is time to expect more. Determine that your work from this point forward will be work that fully expresses and fulfills you, in all your uniqueness.

Partners as Separate Individuals

Again, this step of rediscovering your SELF is a dual process for couples. It is essential that each of you go through this discovery independently. At this point the question is "What are you *like*?" (your type and temperament).

Later you will, again independently, look at: What *engages* you? (your interests); What has *meaning* for you? (your values); What can you *do*? (your skills and productive traits)

After completing this step on your own, it then will be time to discuss with your partner your major findings about your unique self. "Stand together, yet not too near together: For the pillars of the temple stand apart, And the oak tree and the cypress grow not in each other's shadow" (Kahlil Gibran).

SNAPSHOT: Jewel and Harvey

Jewel and Harvey ran a lucrative business throughout their working lives, selling portable hot houses, with all the components necessary to germinate plants successfully in any climate. When they reached a point where they had earned as much money as they would ever need, and then some, they sold their business by posting an ad in the Wall Street Journal with the headline." All the Money We Need..." After interviewing potential buyers until they found one they were willing to entrust with their business—their labor of love—they launched themselves into their next life—racecar driving.

At first only Harvey joined the racing circuit, both working on race cars and racing them. He bought his own racecar and earned the title "Rookie of the Year." One of his most prized possessions was a photo of himself, seated in his racecar wearing his helmet, with fellow racing enthusiast Paul Newman leaning into the cockpit to talk with him.

Jewel soon joined Harvey in the world of racing, owning and racing her own car, of course. They both competed regularly in races until the year Jewell was in a racing accident. Another car rolled up over hers, crushing her hand as it grasped the steering wheel, leaving her in a cast and unable to race until her hand had had time to heal.

At that point, Harvey surprised Jewell with an all-expenses-paid trip to hike the Himalayas. Jewel claimed that the real reason Harvey gave her this incredible gift was that he felt guilty. Why? Because

> *during the time she was out of commission, he had sole use of her racecar as well as his own. According to Jewel, "Harvey always liked my car better than he liked his own."*
>
> *What aspect of Harvey and Jewel's personality types and temperaments were better expressed by their retirement careers than by their earlier ties to their business venture? Likely their Artisan/Experiencer selves—their adventurous temperament—living for action, impulse, and the present moment.*

And So...

What fun you have had analyzing who you actually are versus who you thought you were, or who you should be. What surprises did you uncover about yourself? Perhaps you were a bit caught off guard because your actual psychological profiles did not always align with your conventional, comfortable vision of who you thought you were based on what you have done in your life so far.

Maybe your type and temperament descriptions resonated with what you have suspected about yourself for a while. Or perhaps you are confused now because your results indicate that you seem to have undergone a shift in values or personality. So which version of you are you really?

Did your SELF find expression during your career years? Or were you adapting to work that would have been a better fit for another personality type and temperament?

Now is not the time to abandon ship, to "throw out the baby with the bath," nor to plunge into a deep chasm of denial. Just let the data and facts speak to you for a while. Even better, share your newly discovered persona with a close friend or your partner. And carry your discoveries forward into the remaining steps in the reinvention process.

Open up your heart, mind and psyche to the possibility that perhaps, just perhaps, these descriptions accurately reveal your authentic self, even if this is a re-discovery, or new discovery. Or possibly this self-portrait is still an incomplete picture of who you really are.

Certainly, there is more to be added to your self-portrait. What about the essential ingredients of:

- What engages you? (your interests)
- What has meaning for you? (your values)
- What are your signature character strengths (your core)
- What can you do? (your skills and productive traits)

These three, when combined with your Type and Temperament, will complete your profile, and guide you as you envision and design your own life and work after retirement. So, we will set out to explore and add these remaining four elements in the next chapter.

CHAPTER 6:
Step #4: Rediscover Your WORK

Long before my sister and I understood classical music and opera, my dear Aunt Hannah, who was bent on serving us a healthy dose of "culture" at an early age, dragged us, reluctant though we were, to a series of classical concerts at our local community center. After a few unsuccessful attempts, and several less than pleasant "incidents," she decided that perhaps we were too young or too hopelessly bourgeois to ever have an appreciation for these finer pursuits.

But, never one to abandon her determination to "culturize" us, she decided to try her luck taking us to a Broadway show—*Auntie Mame*. This captivating musical comedy was my first encounter with live theatre, and I was hooked. From then on, I became an ardent fan of all facets of live theatre. This passion has remained with me to this day.

Likewise, my best friend's dad was a classical violinist. She was raised in a home where it was taken for granted that she and her brother would learn, and become proficient at mastering, a musical instrument. She became an expert clarinet player, regularly recruited as a member of various local musical groups. But more, she developed a love and appreciation of all types of classical music—an interest that has become one of the centerpieces of her cultural life.

My friend and I represent examples of *nurture*'s influence over the interests, talents, and passions to which we are introduced early in life and that continue to develop throughout our adulthood. These interests enrich our lives and provide hours of enjoyment. And now they may come to bear on our work rediscovery process.

As we move ahead to *Step #4: Rediscover Your Work*, you will be asked to carry forward the "what you are like" dimension of your SELF from *Step #3*, then reexamine and integrate five other dimensions: your interests, values, character strengths, skills and traits. Whether through nature or nurture, these additional dimensions play a critical role towards forming an authentic, rich, multidimensional picture of your full and essential SELF as they guide your progress towards your rediscovered work and life after retirement.

What *Engages* You? Your Interests

Although you may have had some surprises when you reexplored your personality type and temperament and reinvented your SELF, certainly you already know what your interests are. Or do you? Interests are key to contentment and fulfillment in work as well as life. Time spent in pursuit of your interests is engaging, sometimes to the point where you enter what positive psychologists call "flow," losing all track of time because you are so engrossed.

It is important to understand that your *interests* to date have been heavily influenced by your history. These interests may or may not have been generated by your own unique SELF. "How so?" you ask. Good question. Your parents were your initial window to the discovery of your *interests*. Based on their financial resources, educational and cultural backgrounds, geographical location and time commitments, your parents offered you what they considered to be desirable and worthwhile activities. As a child, you tested these activities, willingly or unwillingly, and formed your own responses to them.

Once you were exposed to an activity that captured you, the degree to which it became an *interest* for you depended heavily on whether your efforts in that direction were reinforced, positively or negatively, or even ignored. Positive reinforcement in the form of praise, accomplished goals, improved self-concept, and sometimes monetary reward, established a particular activity as an interest. Negative reinforcement, including punishment, negative remarks, denial of opportunities, and damage to self-concept, led to a dampening of interest, or even an aversion, to an activity. If your parents ignored your efforts, this had an even more powerful stifling effect than that of negative reinforcement.

Reinforcement, both positive and negative, had a cumulative effect over time, determining which of your explored activities turned into sustained *interests*. Other role models–people whose success you admired and wanted to emulate—were another powerful source of influence as you fashioned your life *interests*. Thus, through a combination of influences–exploration, reinforcement, attention, and modeling–your interests formed and became a part of you.

All of this tells you something important about your SELF and your interests, as you have come to know them. Since you needed *both* the exposure, and also the positive reinforcement and attention to your efforts in order that an activity you experienced became one of your *interests*, this means that some of your *potential* interests you may not have discovered YET. So, although your interests may seem fixed and stable at this point in your life, you may find that they will expand in important ways if you open yourself to exploring and discovering additional ones. And these as yet undiscovered potential interests may turn out to be among your most passionate pursuits.

To identify and measure your interests, and the predominant categories in which they fit, begin by asking yourself what you genuinely like to do. According to Dr. John Holland, there are six principal categories of people according to their interests:

- **Realistic Interests: the DOERS**
  Doers prefer practical, hands-on, physical activities, with tangible results, and generally have athletic or mechanical abilities. They enjoy working with objects, machines, tools, animals or plants—building, fixing, repairing, caring and cultivating.
- **Investigative Interests: the THINKERS**
  Thinkers prefer to solve abstract problems in science-related or engineering subjects. Curious about the physical world including why and how it works, they enjoy intellectual challenge and

original or unconventional ideas. They are engaged by work that involves observing, learning, investigating, analyzing, evaluating, and solving problems.

- **Artistic Interests: the CREATORS**
  Creators prefer unstructured situations that offer them opportunities for self-expression of ideas and concepts through different artistic media such as art, music, theater, film, dance, multimedia, or writing. They have artistic, innovative or intuitional abilities, and enjoy using imagination and creativity.

- **Social Interests: the HELPERS**
  Helpers prefer work that engages them in direct service that helps people—advising, counseling, coaching, mentoring, teaching, guiding. Skilled with words, they are drawn to humanistic or social causes, and like to work with people—to inform, enlighten, help, train, develop, or cure them.

- **Enterprising Interests: the PERSUADERS**
  Persuaders prefer business situations where they engage in persuasion, selling, or otherwise exercise influence over others. They are enthusiastic, energetic, assertive, self-confident, and like working with people, and are drawn to management, leadership or marketing roles.

- **Conventional Interests: the ORGANIZERS**
  Organizers become highly engaged when working in a structured business situation involving data analysis, finance, planning, and organizational tasks. They value efficiency and order, and have an exceptional ability to carry out projects in detail and follow through on instructions.

SNAPSHOT: Sherry

Sherry started out as a secondary art teacher, but her heart wasn't in it. She loved the work of a graphic artist and wanted so much to start her own business. After a few years, her husband convinced her to take the leap to strike out on her own.

As fate would have it, the entire world of graphic design was shifting from an analog to a digital platform. Sherry enrolled in a computer-based graphic design program at her local community college. The rest is history. Sherry developed a web site, advertised locally, and gradually gained a base of clientele.

But that's not the best part of this story. In the meantime, Sherry became interested in restoring antique cars. This endeavor captured her need for challenge and problem solving. Over time, she found herself spending more time finding cars to restore, and less time working as a graphic artist.

At first Sherry outsourced the mechanical aspects of her car restoration projects. But she gradually became adept at performing the aesthetic aspects herself. Twelve years ago, Sherry retired from graphic arts and turned over her business to her two children. She now spends her time on her passion. So far, she has restored seven cars. Her goal is to leave one vehicle to each of her grandchildren. The family teases her whenever a new grandchild is born, asking what she is going to do if her grandchildren begin to outnumber her restored autos. But, so far, Sherry is ahead of schedule!

Self-Assess Your Interests

In order to determine your own current and expanded interests, take some time now to complete the *Interest Self-Assessment* check sheet below and/or the online assessment at the website provided. The purpose of this exercise is to "mine" your past for interests that have emerged so far, and then to envision any further interests you may want to add in the future. These interest categories are the keys to what does or does not, will or will not, engage you.

Self-Assessment Instructions: For each item in the following six tables, check those that describe you *now* in terms of what you *are like*, as well as what you *can do* and what you *like to do*. Then expand your lists, going back to tag anything that you may want to explore in the *future*, but may have not yet experienced.

Use a different color pen for these future items so that you will be able to tell them apart from your past and present ones. Some of your most compelling interests may be ones you added as you expanded your interests list. After checking off items, total up each category. Include in your totals the items you add when you expand your list.

When you have a total for each category of interest, identify the *three* categories that scored the highest. These combine to create the most accurate picture of your interests.

Interests Self-Assessment

REALISTIC (R)					
Are You...		**Can You...**		**Do You Like To...**	
☐	Practical	☐	Fix electrical things	☐	Tinker with mechanics
☐	Athletic	☐	Solve mechanical problems	☐	Work outdoors
☐	Straight forward	☐	Pitch a tent	☐	Be physically active
☐	Mechanically inclined	☐	Play a sport	☐	Use your hands
☐	A nature lover	☐	Read a blueprint	☐	Build things
☐	Good with tools and machinery	☐	Work on cars	☐	Repair things
			R Total =		
INVESTIGATIVE (I)					
Are You...		**Can You...**		**Do You Like To...**	
☐	Inquisitive	☐	Think abstractly	☐	Explore ideas
☐	Analytical	☐	Solve math problems	☐	Use computers
☐	Scientific	☐	Understand physical theories	☐	Work independently
☐	Observant	☐	Do complex calculations	☐	Perform lab experiments
☐	Precise	☐	Work on cars	☐	Read scientific or technical magazines
☐	Curious	☐	Analyze data	☐	Do puzzles
			I Total =		

ARTISTIC (A)		
Are You...	**Can You...**	**Do You Like To...**
☐ Creative	☐ Sketch, draw, paint	☐ Attend concerts, theaters, art exhibits
☐ Intuitive	☐ Sing ,play a musical instrument	☐ Read fiction, plays, poetry
☐ Imaginative	☐ Write stories, plays, poetry	☐ Work on crafts
☐ Innovative	☐ Design fashions or interiors	☐ Take photographs
☐ An individualist	☐ Compose music	☐ Express yourself creatively
☐ Original	☐ Act, dance	☐ Design gardens or landscaping
	A Total =	

SOCIAL (S)		
Are You...	**Can You...**	**Do You Like To...**
☐ Friendly	☐ Teach/train others	☐ Work in groups
☐ Helpful	☐ Express yourself clearly	☐ Help people with problems
☐ Idealistic	☐ Lead a group discussion	☐ Participate in meetings
☐ Insightful	☐ Mediate disputes	☐ Do volunteer service
☐ Outgoing	☐ Plan and supervise an activity	☐ Work with young people
☐ Understanding	☐ Cooperate well with others	☐ Play team sports
	S Total =	

ENTERPRISING (E)		
Are You...	**Can You...**	**Do You Like To...**
☐ Self-confident	☐ Initiate projects	☐ Make decisions affecting others
☐ Assertive	☐ Convince people to do things your way	☐ Be elected to office
☐ Sociable	☐ Sell things	☐ Win a leadership or sales award
☐ Persuasive	☐ Give talks or speeches	☐ Start your own political campaign
☐ Enthusiastic	☐ Organize activities and events	☐ Meet influential people
☐ Energetic	☐ Lead a group	☐ Promote ideas
E Total =		

CONVENTIONAL (C)		
Are You...	**Can You...**	**Do You Like To...**
☐ Well groomed	☐ Work well within a system	☐ Follow clearly defined procedures
☐ Accurate	☐ Do a lot of paper work in a short time	☐ Work with data
☐ Numerically in-clined	☐ Keep accurate rec-ords	☐ Work with numbers
☐ Methodical	☐ Use a computer ef-ficiently	☐ Type or take shorthand
☐ Conscientious	☐ Write effective business letters	☐ Be responsible for details
☐ Efficient	☐ Assure quality and accuracy	☐ Organize
C Total =		

Assess Your Interests Online

To confirm your self-assessment results, complete the free assessment on the Career Zone site at:

https://www.cacareerzone.org/ip/

For each of 180 items, you will be asked to click on "**L**" if you think you would LIKE to do the activity, "**D**" if you think you would DISLIKE the activity and "**?**" If you are not sure. As you select your response to each item, include both your current and your expanded interests. Mark as "Like" tasks that have interested you in the past and also those you think may interest you in the future. When you have completed the online assessment, you will receive immediate results, showing your top three categories of interests.

Compare these results to your self-assessment, then highlight the boxes for each of your three top-scoring categories on the diagram below. The first letter of each of your top three interests will be your *3-Letter Interest Code.*

Interests Diagram

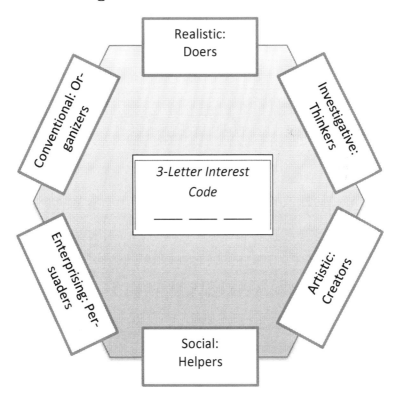

What Your Interest Results Tell You

What do these results reveal about your SELF and your WORK? Your *3-Letter Interest Code* provides essential clarification to ensure that you will be able to choose work that engages and satisfies you. Consider each of your three categories separately, then in combination.

If one part of your interest code is *R (Realistic)*, you need to work with your hands, making, fixing, assembling, or building things, using and operating equipment, tools or machines. If a part of your code is *I (Investigative)*, your work needs to challenge your mind in order to keep you interested. You like to discover and research ideas... To observe, investigate and experiment... To ask questions and solve problems. If a part of your code is *A (Artistic)*, it is essential that your work enables you to express yourself through creating and designing things. You like to use words, art, music, or drama to communicate and perform.

Suppose a part of your code is *S (Social)*. Your work needs to support the well-being and welfare of others, through teaching or training them, informing or helping them, healing or curing them. Is one part of your code *E (Enterprising)*? If so, your work needs to include influencing and encouraging others. You have a need to work with and to lead people. If *C (Conventional)* is part of your code, you are most engaged when working outdoors or when carrying out work that depends on you for the organizing, planning and follow through.

Consider, too, what each opposite indicates. For example, if you are an *Artistic (A)*, but you do routine work that requires that you replicate designs created by others, you will *not* be engaged. If you are a *Social (S)* who operates equipment, tools or machines to complete tasks or produce products, you will *not* be engaged because you are not working with people. If you are an *Investigative (I)* who teaches or trains group after group, repeating the same concepts over and over, you will *not* be engaged unless you are being mentally challenged. In each of these cases you will *not* be fully engaged because the work does not capture your interest at a very fundamental level.

What Has *Meaning* for You? Your Values

Many things are meaningful, in theory. But for each of us, the legacy we choose to leave varies according to what is most uniquely meaningful to *us*. And what is most meaningful is based on our *values*.

The word *"values"* is a broad term that means different things to different people. Most values are qualities that are universally recognized to be worth pursuing in life. But here we are talking about what you, *yourself*, value *most*—what are the values to which you particularly want to dedicate your energies and skills, talents, and time, during your lifetime? What is it that you uniquely care about leaving better than you found it in this world? What will be your legacy?

In order to determine your own values, particularly as they apply to the work you do, take some time now to complete the self-assessment below. Then visit the website provided in the *"Assess Your Values Online"* section that follows to complete a free online assessment.

Self-Assess Your Values

Self-Assessment Instructions: For the statements that follow, circle a number 1 to 5 to indicate how important each item is to you. Many items may seem to be of value in general. But the key question is which are of highest value to you personally? When you have completed this exercise, total up the numbers for each grouping.

> 1 = Unimportant
> 2 = Of Little Importance
> 3 = Moderately Important
> 4 = Important
> 5 = Very Important

Values Self-Assessment

	TOTAL
CREATIVITY: Work that permits me to invent new things, design new products, or develop new ideas. I value the opportunity to create something new. 5 4 3 2 1 I value being able to contribute new ideas. 5 4 3 2 1	

MANAGEMENT: Work that permits me to plan and lay out work for others. I value the opportunity to use leadership abilities. 　　5　4　3　2　1 I value being able to plan and organize the work of others. 　　5　4　3　2　1	**TOTAL**
ACHIEVEMENT: Work that gives me a feeling of accomplishment doing a job well. I value the feeling of doing a good day's work. 　　5　4　3　2　1 I value knowing by results that I have done a good job. 　　5　4　3　2　1	**TOTAL**
WAY OF LIFE: Work that permits me to live the life I choose and be the type of person I wish to be. I value the opportunity to be the kind of person I would like to be. 　　5　4　3　2　1 I value being able to lead the kind of life I most enjoy. 　　5　4　3　2　1	**TOTAL**
ASSOCIATES: Work that brings me into contact with fellow workers I like. I value being able to feel like one of the gang. 　　5　4　3　2　1 I value having good connections with fellow workers. 　　5　4　3　2　1	**TOTAL**

	TOTAL
AESTHETIC: Work that permits me to contribute beauty to the world. I value the opportunity to make use of my artistic ability. 5 4 3 2 1 I value being able to add beauty to the world. 5 4 3 2 1	
INDEPENDENCE: Work that permits me to work my own way, as fast or slow as I wish. I value being able to have freedom in my area. 5 4 3 2 1 I value the opportunity to make my own decisions. 5 4 3 2 1	
VARIETY: Work that provides me an opportunity to do different types of tasks. I value not being required to do the same thing all the time. 5 4 3 2 1 I value the opportunity to work at a variety of tasks. 5 4 3 2 1	
ALTRUISM: Work that enables me to contribute to the welfare of others. I value having opportunities to help others. 5 4 3 2 1 I value adding to the well-being of other people. 5 4 3 2 1	

INTELLECTUAL STIMULATION: Work that provides opportunity for independent thinking and to learn how and why things work. I value being challenged to solve problems. 　　　5　4　3　2　1 I value being required to remain mentally alert. 　　　5　4　3　2　1	TOTAL
SCORE TOTALS: Add together the numbers for each category. 1–4　　　Of Little Importance 5–7　　　Important 8–10　　Very Important	
Highlight your *top five*. Also note any additional categories where your total was in the "Very Important" range (8 to 10).	

Assess Your Values Online

If you would prefer to take a version of this assessment that is self-scoring, or to confirm your results from the self-assessment, use the free assessment at WhatsNext.com (type or copy/paste URL):

https://www.whatsnext.com/life-values-self-assessment-test/

Top Five Values

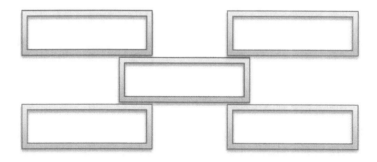

What Are Your Signature Character Strengths?

Determining your *Signature Character Strengths* is essential to designing a retirement life and work in which you will thrive. These characteristics differ from your other strengths, such as skills, talents, and interests. They describe the positive aspects of who you are, reflecting your "core"—the real you.

To the degree that you put these strengths to use, you will be engaged and energized. These strengths underlie your sense of well-being and happiness and enhance your prospects of flourishing. They enable you to overcome problems and improve your relationships by bringing you closer to others and aiding in mutual connection.

The 24 total *Signature Strengths* fall into the six categories of:

1. *Wisdom*
2. *Courage*
3. *Temperance*
4. *Transcendence*
5. *Humanity*
6. *Justice*

WISDOM				
Creativity	Curiosity	Judgment	Love of Learning	Perspective
COURAGE				
Bravery	Perseverance	Honesty	Zest	
TEMPERANCE				
Forgiveness	Humility	Prudence	Self-Regulation	
TRANSCENDENCE				
Appreciation of Beauty	Gratitude	Hope	Humor	Spirituality

HUMANITY				
Love	Kindness	Social Intelligence		
JUSTICE				
Teamwork	Fairness	Leadership		

Assess Your Signature Character Strengths Online

Take a free online assessment of your *Signature Strengths* to determine for yourself the positive aspects of who you are, how you are most engaged and energized, and how you might make the greatest contribution. Use the 15-minute survey on the *Via Character* site:

https://www.viacharacter.org/www/Character-Strengths

Signature Character Strengths

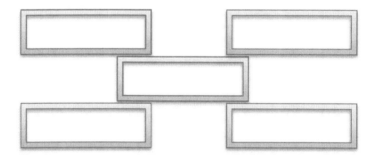

What Can You *Do*? Your Skills, Strengths and Traits

Think about the marketable skills you developed during your career. Make a preliminary list of the skills you already have to offer. Include not only those skills used in your work, but also those you used when you were in school or as a community member or volunteer, as well as those you used as part of your employment. Note your people skills, as well as your mental and physical skills.

People often confuse *skills* with *traits*. If an item is something you can *do*, list it as a *skill*. If it is a positive personal *characteristic*, list it as a *trait*. For example, you may have *skill* at "building," and the *trait* of being "resourceful" when you are building.

Skills Inventory

Using Your Hands					
☐	Assembling	☐	Building	☐	Operating machinery
☐	Fixing	☐	Repairing	☐	Refurbishing
☐		☐		☐	

Using Words					
☐	Writing	☐	Speaking	☐	Training
☐	Reading	☐	Editing	☐	Ghostwriting
☐		☐		☐	

Using Numbers					
☐	Calculating	☐	Computing	☐	Analyzing
☐	Managing money	☐	Taking inventory	☐	Keeping financial records
☐		☐		☐	

Using Intuition					
☐	Sizing up a person	☐	Sizing up a situation	☐	Acting on gut reactions
☐	Showing foresight	☐	Having insight	☐	Sensing what lies ahead
☐		☐		☐	

Using Analytical Thinking					
☐	Researching	☐	Classifying	☐	Organizing
☐	Gathering information	☐	Problem-solving	☐	Diagnosing
☐		☐		☐	

Using Creativity		
☐ Inventing	☐ Creating	☐ Designing
☐ Developing	☐ Improvising	☐ Adapting
☐	☐	☐

Using Helpfulness		
☐ Listening	☐ Counseling	☐ Understanding
☐ Building trust	☐ Developing rapport	☐ Guiding
☐	☐	☐

Using Artistic Abilities		
☐ Acting	☐ Singing/dancing	☐ Painting
☐ Fashioning	☐ Composing music	☐ Playing a musical instrument
☐	☐	☐

Using Leadership		
☐ Organizing	☐ Directing	☐ Making decisions
☐ Negotiating	☐ Persuading	☐ Promoting
☐	☐	☐

Using Follow-Through		
☐ Classifying	☐ Recording data	☐ Filing & retrieving
☐ Carrying out plans	☐ Following instructions	☐ Attending to details
☐	☐	☐

Now think beyond what you currently can do to what you might want to add. Are there skills that you have not developed YET, but have always wanted to acquire? Or are there skills you developed in the past but set aside and now would like to rekindle or expand? Return to your *Skills Inventory* using a different color pen and add these other skills to your list. The skills you add when you expand your list may be the ones that will excite you most in your work ahead.

Skills Sort: What Can I Do That I Want to Do?

Look through your lists of skills, current and future. You will want to carry some forward, while leaving others behind. Just because you *CAN* do something does not necessarily mean you *WANT* to do it now. Sort each skill you checked into one of the *Four Boxes* below:

1) Skills to use,

2) Skills NOT to use,

3) Skills to refresh, or

4) Skills to add.

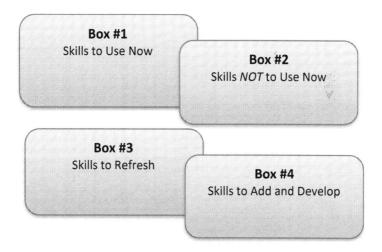

After you have sorted your skills, then focus on those skills you have placed into Box #1, Box #3 or Box #4. Select your *Top 5 Skills of Choice*. These will be your actionable skills—the skills to be carried forward into your action plan for your next phase.

Top Five Skills of Choice

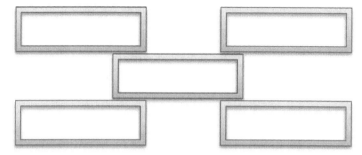

Assuming your Box #3 skills will need to be refreshed, and your Box #4 skills will need to be developed anew. Part of your action plan will need to include opportunities for you to learn and practice these skills in order that you be able to use them competently.

Now Focus on Your Traits

Starting with any items you listed above as *Skills* that actually were personal *traits—*positive personal *characteristics—*compile a list of your strongest traits.

1. Check off ten or more of your strongest traits below.

2. Start with these samples and add others that describe you.

3. Then select your Top Three Positive Personal Traits.

My Positive Personal Traits					
☐	Accurate	☐	Adaptable	☐	Confident
☐	Cooperative	☐	Creative	☐	Diligent
☐	Dynamic	☐	Empowering	☐	Energetic
☐	Flexible	☐	Independent	☐	Innovative
☐	Outgoing	☐	Perceptive	☐	Persevering
☐	Persistent	☐	Professional	☐	Punctual
☐	Resourceful	☐	Self-motivated	☐	Versatile

Top 3 Traits

Now Pull It All Together—The Sum of Your Parts

Your task now is to synthesize these dimensions of your SELF to create a SELF Statement. Taken together, these elements create a picture of your full and unique SELF. The work or pursuits you choose from this point forward will be fulfilling to you to the degree that they express the combined essence of YOU.

- What you are *like?*
- What *engages* you?
- What has *meaning* for you?
- What are your signature character strengths?
- What you can *do?*
- What are your main positive *traits?*

Personal Summary
What Are You LIKE? Your Type & Temperament
<ul><li>The descriptor for your *4-Letter Personality Type* code</li><li>The descriptor for your *2-Letter Temperament* code (Guardian, Artisan, Giver, Thinker)</li><li>Your Compulsion</li></ul>
What ENGAGES You? Your Interests
<ul><li>The names for your top three *Interest Categories*.</li></ul>
What Has MEANING for You? Your Values
<ul><li>Your top five *Values*.</li></ul>
What Are Your Core Character Strengths?
<ul><li>Your dominant 5–6 *Character Strengths*.</li></ul>

What Can You DO? Your Bank of Skills

- Your top five *Skills of Choice*.

What Are Your Positive Personal TRAITS?

- Your top three *Positive Personal Traits.*

Your SELF Statement

Now it is time to bring all these elements of your SELF together into a single *SELF Statement*. This statement will become your guide for the chapters ahead, and for your future life. If you have a partner, there will, naturally, be two SELF Statements.

In the blanks below, fill in the blanks in this order:

1. Your Type
2. Your Temperament
3. Your Compulsion
4. Your Interests (3 categories)
5. Your Values (top 5)
6. Your Signature Character Strengths
7. Your Skills (top 5)
8. Your Positive Personal Traits (top 3)

SELF Statement

I am a ____(1)____, a/an _____(2)____ with a compulsion to ___(3)_____. I am engaged by pursuits that are ___(4)_____, _____, and _____. For a pursuit to have meaning for me, it needs to satisfy my values of: _____(5)____, _____, _____, _____, and _____. My signature character strengths are: _____(6)_____, _____, _____.I am skilled at: ____(7)_____, _____, _____, _____, and _____. My positive traits are that I am: ____(8)_____, _____, _____.

Sample Self Statement

I am a <u>Mastermind,</u> a <u>Thinker</u> with a compulsion to <u>Improve</u>. I am engaged by pursuits that are <u>Investigative, Creative and Enterprising</u>. For a pursuit to have meaning for me, it needs to satisfy my values of: <u>Creativity, Intellectual Stimulation, Achievement, Way of Life, and Variety.</u> My signature character strengths are: Love of Learning, Creativity, and Curiosity. I am skilled at: <u>Researching, Systematizing, Designing, Writing, and Speaking</u>. My positive personal traits are that I am: <u>Insightful, Communicative and Empowering.</u>

And So...

Where does all this leave you, and what needs to happen next? You now have looked at your SELF and have attempted to see yourself more clearly in terms of what you may be uniquely and even passionately ready and able to do next.

You have explored your WORK, reexamining and integrating five other dimensions: your interests, values, character strengths, skills and traits. These are the additional dimensions that are critical to identifying an authentic, rich, multidimensional picture of the full and essential YOU. Together these clarifications and insights about yourself will guide your progress towards your rediscovered work and life after retirement.

All this time that you have invested to take a new look at your SELF and your WORK, and to formulate a profile that combines what you are *like* with your own *interests, values, character strengths, skills* and *traits,* will repay you repeatedly with the gift of the rest of your life well spent. Your recent introspective work now positions you to move happily into your next phase, armed with purpose, focus, and valuable self-knowledge.

The self-exploration, self-reinvention, and rediscovery you have undertaken so far have been challenging. Moving to *Step #5: Make Your Match & Move* will add another layer of complexity, as you hold in the balance all that you have determined so far, and then look at how and where all of it will best fit. Your final step in the process will be to align your reinvented SELF and your rediscovered WORK with actual possibilities for your retirement career.

But before you work through this next critical step, we will take a break in the *5-Step Process* to consider some of the life and work options from which you will be able to choose.

CHAPTER 7: Life & Work Options

Sure, we've all heard it. "There are many roads to Oz." That's the good news. The flip side, which we've all learned, or will soon come to realize, is that once you choose one of those many roads, there often "ain't no turnin' back," at least not without a sliding scale of consequences. We mention this because, as we introduce you to the many options offered in Chapters 8-12, we also want to alert you to a few caveats.

First, just as today you are bombarded by TMI (too much information), you might, as you encounter all the options now available to you, initially be overwhelmed by TMC (too many choices.) Don't be floored by what can be referred to as the "Mall of America Syndrome." Too many shops to navigate, too much dissonant loud music, too many beckoning food kiosks, too many seemingly rudderless crowds—multimedia sensory overload! This assault on the senses can result in confusion, frustration, and the feeling of "what's the use, I can't deal with this today, get me outta here!"

A suggested strategy... Read one of these five chapters per day, highlighting those segments that tend to "light your fire." Then, after you have initially digested all five chapters, one at a time, go back and re-read them all. After all, you are on the brink of embarking on what you hope will be a new, long, fruitful adventure. Doing your due diligence up front is all!

Secondly, ask yourself which of the five work options initially excite you. You might readily eliminate one or more work scenarios. Then, most importantly, re-remember who you are—your type and temperament, your interests, your values, your skills—as well as your available human and material resources, and your non-negotiables. Refer to the processes you underwent in Chapters 5 and 6, and don't deny, shortchange or underestimate what you learned about yourself. If you try to minimize the importance of those criteria, you do so at your own peril. We'll talk more about this in our comments about each of the five work options discussed in Chapters 8 through 12.

Thirdly, let's consider the risks that we may encounter should we change our mind after we embark on one of these five major arteries on that road to Oz. For example, do any of the five highways have a "no U-Turn caveat?" In other words, because of who you are, and/or the circumstances in your life, would one of those chosen paths eliminate your option to reverse your course or change your decision? Or, although you have the option to rethink your course and to try another route, would this choice cause you catastrophic results in the loss of time and resources, both human and material? Alternately, does one or more of these roads provide connecting bridges to others, so that, as you travel in one direction, you have the option to branch out into a different, unexpected adventure, without significant loss in time or money or personal investment? All of these "what if" options need to be explored before we "hit the road running" for this, our last, and hopefully our greatest, opus.

Again, know yourself, your needs, your passions. First and foremost, this is the time in your life when you should do what you love and love what you do.

You Might Want to Work in Cyberspace

For years you drove to work in the dark and returned home in the dark. You never experienced the luxury of seeing the budding spring or the magnificent autumn. You travelled far in foul weather, endured endless road construction delays, traffic jams, accident hazards and dreaded gas prices and shortages, while carpooling and mass transportation proved to be non-existent or totally impractical options.

Then there were the human aspects of working "out there in the real world." At times you needed to muster the tactfulness of an international diplomat to deal with what you perceived as less than intelligent co-workers, or a difficult supervisor, or an inadequate salary, or ungodly and arbitrary hours.

As retirement neared, you fantasized about how great it would be to travel to work upstairs or downstairs in your PJs and robe, a fresh, piping hot pot of coffee or hot chocolate at your disposal, ready to begin your day. Now you're there, ready to explore the possibility of working online.

Not so fast! Let's first do a reality check of what such a choice entails. First, today's cyber jobs demand a high degree of technological skill. And although most on-line companies do, in fact, train prospective employees on their own software processes and programs, these organizations expect and require that candidates have a more than average degree of computer expertise. Also, online employers demand that their workers come prepared with specific hardware, software, and network capability. Would you be prepared to make this financial investment up front?

And speaking of financial considerations, online work compensation presents itself in many forms. Some work is salaried or hourly. Some jobs tie payment to the completion of a project. Other forms of payment are dependent upon your ability to find your own work, to outsource yourself. It's important to know in advance what your expectations are in terms of how much money you need or want to earn working online. Chapter 8 will serve you well in presenting the many options, opportunities and configurations for cyber employment.

Next you need to consider some very personal, human, domestic, family conditions that are bound to impact your decision to work online. For example, do you have the independence and autonomy needed to work in an informal "at home" environment, considering the demands of pets, family members' needs, and social interruptions. And what about the realities of international time changes? Are you willing and able to work in customer service for a company whose clients are internationally based? For example, as an English tutor for Asian students, you would need to accommodate your students according to their time zone, which might prove to be in the middle of your night. Getting up at 3 a.m. each morning to teach might easily wear thin after a while. Or, unless you are a nighthawk, you might not appreciate your phone service job when you find yourself taking orders at two in the morning for the latest Jimmy Choo pair of shoes!

Then there is the aspect of self-discipline and accessibility. Some online positions require that you log in and log out at specific times.

But others assign a task and allow you a fixed, but flexible time period to complete the work. Do you have the self-discipline to work independently, as well as the personal life situation that allows you to do so?

Lastly, whether you realize it or not, working on-line can be lonesome, especially for someone whose claim to fame is that of the "social butterfly," "life of the party," "queen or king of the coffee break." For those of us who are gregarious extroverts, our jobs became, in many instances, sources of social enrichment and meaningful, lasting friendship as well as authentic professional satisfaction. Here's a small, informal, non-scientific self-test to determine whether you might be happy working online and at home. First, if you live alone and find that on a given long weekend you have not spoken to a living person, do you experience a supreme degree of relaxed elation, or do find yourself desperate for human contact by Monday morning? Secondly, during your recent bout with the flu, when you were confined to bed for a week, did you find yourself insisting that the TV remain on throughout the night, just for the sake of hearing human voices? Thirdly, when you were at work during your primary career, were you always the one who initiated and organized the birthday luncheons, the holiday parties, the annual outing? If the answer is "yes" to one or more of these salient scenarios, then perhaps you should have second thoughts about working online.

Now let's flip the coin. There are so many pluses for working online. For one thing, you can do it from almost anywhere! Unless you plan to establish roots in the far ends of Nepal or Antarctica, you and your computer and your Wi-Fi are in business...anytime, anywhere!

And if you plan to work from home, think about the flexibility you will have to walk the dog, do a soccer run, watch your favorite talk show. And more, cyberwork incentivizes your learning new technology skills, thus making you more marketable!

You May Plan to Work in the Workplace

Let's assume that you have successfully spent most of your pre-retirement career in a traditional job environment, with all the conventional trappings and perks of such 20th century work. These included regular hours, steady work, a reliable, comfortable salary, some type of retirement package, sick leave, vacation and holiday guarantees.

This is the only type of work you know, the only career paradigm in which you are comfortable. And that's OK. There are still, and will continue to be many enriching, satisfying job opportunities in the traditional work environment. Chapter 9 is a great place to start to learn of the many fulfilling opportunities available to you if your choice is to work outside your home in a traditional job that may or may not be related to your previous lifetime career.

Just keep in mind your following new realities. Are you willing and able to endure the hardships and inconveniences that you took for granted as "part of the job" when you were younger? This includes travelling distances in sometimes inclement weather and adverse road conditions at possibly odd hours to a job that might not yield a salary commensurate with your experience and expertise. Or are you willing to put up with the frustrations and vicissitudes of airline travel, or even more, the possibility that you might be asked to relocate to a different part of the country?

In other words, at this point in your life, are you in a different place, psychologically? You might want to consider a more leisurely, flexible work environment, one that affords you the opportunity to engage in more personal pursuits—activities that you were required to put on hold until today. Or your retirement plans might include wanting to stay near immediate family, children, grandchildren, and close friends. In other words, in no way is re-location a blip on your retirement radar screen!

All is not gloom, doom and hardship if you decide to take on the world of brick and mortar. Remember all the pitfalls of loneliness and isolation you risk falling into if you decide to work from home? Gone! You'll experience all the comradery and social interaction you were accustomed to enjoy in your previous work environment.

And as for the males among you, you'll find a whole new cadre of friends to share your love of football, golf, and Friday afternoons at the local watering hole! And as for you lovely ladies, now you can wear all those expensive outfits you justifiably purchased when you were previously focused on "dressing for success!" And you'll no more be out of the latest gossip loop!

What you can take heart in is the fact that many employers are eager to hire seniors who are financially comfortable, who don't need such perks as medical insurance or retirement benefits, and who are willing to work a limited number of flexible hours for a moderate supplemental income. In fact, the data shows that this whole cadre of seniors prove to be exceptionally reliable and competent—qualities in high demand among employers.

Do You Wish to Work for Yourself or Partner Up?

It looks so easy! We see it every day on TV! So many different personality types concocting so many common sense or outlandish money-engendering ideas. The perfect pillow, untuckable shirt, magic exercise gizmo—each convincing you that you are perfectly capable of launching that innovative, appealing, labor and cost saving idea that you have had brewing for these many years. Now it's your turn for that secret entrepreneur that lies within to blossom.

Not so fast! Here's where reality trumps fantasy. Let's start with who you are. Are you the "Nervous Nelly" type, a worry wart who not only anticipates everything that could go wrong, but who falls apart at the slightest setback? In other words, what's your "risk tolerance IQ?" If you plan to start your own business, you must be ready to deal with uncertainty, unevenness, unanticipated glitches, and the realities of Murphy's Law.

How much stick-to-itiveness do you have in the face of adversity? Do you have the persistence of a bulldog with a bone, or do you shrivel up and wither away at the first sign of an unanticipated difficulty? When there is a problem to be solved, are you the last person standing, the one whose determination yields ultimate success?

Then there is the issue of resources, both material and human. The ability to read others, to assess each would-be team member's strengths and potential contribution to the cause, to determine whether he/she would be a positive fit within the group... The success or failure of many a promising venture rests on the right combination of human talent.

Never underestimate the power of the purse. A good rule of thumb for a potential business startup is—decide how much time and money you realistically think you will need to launch your idea, then take half that figure and add it to your original business plan. Assure that your financial resources are firm and guaranteed and remember that time equals money.

And speaking of time... Ask anyone you know who has had the courage to strike out on their own: "How much time have you found you need to invest in establishing and shepherding your own business as compared with the hours you spent working in your former traditional job?" Don't be surprised if the response is: "Are you joking? There's no comparison! Entrepreneurship does not allow for 9 to 5 limitations! My best ideas sometimes emerge in the middle of the night! I always need to be the first one on the job and the last one to leave! When plans or projects go awry, everyone relies on me to cast the deciding vote!"

However, nothing can compare with the self-satisfaction as well as the monetary reward that accrues to the successful entrepreneur. The courage and energy to take a dream and turn it into a tangible reality is what fuels the engine of our capitalist economy. The NASDEQ is proof positive of the opportunities and results that are yours for the earning if and when all your stars align at the right time and in the right place.

Entrepreneurship is not for the fainthearted. This is why the government provides all types of incentives for those who have the courage and mettle to follow their dream of self-employment. Chapter 10 discusses strategies and tools that will be your best friends as you start out on your venture of choice.

Would You Want to Work for Other Seniors?

Ask yourself: "Who better than another senior to determine and meet the needs and wants of this tsunami of seniors who are now, and who will continue to, flood our cities, our suburbs, our restaurants, theaters, museums, malls and places of employment?" In fact, many of us have a ready-made cadre of clients within our own circle of family and friends. We are finding that the very products and services that we ourselves are wanting and needing are those we can provide to others of our own generation.

In Chapter 11, we differentiate among the "young-old, middle old, and older old." Each of these groups has a different set and degree of requirements and desires. And because we ourselves are members of one of these sets, we can empathize with our colleagues, with an almost intuitive sense of how best to serve this population. After all, even though we may have joined the ranks of those who have left behind a major life passage—what was a long and fruitful profession, avocation, or career—we still plan to thrive in and through our recreational, social, intellectual, and work lives, sharing our energy, talent and skills with our contemporary senior colleagues.

The dynamics of our various senior groups provide for an interesting and challenging set of possibilities. For example, those in the "young-old" group are physically more in a position to offer a whole variety of goods and services to those in the "older old" category. Simultaneously, those among the young senior group, as they develop these necessary goods and services, can all the while be preparing for the day when they, too, will be utilizing some form of these things.

As with all the options you will consider for this, your last hurrah, there are some realistic considerations to be aware of. If your current life's circumstances find you spending most of your time with members of your own generation, you may decide that the last thing you want to do is to work in an environment populated mostly by the elder generation. In fact, you might make a conscious decision to place yourself in a multigenerational environment, where a variety of age groups occupy your time and energy. That's perfectly acceptable.

Undoubtedly, you have already had the opportunity to provide some type of services or products to various members of senior groups. Whether you have visited someone in a senior full-service residence, driven them to a doctor's appointment, treated them to a local performance of some type, introduced them to a local gym membership, invited them to play cribbage with a group of friends, you have experienced the gratitude and enjoyment these seniors have expressed. Admittedly, you have probably felt an inner connection, too, knowing that someday, perhaps soon, you might be the recipient, instead of the giver of such amenities.

As retirees, those of us in the younger group of seniors are finding that the lines of aging are blurring. As we move among members of our own group, we see that, in truth, age is only a number. We might even blushingly admit that some older members are physically spryer and intellectually sharper than ourselves!

Is Volunteerism How You Plan to Spend Your Time?

Volunteering is more in vogue than ever for several reasons. The need seems to be greater than ever. As the gap between rich and poor is ever widening, those in the latter category are more at risk of being forgotten than ever. And we are not referring just to material need. The ranks of the mentally ill, the homeless, the substance addicted, the poorly educated, the physically handicapped, and the extremely old are increasing exponentially.

Here are some sobering statistics to inform the critical degree of need that volunteerism can fill:

- On a single night in January 2015, 564,708 people were experiencing homelessness—meaning they were sleeping outside or in an emergency shelter or transitional housing program. (*Report: The State of Homelessness in America*, National Alliance to End Homelessness, 2016)
- Approximately 32 million adults in America are illiterate; about 14% of the entire adult population cannot read. 1 in 4 children in America grow up without learning how to read. Nearly 85% of the juveniles who face trial in the juvenile court

system are functionally illiterate, proving that there is a close relationship between illiteracy and crime. More than 60% of all inmates are functionally illiterate. (*Report: 11 Facts About Literacy in America*, DoSomething.org)

- About 56.7 million people—19% of the population—had a disability in 2010. The *2012 U.S. Census* reported nearly 1 in 5 people as having a disability.
- According to the Substance Abuse and Mental Health Services Administration's (SAMHSA's) *National Survey on Drug Use and Health*, 23.5 million persons aged 12 or older needed treatment for an illicit drug or alcohol abuse problem in 2009 (9.3% of persons aged 12 or older). Of these, only 2.6 million— 11.2% of those who needed treatment—received it at a specialty facility. (National Institute on Drug Abuse, 2011.)
- According to the US Bureau of Justice Statistics (BJS), 2,220,300 adults were incarcerated in US federal and state prisons, and county jails in 2013—about 0.91% of all adults (1 in 110) in the U.S. resident population.

The good news is that, while the need for volunteers is greater than ever, so, too, are there more seniors ready, willing, and able to fill these needs. Consider that group of seniors who do not have the financial need to work and thus have more leisure time to fill with meaningful activity. These members have talents, energy and skills that can and should be shared. Ironically, as you talk to senior volunteers, they insist that they, rather than those they serve, are the greater beneficiaries. The eternal paradox holds true with this group: The more you give, and more you receive in return.

However, the decision to volunteer is not an arbitrary capricious one to be assumed lightly. Nor is it one to be taken on with the attitude that "they're lucky to have me, so I can show up whenever I feel like it." Quite the contrary. In fact, it might be argued that, in some ways, volunteering demands more of a commitment than a paying job. And why is that so?

Many organizations that solicit volunteers are understaffed and underfunded. They count on volunteers to supplement and complement their organization. But these institutions, to operate credibly and effectively, need to be able to rely on specific commitments from their volunteers, whether this commitment be in the form of donated time frames, types of activities, or monetary support. So, it behooves would-be volunteers to consider in advance how much time and energy and resources they are willing and able to commit on a regular basis.

Volunteerism sheds light on a universal paradox—the question of who receives the most in terms of joy, satisfaction, happiness—the giver or the recipient? Ask any volunteer you know, and they will unequivocally declare that they, in fact, are the greater receiver. That is why they become so faithful to their commitment. Volunteering elicits the best of ourselves. It forces us to focus on others, as it becomes evident how much more fortunate we are to experience our own life's advantages, whether they be mental or physical health, monetary comfort, family stability, or a privileged education or career.

In a word, volunteerism sobers us. In this sense, it enriches us, makes us more human and empathetic with the human condition of those less fortunate than we are. Chapter 12 will offer information and guidance about the option of volunteerism as part or all your retirement plan.

So… as you start off on your journey, it behooves you to "follow the rules of the road." Do your research. Plot your route. Check, double-check, and re-check the soundness of your vehicle. Make sure you choose compatible travel companions. Allow for detours and side trips. Don't speed. Savor the journey, while keeping your destination in mind.

Voila! You're practically guaranteed a foolproof adventure on this, your last, best life journey.

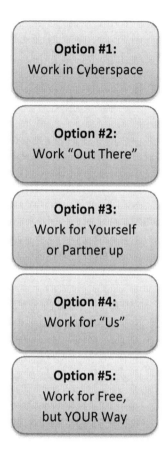

CHAPTER 8:
Option #1: Work in Cyber Space

Where, oh, where have all the jobs gone? One answer: *online*. According to many sources, there has been a *structural change* in traditional employment, as more businesses have adopted online and "freelance" hiring as a core business strategy. Businesses have developed innovative workforce models that blend full-time and part-time, local and online, permanent and contract workers. The ability of businesses to gain instant access to qualified talent with in-demand skills, regardless of location, is a global trend that has changed the way businesses and people work.

These demands have enabled knowledge workers to build independent careers working online, for one or multiple clients, from their home office, from public spaces, or from a co-located office (at home and on site combined). Technology, such as the proliferating number of freelance platforms and apps, is improving access, matching employers to freelancers to carry out freelance gigs.

A large-scale 2016 study of more than 6,000 U.S. working adults over the age of 18, conducted online by the independent research firm Edelman Intelligence, found that more people are creating their own jobs today than ever before. The number of freelance workers hit 55 million in 2016. Freelancers now made up 35% of the U.S. workforce, and collectively earned $1 trillion, in 2016. The Freelancers Union represents 300,000 members.

This employment survey also showed that freelancers are earning more; 46% reported receiving raised rates in the past year. Among those who quit a traditional job to freelance, more than half are earning more than they did when they were getting a steady paycheck. And 53% of freelancers believe that having a diverse portfolio of clients is more economically secure than having a single employer.

WOW FACTOR

The online contract work segment is growing at twice the rate of the standard workforce. For one agency,

> monthly demand for online workers has surpassed sup-
> ply by over 30%, leaving thousands of contract jobs un-
> filled.

Just as online shopping has transformed our habits and expectations as consumers, online employment has profoundly changed the
landscape of employment and work. Savio Rosati, CEO of *eLance*
(now *UpWork*) summarizes these changes: "Fueled by technology,
work is no longer confined to the 9-to-5 office environment."

Job Shortages or Worker Shortages?

While global economies have continued to struggle with job creation,
online work has thrived. The merged oDesk/eLance enterprise, now
renamed "*UpWork*" (*https://www.upwork.com/*), serves more than
2 million businesses to find, hire, and pay over 9.7 million freelancers
from over 180 countries, making it easier than ever to build successful companies as well as thriving online careers.

The *Future Workforce Report*, commissioned by *UpWork* and
conducted by an independent research firm *Inavero*, set out to establish a blueprint for the evolution of work by surveying more than
1,000 U.S. hiring managers. The picture that emerged showed how
businesses are adapting to keep up with the rapid pace of change,
where in just a few years, a third of the skills needed in our workforce
will be brand new. *UpWork* CEO, Stephane Kasriel describes the difficulty: "Traditional models of hiring no longer provide the agility
businesses must have to access in-demand skills when and where
they're needed. With 55 million Americans freelancing, businesses
are thinking beyond archaic Industrial Era-approaches and turning
towards flexible hiring to get work done."

Even during these recent years that have been marked by widespread concerns about unemployment, the demand for online employees has exceeded the supply. A reasonable conclusion is that the
quantity of total jobs is sufficient, but that many of these jobs now
have moved online.

Job *Gains* Overseas

In addition to providing the connections that make possible plentiful online work opportunities in the US, online employment platforms also have broken down global barriers, and opened up opportunities for working abroad. In 2011, US-based contract workers exported their services to more than 140 countries.

This work trend is the opposite of the trend that has persisted over the past four decades, where American jobs were *lost* to workers overseas. Now, increasingly, Americans are *gaining* jobs from overseas, while working from home—online.

The emerging workplace is one where the work is brought to the worker instead of the worker being brought to the work. Businesses gain from this the results they need, when they need them. Workers gain the considerable benefit of being able to work where and when they choose.

Gary Swart, CEO of *oDesk* (now *UpWork*), summarizes the transformation of the workplace, and the shift in expectations as follows:

> *"The Internet has catalyzed job creation across the board by eliminating geographic barriers—and not just in industries that deal with new technologies. Even in age-old professions such as legal work and writing, the Internet has brought growth to countless industries by creating opportunities that didn't exist before, that are unrestricted by geography... Today, it's about enabling the best minds to work together, regardless of where they happen to be. Technology makes this possible. And we predict increasing connectivity and Internet savvy is going to continue to fuel this employment revolution, with one in three workers hired to work online by 2020. Now that is what I call an employment revolution."*

Why Work Online in Retirement?

Think about it. Online opportunities are *growing at twice the rate* of the standard workforce, and non-traditional contract workers make up *more than 1/3 of the US workforce*. What better place could you consider for your own retirement work?

There are many possibilities for working online, with openings and possibilities that include, but are not limited to:

- ☐ Web Development
- ☐ Software Development
- ☐ Networking & Information Systems
- ☐ Writing & Translation
- ☐ Administrative Support
- ☐ Design & Multimedia
- ☐ Desktop Publishing
- ☐ Research
- ☐ Teaching
- ☐ Customer Service
- ☐ Sales & Marketing
- ☐ Business Services

Pause now to check off any of these online work areas that may be a potential match for you.

Three Major Advantages of Working Online

Whatever hesitations and trepidations you may have about working online, consider these advantages:

- Freedom of location
- Broader options for employment
- Fewer expenses, resulting in more take-home pay

Freedom of Location

Undoubtedly, accepting employment in the brick-and-mortar workplace confines your movements. Not so with online work that generally can be done from any location you choose—the mountains, the beach, or a condo on the coast of France, with a view of the Mediterranean. The only essential need is to have access to a Wi-Fi hot spot. And in today's cyber world, access is ubiquitous. Based on personal experience, I can even report that it is possible for you to work online via satellite from the middle of the Atlantic Ocean while cruising transatlantic to Europe.

Would you consider working online in order to free yourself? Have laptop, will travel! The new reality is that conducting business online now may be as simple as waking up in the morning wherever you happen to be at the moment, donning your shorts, T-shirt and flip flops, and heading out for breakfast at the nearest café.

If you are designing a retirement that combines several pathways—like perhaps work plus travel or work plus leisure or work plus study (possibly with the one providing funding for the other)—online work could be the answer to your question "How can I have my cake and eat it too?"

Broader Options for Employment

Another major reason for working online is to expand your options beyond your own geographical area. Locating work in your surrounding geographic area can be very limiting. You may even find that in order to expand your options to find a job "out there," you will be forced to factor in a move. These opportunity-versus-location constraints increase exponentially if you are married and need to consider two sets of location and relocation needs in order that both partners have the opportunity to work at engaging jobs.

You may think that if you decide to work during retirement, you will be forced to make difficult choices and compromises, based on how far you are willing or able to drive to work every day. Even if you aspire to starting your own business, you may feel confined to offering something in your own town that hopefully will generate enough local traffic and commerce to become profitable.

If your options are limited near home, working online may be the answer that will expand your potential "workplace." By shortening your commute to a walk up the stairs or down the hall, you will widen your customer base to encompass the entire world! Talk about significantly increasing your target market!

When you work online, you can work where you want to work and live where you want to live. Yes, you *can* have the best of both worlds. If you wish, you can even live in multiple places over the course of the year, following "snow bird" or other migratory patterns. You could summer in Colorado and winter in Key West—while still working on the same projects, for the same employer and/or clients, year-round.

Fewer Expenses Means More Take-Home Pay

Working online also results in more money in your pocket, and less money lost to expenses. While flexibility is appealing, increased profits can prove to be even more enticing.

According to the reported results of an online workers' survey, nearly 50% of online workers said they made more money working from home than if they had continued to commute to a traditional job. Of those who reported that they made more money working from home, 25% said they made *significantly* more money.

Looking purely at the math, and factoring in driving time, commute distance, dress codes, lunch and break expenses, and parking, a *$20/hour* in-town job can quickly shrink down to the equivalent of a *$12/hour* job working online from home.

Looking at the obverse—a *$20/hour* online job can translate to the take-home pay of a *$33/hour* job in town, while earning *$25/hour* online will put as much money in your pocket as earning *$42/hour* "out there."

How to Work Online in Retirement

Working online from home may sound ideal. But exactly where do you find your next job, client, or commission? Where in the worldwide web do you GO to find the employers or customers who will want to pay you to do what you do best?

That is, without a doubt, the most common question raised by those who are thinking about hanging up those car keys, or cashing in those subway tokens, for a morning walk into the den. The Web is big. REALLY big! Finding a place to start when you do decide that, yes, you want to work online, can initially seem overwhelming. But there are ways to tame what may at first seem to be a vast and new frontier, fraught with unknowns.

So how *will* you and your potential employers find each other in the vastness of Cyberspace?" And when you do find each other, how will *they* know that *you* are the very one they need to hire? What evidence will *show* them that you will produce for them at the quality level that is essential to their reputation, while fostering the life and growth of their business?

Although the enormous size and anonymity of the Web may indeed seem intimidating to you at the outset, you *will* be able to make its vastness work *for* you, not *against* you.

Translate Your To-Dos from "Out There" to Online

Start by thinking about how you searched for and found jobs in the past "out there" in the brick-and-mortar work world. Then plan how you will replicate what you did then, but this time do it "virtually."

Out there you would:

- Knock on doors
- Provide résumés that show your value to potential employers
- Look for tasks that need to be done and offer to do them
- Scan the classified ads
- Register with job placement agencies
- Network with business people who might "know someone who knows someone" with a potential need or opening

Online, the "doors" that you knock on will be websites. So, as with the agencies you would approach in town, you will need to keep track of the web addresses you visit online. Start a notebook, or even an Address Book, to record all your important addresses in one place, as you would if you were looking for work "out there."

In order to *provide résumés and show your value* to potential employers, you now will post those résumés online, electronically. And now, since your résumé can be easily adapted, you would do well to customize it, as well as the cover letter that accompanies it, so that it fits, hand-in-glove, the specific job you are addressing. Since these communications will be the only "face" potential employers will see, every word of every communication you send will need to be 100% perfect. If you are not confident in your own ability to express yourself in writing, enlist an editor to work with you to achieve the perfection required to make a good impression.

The equivalent of *looking for work tasks that need to be done and then offering to do them*, will be consulting online job boards, signing up with freelance sites, and doing web searches. To *scan the classified ads* and *register with agencies*, you will be doing much the same as you would in the brick-and-mortar world, except that you will be doing these things online. The same is true for *networking with business people who may know someone who knows someone* to discover potential openings. Again, you will be doing this online. Only now every contact you know, regardless of where they live, may potentially have a valuable lead for you.

These and other job-search activities will open up many possibilities beyond your local geographical area. Once you have made the translations from "out there" to online, create an action list for yourself, including, at a minimum, a virtual form of everything you would be doing if you were looking for work the old way. Then get started, beginning with the links and resources provided later in this chapter.

This might be a good time to think ahead and establish a Word file with blanks where you will record whatever data you might find useful in the future, including:

- Date
- Website name
- Web address
- Description of actions taken
- Response date and content
- Contact: Name, e-mail, phone

Consider the Three Ways to Work Online

As you get down to the business of finding online work, begin by considering these three primary ways to work and earn money online:

- **Employment:** *Find contract work through an agency;*
- **Self-Employment:** *Offer services and find your own clients;*
- **Your Own Business:** *Set up an online business.*

You also may think in terms of combining two, or even all three, of these three primary ways to work online. If you elect to seek employment doing contract work online, you also may want to set up a business through which you do that contract work (think tax benefits). If you offer your services through self-employment, attempting to gain clients through your own enterprises, you also may seek out contracts that have already been posted through the online employment brokers. If you open a business online, you may combine the online element with a local off-line component.

Think "Work," Not "Job"

Consider some of the types of services that are always needed and are typical for online work. Each agency or employment service site has such a *Needed Services List*. These lists can be valuable as you make your plans.

For example, ClickNWork (*https://www.clicknwork.com/*) is one outsourcing agency that enables experienced online professionals to deliver business services to companies worldwide. The job categories on the ClickNWork "Always Needed Services List" include:

- **Analysts/consultants**—with skills specific to an industry or trade: MBAs, CPAs, CFAs, and so forth.

- **Information professionals/specialists**—with strong track records and proficiency at a range of information sources (e.g., Factiva, Lexis, Dialog researchers).

- **Writers/editors**—experienced at high quality business, technical, marketing, or personal writing.

- **Web searchers**—proficient at quickly locating information on the web in answer to specific business questions.

- **Data entry specialists**—skilled at rapid and accurate data entry and reporting.

- **Shoppers, Trend spotters, Social observers**—adept at seeing trends, drawing parallels and generating valuable commercial insight.

- **Telephone interviewers**—skilled at conducting interviews to surface opinions, needs and/or preferences.

- **Photographers**—skilled at photographing buildings, real estate, stores, and products.

- **Translators**—able to translate accurately between languages commonly used for business.

Here's a sample of an actual online job listing seeking to hire a telecommuting contract worker.

Sample Job Post for Content Writer with Fitness Background

Work at home: Telecommute. 20-40 hours per week.

We are looking for a candidate to write content for an online company selling nutritional supplements. This candidate should:

- Have a working knowledge of fitness and supplement practices.
- Be able to produce high quality content & maintain social network sites.
- Creativity is a MUST.

Job Requirements: The candidate will create content for new products and post blogs, Twitter, and Facebook updates to help increase product awareness and boost page rankings. A broad knowledge of general fitness, popular supplements and their ingredients are needed, as well as the ability to transfer this understanding into quality online content.

Six Types of Places to Look for Online Work

So where do you start? Finding contract work online is something of a treasure hunt. Depending upon what you have to offer, your task will be to locate potential clients and or employers who need you, and then to demonstrate to them that you are the one they need. They are looking for you. You are looking for them. And the meeting ground for both of you is the Web.

So where exactly in the vastness of cyberspace do you "go" to seek out and find each other, then check each other out, and ultimately form a match? There are six common hunting grounds where the millions of online employment matches are made. Plan to explore all six types. Record the URL addresses for sites you plan to use regularly:

1. Sites for Online Employment

2. Online options through sites for jobs "out there"

3. Online job boards

4. Online classifieds

5. Newsletters and newsgroups

6. Freelance networks

Work Source #1: Sites for Online Employment

There are many online agencies that focus on hiring online workers. These agencies fall into three main types:

- Outsourcing Services for Online Employment

- Employment Agencies for Online Jobs

- Staffing Services for Online Employment

We will consider each of these types of agencies here, with examples and URLs for you to pursue.

Outsourcing Services for Online Employment

Outsourcing is the business practice of contracting out services that previously would have been performed by internal employees of an organization. The most common reasons why companies decide to outsource work include: cost savings; the ability to focus internal staff on its core business; access to a broader range of knowledge, talent and experience; increased profits.

Online outsourcing service agencies recruit a network of workers with a variety of capabilities and make optimum matches between these workers and a range of business and corporate accounts, based on the specific project work needed. Then, on a project-by-project basis, the agency identifies from its network a list of people capable of completing each client request, accurately and reliably. Project assignments may be permanent, temporary, full-time, part-time or *ad hoc*.

Start with these eight *Outsourcing Services*. Add additional services to this list by searching Google, or another search engine, using the search term: "outsourcing services."

Outsourcing Services	
UpWork (eLance/ODesk) *www.Upwork.com*	**ClickNWork** *ClickNWork.com*
IQ BackOffice *www.IQBackOffice.com*	**VIP Desk Connect** *VIPDeskConnect.com*
AccounTemps *AccounTemps.com*	**Balance Your Books** *BalanceYourBooks.com*
ABGlobal Translations *ABGlobal.net/joining.htm*	**OutSource Your Books** *OSYB.com*

Select three or more of these Outsourcing Services to explore now. Make hand-written (or copy/paste) notes about:

- categories of work assignments,
- requirements,
- the application/registration process.

Add these three resources to your notebook of URL addresses, plus any others you may want to use regularly. If you register for any of these services, record your login information in your notebook as well. The importance of keeping accurate, correct notes during this process cannot be overestimated.

An Example: Working for an Outsourcing Service

As an example of what your experience would be working for an outsourcing service, we will explore here the specifics of *ClickNWork*, an outsourcing company that "partners with companies to see what work their online workforce can complete for them remotely." *ClickNWork* recruits a network of workers with a variety of capabilities. Companies post project requests for tasks such as:

- research
- report preparation
- data entry

- writing
- analysis
- customer service

Then, on a project-by-project basis, *ClickNWork* identifies from its network people capable of completing each specific client request and posts unallocated tasks that are available for them to select. Assignments may be permanent, temporary, full-time, part-time, or *ad hoc*. Sometimes clients require that contractors live in a particular country or time zone. Otherwise contractors complete the project work from a location of their choice. To become part of the *ClickNWork* network and be assigned project work, you first must pass rigorous tests and submit references as part of your background check. All applicants must have a reliable broadband-connected PC and speak excellent English.

Performance is tracked for all assigned work through automated systems or expert reviewers. If individuals fail to meet the quality standards, they are quickly replaced on that project. This competitive approach to project work ensures that companies will get their work done and delivered at a high-quality level, and on schedule.

Some assigned contractors work by accessing the client's server through a secure remote connection, and thus can complete the work project without data ever leaving the client's server. Some clients provide laptops to individuals to give them access to internal systems and to integrate them more seamlessly into the work of the company. Here is a sample posting for contract work.

Sample Online Contract Work

Customer Service Rep

Location: Virtual (Anywhere)

Shift availability: Must be flexible to work at least 8 hours between the hours of 7:00AM to 2:00AM, as schedules will be based on performance and tenure. Shifts may not include weekend days off.

Purpose: To represent American Support and their clients by ensuring cable entertainment satisfaction through excellent customer service, offering courteous problem solving, quality information and other services in response to customer needs.

Major Duties and Responsibilities:

1. Sign in and out for scheduled shifts at appointed times.

2. Access customer information and convey necessary information to customers.

3. Answer customer questions (basic information such as prices, programming, installation of services, billing).

4. Communicate effectively, both verbally and in writing.

5. Resolve basic customer problems/complaints promptly and refer complex issues and concerned customers to the appropriate lead representative or supervisor.

6. Acquire and maintain current up-to-date cable product knowledge and provide it using appropriate persuasive communication skills.

7. Determine service outages (using Knowledge Base and other systems).

Employment Agencies for Online Jobs

Online employment agencies, also called virtual employment agencies, undertake the hiring process for corporate and business clients in order to guarantee quality of work, and to match expert workers with serious employers. These agencies remove some of the risk for employers who have actual work that must be accomplished, and deadlines that are essential to success.

To increase employer confidence, these agencies provide money-back guarantees, and carry out expert hiring practices on behalf of their clients, selecting the right workers that are so crucial to the success of client projects. If the employee will have access to company trade secrets, the agency arranges for non-disclosure agreements.

Also, the agency serves as a payment go between, creating escrow accounts that are released to virtual workers upon successful delivery of the work. Thus, employees are guaranteed being paid, and employers are guaranteed to receive high quality work in a timely manner.

To make such assurances and guarantees, these virtual employment agencies practice expert hiring techniques. They verify certifications, obtain performance ratings for potential workers, and participate actively in mediation and arbitration, when necessary.

Although these agencies generally do offer employers the option of hiring international workers from emerging economies, they also disclose the pros and cons of employing these types of workers. At the top of the list of cons are: legal issues, where the protection of intellectual property may not be enforceable; time zone issues; and the English proficiency of non-native speakers, with the resultant potential for communications breakdowns.

Explore these six *Employment Agencies for Online Jobs*. Again, add additional agencies to this list by searching Google or another search engine using the search terms: "online employment agencies" or "virtual employment agencies."

Employment Agencies for Online Jobs	
AssistU *AssistU.com*	**Transcribe 1-2-3** *YouDictate.net*
"Desktop Staff" (Search) *LinkedIn.com*	**HireAbility** *HireAbility.com*
The Recruiter Network *TheRecruiterNetwork.com*	**Virtual Vocations** *VirtualVocations.com*

Select three or more of these *Employment Agencies for Online Jobs* to explore more completely and make notes about categories of work assignments, work requirements, and the application or registration process. Don't forget to add to your URL address notebook those agencies you will revisit.

Staffing Services for Online Employment

Staffing Services for Online Employment help small businesses meet their staffing requirements using a virtual workforce. This relieves smaller businesses of major expenses such as renting office space, providing computer equipment, and paying staff when no work is available. Advantages from the viewpoint of an employer, include:

- No additional infrastructure is required in your office;
- Your own personal presence in the office is not necessary;
- Quick and efficient startups of new projects are possible;
- Access to a large, skilled and viable work force yields higher-performance workers;
- You are enabled to focus on your core business;
- A virtual workforce can provide great support to your existing team, when needed;
- You have no long-term payroll commitments;
- Costs are reduced;
- Quality of results is increased and turn-around is quicker;
- Your business can offer 24/7 service by hiring across time zones.

Now explore these six *Virtual Staffing Services*. Add additional staffing services sites to this list by searching Google or another search engine using the search term: "Virtual Staffing Services."

Virtual Staffing Services	
Global Staffing *Global-StaffingSolutions.com*	**B & V Staffing** *BVStaffing.com/*
Virtual Corp *Virtual-Corp.com/*	**Virtual Office Temps** *VirtualAssistantJobs.com*
Virtual Staffing Source *VirtualStaffingSource.com*	**Virtual Staffing Partners** *VirtualStaffingPartners.com/*

Select three or more of these Virtual Staffing Services to explore and make notes. Be sure to make additions to your URL notebook for follow-up.

If you are not already familiar with an agency you find through a web search, then "buyer beware." The website www.scam.com is a good resource for determining whether an agency is offering legitimate employment options or is selling employment "opportunities." Unfortunately, the word "opportunity" sometimes translates to the word "SCAM." Avoid any "offer" that will make you "rich quick," or that otherwise sounds too good to be true.

Work Source #2: Telecommuting Posts on Job Sites

In addition to conducting searches on Google and other search engines, you can find another important source of online work leads buried within job search sites for work "out there." Some of these sites do include jobs that can be done via telecommuting. Explore these six sites first...

Major Job Search Sites	
Monster *www.Monster.com*	**Employment911.com** *Employment911.com*
Job.com *www.Job.com*	**Jobvertise** *www.Jobvertise.com*
Flex Jobs *www.FlexJobs.com/*	**Indeed** *Indeed.com*

From within each of these job sites, search using terms such as:

- telecommute/telecommuting
- remote

The *FlexJobs.com* site dedicates an entire section to "Telecommuting, Part-time and Flexible Jobs," with links to job leads in over 50 different job categories, from entry-level to executive positions, and ranging from freelance to employee jobs. All jobs included have been hand-screened and researched so that there are no scams, too-good-to-be-true business "opportunities" or ads on the site.

Work Source #3: Online Job Boards

For many individuals who work online, trawling the online job boards is one of the most common methods of looking for project work. Even those who plan to open their own business, or to be self-employed, use these job boards to assist them with "cash flow" until they have attracted enough clients of their own. Online workers have found that job boards are an effective source of employment.

Looking through the online job boards works well as you build a cadre of clients who use you regularly. When you have gained more regular, repeat customers, you may become less dependent on this method. But no matter how successful you become, it is always wise to return to these locations to see if you can find a few new clients.

Some job board sites are run as auctions, where a potential employer places a job on the board, and a potential contract employee (that would be you) bids against others to get hired. This sounds great in theory. But an unfortunate byproduct of this type of board is that its competitive nature can actually drive down pay rates for the work.

Check out these websites for starters, listed here, then described below. Once you have become familiar with what each of these sites has to offer, select three to visit in depth.

Online Job Boards	
Genuine Jobs *GenuineJobs.com*	**Guru.com** *Guru.com*
Live Career *LiveCareer.com/*	**Job Accept** *JobAccept.com*
JuJu Job Search Engine *JuJu.com*	**Job Line International** *Jobline.net/*
Home Job Stop *HomeJobStop.com*	**Homeworkers** *Homeworkers.org*

Genuine Jobs: *https://www.GenuineJobs.com/*
Sign up as a free member to gain access to their work from home and freelance job listings. You will receive an email whenever new jobs are added to the Members Only database.

Guru.com: *https://www.Guru.com/*
Jobs and more jobs to bid on, including jobs in:

- Websites, software & IT
- Design, art & multimedia
- Writing & translation
- Sales & marketing
- Management & finance
- Engineering & architecture

Live Career: *https://www.LiveCareer.com/*
Use the search feature. This site also offers free expert career and job-hunting advice (through articles, tools, tips, and tutorials), as well as links to many of the best job sites.

Job Accept: *https://www.JobAccept.com*
Posting millions of jobs. Serving millions of candidates. Search using the term "telecommute."

JuJu Job Search Engine: *https://www.JuJu.com*
An extensive search engine by job title, company, location or key-word. Search for "telecommute" and sign up for e-mail Job Alerts.

Job Line International: *http://Jobline.net/*
Use the search tool to check many national and international job boards. Services include how to get international work permits.

Home Job Stop: *https://www.HomeJobStop.com/*
Job board specializing in telecommuting jobs. All content is manu-ally verified and approved before appearing in the Job Bank.

Homeworkers: *http://www.Homeworkers.org*
There are no fees associated in using the Homeworkers jobs data-base. To assure that job listings are as "fresh" as possible, the site archives job listings older than 3 months.

Sample Job Board Post
Virtual Assistant to Fine Artist
Company: iHARTphotography@gmail.com
Address: 637 St Marks Ave, Brooklyn, NY

May Work Remotely

Position: Part-Time, Paid

Hours: 60 Hours/Month Long Term

BONUS: 15% COMMISSION FOR BOOSTING SALES

For this position you MUST be self-directed and committed to meeting deadlines as well as showing initiative.

Major Duties and Responsibilities

- Web Search, Information Sourcing/Collection,
- Content Writing/Creation,
- Data Entry and Order Processing,
- Customer Support,
- Sending Emails, Uploading Content/Videos,
- Miscellaneous tasks including, but not limited to, Personal Assistant work.

Work Source #4: Online Classified Ads

Another excellent place to look for online work is in the *online classified ads*. The most heavily used of *online classified ads* resource is Craigslist (*https://www.Craigslist.org/about/sites*). Many of the work-at-home leads listed on other websites have been taken from *CraigsList*. Each geographic area has its own CraigsList, where every type of classified ad is posted, including job openings, organized into 32 categories. Employment categories range from "Art/Media/Design" to "Accounting & Finance" to "Writing & Editing" to "Web & Info Design" to "Skilled Trades & Crafts."

The CraigsList site will request to access your location and redirect you to the CraigsList for your own area. Scan the categories under the word JOBS and select those that may appeal to you. Check the box labeled "telecommute." Start with your own city, but don't stop there. Since the work you are looking for can be done remotely, you are not by any means limited to your own "neighborhood." So, feel free to check out CraigsList for other cities to find additional telecommuting job options.

Stepping beyond the boundaries of your own local area to look for work can be a difficult mental leap to make as you first enter the worldwide work world. You will need to grow accustomed to new ways of thinking when all those preconceived notions are removed.

Here is a sample telecommuting listing on Craigslist:

RN Telephone Triage: Work from Home

Carenet Healthcare Services is currently seeking highly motivated, caring, compassionate, committed, and talented Registered Nurses to join Carenet's Clinical Team. If you have greater than average flexibility, you'll thrive as a Carenet *Care Advisor*. Carenet provides 24/7 telephone *Demand Management* services that include Nurse Triage, Medical Decision Support, Medical Device Monitoring Services, Member Engagement Initiatives and Healthcare Support programs.

Job Requirements:

- Unrestricted RN license with the ability to become licensed in additional States, as required.

- Recent 3 years clinical experience in areas of Med/Surg, Pediatrics or Emergency Nursing desired.

- Minimum of an Associate degree from a two-year college or technical school or Diploma Nursing Program

- Strong critical thinking skills and desire to provide outstanding customer service

- Ability to work as part of a team

- Effective communication skills to interact with members, patients, and physicians, both oral and written communications

- Proficient computer skills with the ability to use multiple programs simultaneously

---

Also, some newspapers include *Online Employment* sections in their online editions. These are usually unique listings, specific to the location. It is worth checking out your local newspaper's website to see if they post their own classified job ads on their website.

Local businesses like dentists' or doctors' offices, car dealers, and apartment complexes that have always advertised in the Help Wanted are still advertising there, but probably reaching a smaller audience. Often, those are the only places you will find those particular job postings online.

Sometimes the ads are presented as un-searchable images, organized into the traditional classifieds categories – perfect duplicates of the printed paper. Sometimes the printed classifieds are converted into searchable text.

Sadly, the number of those "classic" classifieds actually being published online seems to be declining. Many newspapers, including the largest, adapted to the new competition from large job sites by outsourcing the "Jobs" portion of their website to those same employment super sites, often Indeed, CareerBuilder, or Monster. Essentially, they provide a window into the existing database of jobs at a different site, quite disconnected from the "real" Help Wanted ads appearing in the printed editions of the paper.

Make a note on your *To Do List* to monitor newspaper sites regularly. Job listings change on a daily, even an hourly, basis. Bookmark your "finds" as you go. Record URLs in your notebook and keep notes on all actions that you take so that you can efficiently return to sites of particular interest. Return several times weekly to view updates.

Online Work Source #5: Newsletters & Newsgroups

There are many helpful work-online websites that will send you recent job advertisements regularly. Join their mailing lists, subscribe to their newsletters, and sign up for job alerts.

Some examples are:

- Home Job Stop: *HomeJobStop.com*
- Career Builder: *CareerBuilder.com*
- Indeed: *Indeed.com*
- Monster: *Monster.com*

Work Source #6: Freelance Networks

Working as a freelancer means that you are self-employed, and that you charge by the hour, day, or project. Typically, on a freelance network site, an employer posts a project to be completed, and freelancers from within the network express interest in completing the project, usually through a bidding process, with the lowest bid usually winning.

Freelance networks allow freelancers to look for work within their own field, or even to break into a new career market, through access to hundreds, even thousands, of potential income opportunities. Check out some of the freelancer networks. Select those you may want to join to work as a freelancer, perhaps in combination with a more long-term online job, or if you aspire to expand your work experience into new areas.

UpWork.com (formerly eLance and oDesk) is one major freelancer site, with job opportunities in a range of categories, including:

- Web Developers
- Mobile Developers
- Designers & Creatives
- Writers
- Sales & Marketing
- Virtual Assistants
- Customer Service Agents
- Accountants and Bookkeepers

Freelancers.net is another freelancer network that has been matching freelancers seeking work with clients needing their services since 1999. *Freelancers.net* is focused on the United Kingdom but lists many jobs from across the globe that regularly use freelancers from outside Great Britain. Listing yourself on *freelancers.net* is free, both for freelancers and for potential employers.

Another freelancer network is: *https://www.freelancer.com/,* with jobs listed in all the usual categories, plus: Product Sourcing & Manufacturing, Translation & Languages, and Data Entry & Admin.

Three Tips for Finding Online Work

Stay Organized While Searching

Throughout the search process, keep URLs and Login information organized in a small notebook. Keep an updated log of sites where you post your résumé and portfolio or apply for a job, leaving space to record the results when you hear back. Use index cards or an online calendar to keep track of what you are sending to whom, when, and with what results. Also, take excellent notes. Save bookmarks, organized into folders, for sites to which you plan to return regularly.

Request Feedback

When you receive a response, request additional feedback on any application for which you are not selected. Sometimes even small changes to your résumé or cover letter could make all the difference. Adding one piece of equipment to your home office or finding a way to create a quieter work environment, or taking a class, or adding a certification could be the key that changes a "no" to a "yes" response. Find out what you need to be doing better or differently, then do it.

Knowing how to improve your game and become more marketable is itself a valuable skill as you go through the job hunting process. The more you invest in yourself through ongoing learning, the more valuable you become to potential employers.

Know How Much Action Is Enough

How much job search activity is *enough* to locate the optimum online work for you? Use the same "job search math" as you would if you were looking for a job "out there." The magic number cited by job hunting experts is 100. Roughly stated, assume that it will require 100 genuine actions on your part to yield 10 responses, that will turn into 5 serious possibilities, that will result in the one job (or set of clients) that will be perfect for you.

What constitutes an action? Blanketing a hundred employers with a generic résumé that does not specifically show how you match their needs… This does *not* count as an action. E-mailing everyone in your e-mail address book that you are "looking for a job"… This does *not* qualify either. These typical patterns are known *not* to work.

What *does* count are actions where you actively attend to the matchmaking process. Since you are the one who knows best why you would be great at doing a particular job, it is your task to take the lead in making your own matches. Some actions that *do* count towards your goal of 100 include:

- Applying for a specific job, following the application guidelines and requirements;
- Sending a customized cover letter and résumé to a contract employer that is seeking additional expertise and talent;
- Presenting yourself and your portfolio to someone who needs what you can do;
- Listing yourself with an online agency and responding to a specific work posting.

To determine how many actions to take each week, think of how many weeks you have available to locate work, then do the math. If you take one action a week, for example, how long will it take you to complete 100 actions? That would be 52 actions a year. So, to get to 100 would take you almost *two years*!

$$\frac{100\ actions}{52\ actions/year} = 2 \text{ years}$$

Too long? Then work the numbers in the other direction. Five genuine actions a week would bring you to 100, and the culmination of the process, within *20 weeks*.

$$\frac{100\ actions}{5\ actions/week} = 20 \text{ weeks}$$

Even better, 20 actions a week would bring you to the culmination within *five weeks*. Sound good?

$$\frac{100\ actions}{20\ actions/week} = 5 \text{ weeks}$$

Of course, these numbers are guidelines only, not absolutes. The specifics may vary somewhat, depending on several factors. But the concept holds. Decreased activity increases the duration of the job search timeline. Increased activity decreases that duration. The key is to plan *enough* activity to meet your goals within the timeframe you have in mind. So go for 100! Job hunting is an action sport. 100 yards to a football field. 100 actions to get your ideal job. Play ball!

Now What About You?

So many possibilities for working online... And so many types of interesting work you could be doing, while preserving part of your time for other retirement pursuits. Select three specific actionable ideas for working in cyberspace to add to what you will consider later when you "make your match and move."

And So...

You now know something about working online in retirement. This may be the ideal plan for you as you set out on your own combination of pathways, expressing your own unique self and talents in ways that engage you and make full use of what you have to offer. But, wait, there's more. In the next chapter, we will look at some of the many, many options for working "out there," wherever "there" is, in ways that are engaging and new... or that at the very least are new to *you*. Again, prepare to think outside the box... or at least to think outside YOUR box. For starters, have you ever considered a career as Santa Claus?

Read on to learn about retirement work "out there." There are many, many more options beyond becoming the stereotypical Wal-Mart greeter. And there are important ways to choose among these options in ways that optimally suit your reinvented SELF.

CHAPTER 9:
Option #2: Work "Out There"

Well now you are confused. Why would you consider working "out there" when retiring just recently freed you from all that? If you wanted to stay "out there," working at a job, why were you counting the days until your retirement? After a lifetime of work, culminating in the eventual "promised land" of retirement, isn't work "out there" exactly what you DON'T want to do?

Yes and no. Yes, it is probably true that you do *not* want to work as much you did before—too many hours, too much time away from home, too much all-out effort. And, yes, you may *not* want to work at the same type of job you held during your lifetime career—too much compromise, too much being defined by the job and not by your unique self, too much feeling drained and exhausted by the end of the day. Also, you may wish for more balance and more freedom in your life after 30 or 40 years of too much stress and too many constraints.

What's New About Working "Out There"?

In order for you to consider working "out there" again, you likely will want, to some degree, to keep control of the where, the what and the when. You will want your work to fit in with your life, and not the other way around as it was before. And you will want assurance that your life will continue to "belong" to you, not to your employer. Remember, this is YOUR time. Work YOUR way.

Now that you are "retired," the essence of what will be new and different about working "out there," if you do decide to do it, is mainly a change in your mindset about who is in charge of what. Then it was them, now it is you!

When you entered your career three or four decades ago as a young and upcoming worker, you may have been willing and content to find a job and to let that job define you—what you did, when you did it, and how it meshed with your personal life. But now you are apt to be more demanding. You expect to be the one to determine for yourself who you are, what you will do, when you will do it, and how it will fit in with the rest of your life. Most importantly, you will want any work that you take on next to match and to engage your reinvented, or reawakened, SELF.

Another important difference—now at least some of your income needs are already being met through some combination of retirement benefits, Social Security, and retirement savings. And you are paying less income tax. You may have additional significant financial advantages, such as a home that is fully paid for, children who are fully launched and financially independent, and possibly a simpler lifestyle.

The sum of these changes in your financial reality is that if you do work "out there" again, you will be less driven by how much income your choice of work generates. Where once you may have set aside as impractical career options that you thought would not earn you a full living, now that you have a somewhat adequate retirement income, those previous options are back on the table.

Furthermore, now any new income will supplement, and not replace, the retirement benefits and Social Security to which you are entitled as a result of your lifetime of hard work. So, it is highly likely that if you do consider working "out there" again, you may want that work to be on a part-time basis.

SNAPSHOT: Kathleen

Kathleen studied nursing after her children were grown and rose to the level of supervisor of the oncology unit at the hospital where she worked. Her many accomplishments included designing and implementing an innovative patient care model that assigned a regular team of doctors and nurses to remain with an individual patient throughout their treatment period.

In a late career change, Kathleen went back to school to study medical ethics. She then became the Director of Medical Ethics at a major university medical school, a job that she found highly fulfilling.

When her husband was incapacitated from a stroke, Kathleen retired from the University to be able to stay home with him. After he passed away, she found that she was still interested in working some of the time but not all of the time, so she considered what she wanted to do next.

Although she did decide to respond to the University's fervent plea that she return to work, she made it clear that she would do this only on the condition that she set her own schedule in a way that would not impact either her University retirement income or her Social Security.

She now works two or three days a week, except for the months of October and May, which she keeps free to pursue her own interests. She also takes off major blocks of time during the Christmas and Easter holiday seasons.

In addition to her work, Kathleen's list of retirement priorities includes continuing as a Guardian Ad Litem and also spending blocks of quality time with her children and grandchildren. She travels to London each year, taking up residence in the same flat, where she devotes herself to reading, exploring the city she loves, and creating lovely miniature watercolors.

Do Employers Want You?

The short answer to the question "Do employers want you?" is "Certainly yes!" Whatever factors led to your retirement from your previous work, they likely had nothing to do with your capabilities. Even if you did not anticipate or actively seek your retirement, in many cases you were still highly valuable to your employer. But you also were very expensive. Many of us have had our lives changed because of an employer's budget decisions.

Or maybe you instigated your retirement yourself, for one reason or another. Even so, you may be willing to continue to work, only not at that job, with that level of stress, and that level of time and energy commitment. Retiring from one job can open the way for another. And there are many employers "out there" who do want you and need what you have to offer.

What Do You Have to Offer an Employer?

Before setting out to navigate the job jungle "out there," consider what you have to offer specifically due to your age and status. Your years of professional experience are invaluable, and can only be gained with time, thus setting you apart from younger job seekers and recent college graduates. In addition to professional experience, you are seasoned in the ways of the world. From decision-making to people skills, your wisdom is a huge asset to companies.

And as a senior employee, you are more likely to feel a sense of commitment and loyalty to the company. Because of this, employers know that you are less likely to jump from one job to another in hopes of advancing your career. Instead, you will want to make the most of the job that you have.

WOW FACTOR

By 2017, over 28 million Baby Boomers 55+ will be employed out of a total of 77 million. That is more than 1 out of every 3 of us.

Four Views of Working "Out There"

To navigate this new world of defining, then finding, your "intentional" work, consider the possibilities "out there" from four viewpoints:

1. **Work that is Available to Us**: What jobs are out there for 55+ workers?
2. **Work that Appeals to Us:** What kinds of work do 55+ workers most want to do?
3. **Work that Engages Us**: What kinds of jobs best fit us, based on the temperaments we fall into—Guardian (SJ), Artisan (SP), Giver (NF), Thinker (NT)—to ensure that our new work engages our authentic selves?
4. **Work that Balances with Our Lives**: What work complements the rest of our retirement lives, without confining us, or exhausting us, or otherwise consuming us?

We will discuss each of these, with an eye to what actions to take to ensure that if you do seek out and sign on to work "out there," the outcome will be one that fully suits you and enhances your life.

View #1: Work that is Available to Us

Times have changed in terms of what work is available to us after we retire. Data from the *Bureau of Labor Statistics* and the *Census Bureau* estimates that most of the job growth between now and 2018 will be in the "social sector," adding 7 million new jobs. Many of these jobs (about 5.9 million) are particularly well suited for older workers.

Some types of work are particularly likely to be performed by "mature" workers. Work areas where 20% or more positions will be held by workers who are 55+ include a range of jobs, from Tour/Travel Guide to Archivist/Curator to Social/Community Service Manager to Animal Trainer or even Private Investigator. A fuller list of those work areas where mature workers will hold 20% or more of the jobs is shown in the table below, again based on data from the *Bureau of Labor Statistics* and the *Census Bureau*.

As you look through this list, highlight any you would consider if you were qualified, or could become qualified, and if you could find a good placement that fits in with your other retirement priorities.

Over 20% of Jobs Held By 55+Workers	
Promotional worker 44%	Entertainment worker 23%
Instructional coordinator 32%	Cost estimator 23%
Clergy 32%	Transportation inspector 23%
Brokerage clerk 30%	Animal trainer 23%
Religious activities director 28%	Personal assistant 23%
Tour/travel guide 27%	Veterinarian 22%

Management analyst 27%	Writer 22%
Postsecondary teacher 27%	Engineer 22%
Construction inspector 26%	Usher/lobby attendant 21%
Locksmith/safe repairer 25%	Pharmacist 21%
Archivist, curator 25%	Ambulance driver/EMT 21%
Correspondence clerk 25%	Environmental scientist 20%
Social service manager 24%	Private investigator 20%

Job Growth Projections for 55+

Looking at a complete list of job areas that will grow substantially in the next five years, then combining them into 40 job groupings, reveals hundreds of thousands of openings, in dozens of interesting areas of work, including many where substantial numbers of those jobs are predicted to go to seniors. The largest numbers of jobs for 55+, factoring in the associated growth in the job market for these areas by 2017, and the proportion of those jobs that will be filled by seniors, range from community service, computers, or social work, each with around 160,000 jobs for seniors, to medical or instructional jobs, each with over 600,000 jobs for seniors.

Top 15 Job Groups for Seniors	
AREA	JOBS FOR SENIORS
1. Medical	636,145
2. Instructional	617,454
3. Financial	501,060
4. Health	475,878
5. Children	399,714

6. Information	355,465
7. Customer Service	326,846
8. Personal Assistance	280,293
9. Religious	230,525
10. Management	214,341
11. Landscaping	211,378
12. Sales	211,168
13. Community Service	162,424
14. Computers	158,685
15. Social Work	155,786

The table below shows all 40 groupings of high growth areas of work, with projections of how many people aged 55+ will be employed in each by 2017. Look through these groupings and highlight any that may appeal to, challenge, and interest you. Include those you would consider only if the work could be done on a part-time basis.

High Growth Job Groupings for Seniors			
Grouping	**Sample Job Titles**	**Growth by 2017**	**55+ Employed**
Animal Service	Animal Trainer, Veterinarian Assistant	23-36%	33,064
Archiving	Archivist, Curator, Museum technician	22%	17,022
Business	Operations Specialist	21%	22,813
Children	Childcare, Preschool teacher, Kindergarten teacher	18-24%	399,714
Communications	Correspondence, Media	18%	19,420
Community service	Community specialist; Manager	25-28%	162,424

Groupings	Sample Job Titles	Growth by 2017	55+ Employed
Computers	Software engineer, Systems analyst	29-38%	158,685
Counseling	Counselor	21%	156,327
Customer service	Counter clerk, Service rep	23-25%	326,846
Data systems	Network Systems, Data communication	53%	33,432
Design	Architect	18%	47,347
Diagnostics	Technologist, Technician	17%	41,114
Engineering	All types	18%	112,363
Entertainment	Usher, Lobby attendant	18-24%	54,031
Estimation	Cost estimator	19%	30,595
Financial	Accountant, Auditor	18-41%	501,060
Food	Preparing, Serving	18%	62,494
Gaming	Supervisor, Manager	19%	32,657
Health	EMT, Practitioner, Physical therapist	18-28%	475,878
Information	Receptionist, Information clerk	17%	355,465
Inspection	Building, Transportation	18-19%	39,727
Instructional	Training Coordinator, Adjunct	18-23%	617,454

Groupings	Sample Job Titles	Growth by 2017	55+ Employed
Investigation	Private investigator	17%	21,280
Landscaping	Supervisor/Manager, Greenskeeper	18%	211,378
Legal	Paralegal, Legal assistant	22%	43,601
Management	Analyst, Consultant	22%	214,341
Medical	Pharmacist, Nurse	23%	636,145
Personal Assistance	Personal aide, Homecare aide	51%	280,293
Planning	Meeting planner, Convention planner	20%	9,188
Promotion	Model, Demonstrator	18%	41,337
Recreation	Recreation worker, Fitness worker	19%	47,173
Religious	Clergy, Religious activities, Religious education	19-21%	230,525
Repairs	Locksmith, Safe repairs, Other repairs	23%	7,832
Research	Computer research, Information research	24%	36,938
Sales	Advertising sales, Service sales, Product sales	21-28%	211,168
Science	Environmental, Geoscience	24%	25,658
Social Work	Social worker	22%	155,786

Groupings	Sample Job Titles	Growth by 2017	55+ Employed
Surveying	Cartographer, Photogrammetrist	24%	8,800
Travel	Tours, Travel guides	20%	12,798
Writing	Technical, Web content, Ghostwriter	20%	13,809

View #2: Work that Appeals to Us

Another way to look at working "out there" from a new viewpoint, is to consider what fields appeal to us. Interestingly, many of the fields that are of particular interest to 55 and over are in the social domain—a domain that promises some of the highest growth and personal satisfaction over the years ahead. In fact, the list of job areas experiencing the most growth is remarkably parallel to the top fields of interest to 55+ workers.

For example, 31% of workers 55+ are interested in working in the instructional area, a domain that is predicted to grow by 18%-23% by 2014, with over 600,000 jobs for older workers. Almost one third (32%) are interested in working with children, an area that promises 18%-24% growth, with almost 400,000 jobs for older workers. So, too, the fields of healthcare, spiritual/religious work, and working with older people. Senior workers have high proportions interested in these areas, matched by projections of strong employment growth, and high numbers of jobs that will go to this group.

Study the chart below showing top fields of interest for 55+ workers. Highlight those areas that may be of interest to you.

Top Fields of Interest for 55+ Workers	
MOST DESIRED FIELDS	PERCENT INTERESTED
Advocacy	36%
Work with children/youth	32%

Conservation	31%
Instruction	31%
Community safety	24%
Local or global poverty alleviation	24%
Spiritual/religious work	23%
Work with older people	17%
Health care: hospital, hospice	17%

View #3: Work that Engages Us

A third way to view work "out there" is to consider the best fit according to your temperament—what area may be a good match for you?

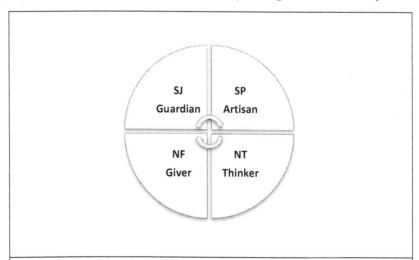

Guardian/Traditionalist: SJ (Sensing/Judging)

Keeper of Service and Duty.
Compulsion: to be useful.
[Inspector. Protector. Supervisor. Provider.]

Artisan/Experiencer: SP (Sensing/Perceiving)

Teacher of Freedom and Joy.
Compulsion: to act freely.
[Crafter. Composer. Promoter. Performer.]

Idealist/Giver: NF (iNtuitive/Feeling)

Bearer of Truth and Meaning.
Compulsion: to "BE."
[Counselor. Healer. Champion. Teacher.]

Thinker: NT (iNtuitive/Thinking)

Provider of Logic and Understanding.
Compulsion: to improve.
[Mastermind. Architect. Inventor. Field Marshal.]

Although you may expect that the best fit for your reinvented SELF will be work in your own temperament category, look also at the work areas for the other three temperaments. Determine if there are other areas that may spark your interest.

Retirement Work for Guardians (SJ)

If you are a *Guardian*—a "keeper of service and duty," compelled to be useful—below are four possible types of new work that you may consider. Picture yourself in each of them and highlight any that look interesting. Fuller information about each of these types of work follows the graphic.

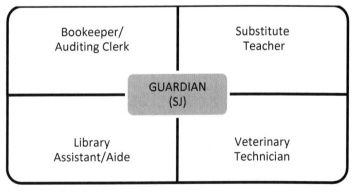

Guardian Job #1: Bookkeeper/Auditing Clerk

As a *Bookkeeper* for a small business, you would handle all financial recordkeeping. Also, you might purchase supplies, process payroll, establish and maintain inventory database systems, track accounts receivable and accounts payable, maintain checking and savings accounts, produce financial reports, follow up on delinquent accounts, oversee audits and reviews, and create quarterly and year end reports.

The hours: Vary by business. Frequently limited to weekly, mid-month and end-of-month, for invoicing or bill-paying functions.

Median pay range: $10.23 to $24.25/hour.

Qualifications: *Certified Public Accountant* (CPA) certification is best. Relevant experience or formal training in accounting/auditing services is a plus. Also: data entry skills, attention to details, working knowledge of financial software such as QuickBooks and Excel, and a calculator.

Guardian Job #2: Substitute Teacher

As a *Substitute Teacher*, you would assume classes midstream, sometimes working from a lesson plan and at other times called upon to improvise. Depending on your background, you may be tapped to teach a range of subjects in grade levels from Kindergarten through Grade 12. If you work with special needs children, you may be more in demand.

Flexibility is essential. School districts typically keep an active roster of substitutes on call who are willing to step into a classroom with little advance notice.

The hours: Ranging from flexible half-days to several weeks of full days. Assignments may become available on a fairly regular basis, but it is your prerogative to refuse a request.

Median pay range: Each school district sets its own pay scale. According to the *National Substitute Teachers Alliance,* the current pay rate for substitutes averages around $105/day.

Qualifications: Most substitute teaching jobs require a BA or BS. For a *State-By-State Summary* of requirements, check out *www.NEA.org/home/14813.htm (NEA)*. For more requirements for your state, and also average salaries, by state, consult the *Substitute Teacher* page of the www.Teacher.org website at *https://www.teacher.org/career/substitute-teacher/*.

Guardian Job #3: Librarian Assistant/Aide

As a *Librarian's Assistant* you would field questions, shelve books, help patrons check out materials, track overdue titles and send notices, as well as process and keep an eye out for lost and damaged items. Most libraries now also include computer workstations, so you may have additional duties of assisting people with conducting online searches to obtain the materials and information they need.

The hours: Schedules vary widely. Large libraries, or those on university campuses, tend to stay open 24 hours a day, while smaller libraries offer more limited daytime and evening hours.

Median pay range: Smaller libraries may rely on volunteers. College, large city, and specialty niche libraries range from $7.69 to $17.82 per hour.

Qualifications: Experience working in libraries is desirable, as is an undergraduate or master's degree. Larger libraries favor research skills using databases and other tools. Other needed skills include: word processing, online searching, accurate recordkeeping, and understanding library operations.

Guardian Job #4: Veterinary Technician

As a *Veterinary Technician*, you would work alongside primarily small animal vets. Your duties might include: preparing pets for surgery, performing lab tests, administering medication and vaccines, emergency nursing care, collecting blood and samples, and the more mundane tasks of recording pet histories and checking their weights. Employment of veterinary technicians is expected to grow 14% by 2020.

Median pay: $10.60 an hour.

Qualifications: A two-year associate degree in veterinary technology is desirable. In 2011, there were 191 veterinary technology programs accredited by the *American Veterinary Medical Association.* Although each state regulates *Veterinary Technicians* differently, most require you to take the *Veterinary Technician National Examination* for credentialing purposes. Clear and calm communication skills are essential.

Retirement Work for Artisans (SP)

If you are an *Artisan*—a "teacher of freedom and joy," compelled to act freely—one of the work areas below may be potentially engaging for you. Picture yourself in each of them and highlight any that you would consider.

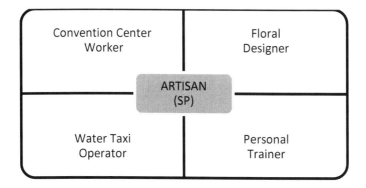

Artisan Job #1: Convention Center Worker

Convention centers in major cities can be wellsprings for a range of part-time jobs with varying skill requirements. Each week, convention venues play host to various industry events, from home to car to boat shows, as well as to concerts and sports competitions.

As a *Convention Center Worker,* you would help with the various tasks of setting up, running, and dismantling conventions.

Part-time jobs include: nurse, parking lot attendant, registration desk, set-up worker, usher, information, or vendor booth attendant. Many jobs require little to no physical labor.

The hours: Work schedules are irregular, and no minimum number of hours is guaranteed. Work is typically available on all days of the year, including holidays. Evening and night hours may be required, depending on the job.

Median pay range: Typically, $10 to $20 an hour.

Qualifications: People skills essential. Working knowledge of the event industry—trade shows, conventions, consumer shows, concerts, athletic events—is a plus for some positions. Pre-employment drug screening and background checks are common.

Artisan Job #2: Floral Designer

As a *Floral Designer* you would use your artistry to cut and arrange live, dried, or silk flowers and greenery into decorative displays. You would help customers select flowers, containers, ribbons, and other accessories, adjusting to their budget, and considering the sentiment or style of the occasion.

Other duties may include: growing flowers; ordering flowers from wholesalers; ensuring adequate supplies to meet customer needs; determining arrangement types, occasions, dates, times, and locations; answering phones and taking orders.

The hours: Hours vary. Most (46%) floral designers work for florists that are open during normal business hours. Another 11% work for grocery stores, where the hours can be longer. Part-time or seasonal opportunities abound, particularly around holidays such as Christmas, Valentine's Day, and Mother's Day.

Median pay: $11.35 per hour.

Qualifications: Artistic ability and knowledge of design are crucial. Also important are customer service, communication and organizational skills.

Artisan Job #3: Water Taxi Operator

As a *Water Taxi Operator*, you would operate a small, motor driven private boat, generally carrying 6 to 20 passengers, providing tours of harbors, canals, or rivers, and possibly also offering commentary on the environs. Employment of motor-boat operators is projected to grow 15% from 2010 to 2020, about as fast as the average for all occupations, driven by the growth in tourism and recreational activities.

The hours: Hours can be daylight as well as evening, and generally include weekends. Many water taxi operators service vacation destinations and have seasonal schedules.

Median pay: Average pay across all water transportation occupations is $22.81 an hour.

Qualifications: Most water transportation jobs require the *Transportation Worker Identification Credential* (TWIC) from the *US Department of Homeland Security*. Most mariners also must have a *Merchant Marine Credential* (MMC). Boat pilots are licensed by the state in which they work; requirements vary.

Other essential qualities include: customer service skills, hand-eye coordination, mechanical ability, and visual acuity.

Artisan Job #4: Personal Trainer

As a *Personal Trainer*, you will demonstrate exercise techniques, adjust machine settings, help clients gauge their physical fitness level, set reasonable goals, and design course plans for your clients' workouts. You also will need grounding in nutrition and diet issues that go hand-in-hand with a fit physique. Most trainers work at health and fitness club facilities. Some offer one-on-one training at clients' homes.

Senior living communities, wellness centers, civic associations, and nonprofits like the *Arthritis Foundation* are often on the lookout for individual or small group trainers.

The hours: Flexible. Mornings, evenings, weekends, according to clients' needs.

Median pay range: $17 to $30 an hour. In larger cities, hourly rates can be $60 to $100 or more. Most health clubs collect payment for sessions, then pay a percentage to you.

Qualifications: Certification is not required by law, but most fitness clubs prefer it. Several national groups offer credentials, including the *American Council on Exercise (ACE)*, the *International Sports Sciences Association* and the *National Strength and Conditioning Association.*

Also, you must be certified in *Cardiopulmonary Resuscitation* (CPR). People skills are essential, as well as a physique that shows that you practice what you preach.

Retirement Work for Givers (NF)

If you are a *Giver*—a "bearer of truth and meaning," with a compulsion to "BE"—the four work areas below may be some possibilities for you. Picture yourself in each of them. Highlight and make notes about any that you might consider.

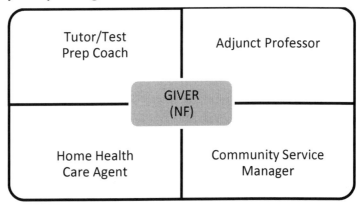

Giver Job #1: Tutor/Test Preparation Coach

As a *Tutor/Test Preparation Coach,* you will work one-on-one with individual students, tutoring them in their areas of need—core curriculum subjects such as world history, physics, science, math, English, and world language, or test prep review—at the student's home or a local library. Public and private schools often pass along tutor referrals to parents.

Online tutoring and test prep jobs, arranged through a tutoring website such as *Tutor.com* or *SmarThinking.com* enable you to work with students inside a secure online "classroom." Teaching and coaching are done using a combination of instant messaging for dialog, interactive whiteboard to draw and work problems, and email attachments to send work back and forth.

The hours: Online sessions may be as short as 25 minutes, but most in-person tutoring sessions range from one to three hours per session, with one to three sessions per week. Most tutoring takes place during the school year, although some parents continue tutoring for their children throughout the summer. Fall and spring are the prime times for test prep tutoring for college-bound students scheduled to take the SAT and ACT aptitude tests. Prep for a range of other standardized tests, such as the GDE, GRE, LSAT and others, are in demand year-round.

Median pay range: $10.27 to $24.21 an hour.

Qualifications: A college degree, background in education and experience working with students is generally preferred. Subject matter expertise, communication skills and an ability to help others succeed, are also essential.

Giver Job #2: Adjunct Professor

As an ***Adjunct Professor,*** you will teach in a University or a 2-year community or technical college classroom, on a class-by-class basis, in your area of expertise. Your students will range from recent high school graduates to career-transitioning adults who are adding new skills or updating old ones.

WOW FACTOR
Adjunct and "contingent" faculty now make up more than half of all faculty positions in the United States.

The *Bureau of Labor Statistics* anticipates that over 523,000 more adjunct teaching jobs will be created in the next few years.

Because adjunct professors are paid considerably lower salaries than permanent faculty, and receive no benefits, many colleges are recruiting more adjuncts on a contractual basis in favor of hiring full-time faculty.

Go online to obtain a copy of current course listings from the college where you would like to teach. Most colleges offer online courses, which may be another option if you have technology savvy and would be at ease teaching classes via computer.

The hours: Vary widely, depending on the number of courses you teach. Summer courses are common. Night and weekend classes are standard. Expect one to three hours of classroom time per week per class, plus preparation and grading time.

Median pay range: Pay rates vary according to the course taught, ranging from $2,500 to $5,000 per course, depending on the number of credit hours, your degree level and teaching experience, and the department for which you will be teaching.

Qualifications: Master's degree in your discipline preferred.

Giver Job #3: Home Health Care Agent

As a *Home-Care Agent*, you will help elderly, ill or disabled people with everyday activities, ranging from bathing and getting dressed, to running errands. Other duties may include: light housekeeping, companionship, grocery shopping, meal preparation and monitoring medications.

WOW FACTOR
Employment of home health care aides is expected to grow by 70% from 2010 to 2020, much faster than the average for all occupations.

The Hours: In-home care jobs can average three to four hours a day, two to three days a week, per client, according to his/her needs. These jobs are often booked through a home-care agency. If you opt for a part-time position in an assisted living facility or hospice, hours will be assigned.

Median pay range: Median pay is $9.70/hour, ranging from $7.36 to $12.45, depending on experience and certification.

Qualifications: Some employers may require a Certified Nurse Assistant (CNA) certification. CPR training is preferred. Good bedside manner is a must. Some positions require transferring or lifting patients and many hours spent on your feet.

Giver Job #4: Community Service Manager

As a *Community Service Manager*, you would coordinate and supervise social service programs and community organizations, directing and leading the staff who provide social services to the public through organizations dedicated to a particular population—such as children, homeless people, or veterans—or that focus on helping people with particular challenges—such as hunger or joblessness. Duties may include:

- Confer with members of the community to determine what types of programs and services are needed.
- Design and oversee programs to meet the needs of the target audience or community.
- Create methods to gather and analyze data to evaluate program impact and effectiveness.
- Report findings to administrators or funders.
- Identify areas that need improvement.
- Develop and manage program and organization budgets.
- Raise funds for programs though the agency's budget process or fundraising campaigns.

WOW FACTOR

Employment of Community Service Managers is expected to grow by 27% from 2010 to 2020, faster than the average for all occupations.

The growth of an aging population accounts for the increased needs for *Community Service Managers*. Other growth factors include the fact that more people with addictions are seeking treatment, and drug offenders are increasingly being sent to treatment programs rather than to jail.

The hours: In larger agencies, *Social and Community Service Managers* typically work full time. Smaller organizations may have part-time positions. Job sharing may be an option.

Median pay: $27.86 an hour.

Qualifications: A bachelor's degree in social work, urban studies, public administration, or a related field is the minimum, with a master's preferred. With a bachelor's degree only, work experience is generally required as well. Also important are analytical, communications, leadership, managerial, and people skills.

Retirement Work for Thinkers (NT)

If you are a *Thinker*—a "provider of logic and understanding," with a compulsion to *improve*—the four areas below may interest you. Picture yourself in each of them; highlight any that may be a possibility.

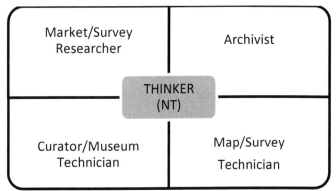

Thinker Job #1: Market/Survey Researcher

As a *Market/Survey Researcher*, you will participate in research tasks conducting surveys (phone, online, mail or door-to-door), analyzing and reporting results. *Market Research* projects vary—evaluating potential sales of a product or service, gathering statistical data on competitors, measuring the effectiveness of a program or service. Potential employers include consumer products firms, university research centers, financial services organizations, government agencies, health care institutions and advertising firms. *Survey Researchers* work in research firms, polling organizations, nonprofits, government agencies, colleges and universities.

WOW FACTOR

Employment of *Market Research Analysts* is expected to grow 41% from 2010 to 2020, much faster than the average for all occupations.

Employment growth of *Market Researchers* will be driven by an increased use of data and market research across all industries in order to understand the needs and wants of customers and measure the effectiveness of marketing and business strategies. *Survey Research* is expected to grow 24%.

For information about careers and salaries in market and survey research, contact the *Council of American Survey Research Organizations* (*CASRO*) and the (MRA), now merged into *Insights Association* (*https://www.InsightsAssociation.org*).

The hours: Flexible, project-based, full time or short assignments.

Median pay: $17.33 an hour for *Survey Research*; $29.10 an hour for *Market Research*.

Qualifications: Both *Market Researchers* and *Survey Researchers* need a combination of research and people skills. A bachelor's degree is the baseline, with a background in liberal arts and social science, including economics, psychology, and sociology. Employers generally prefer candidates who have previous work experience using statistics, analyzing data, or conducting interviews or surveys.

Quantitative skills are important, so courses in mathematics, statistics, sampling theory and survey design, and computer science are helpful. Curiosity and being a stickler for details are positives, since this kind of work relies on precision.

Thinker Job #2: Archivist

As an *Archivist* you will appraise, edit, and maintain permanent records and historically valuable documents, perform research on archival material, and preserve and assess documents and records for their importance, potential value, or historical significance. Also, you may coordinate and offer educational and public outreach programs, such as tours, workshops, lectures, and classes relevant to your collections.

Some *Archivists* specialize in an area of history, such as colonial history, to determine more accurately which records should become part of the archive. Other archivists specialize in one record format such as manuscripts, maps, electronic records, websites, photographs, motion pictures, or sound recordings.

Employment of *Archivists* is projected to grow 12% from 2010 to 2020, based on needs for greater organization of, and access to, increasing volumes of electronic records and information.

Duties may include:

- Preserve and maintain documents and objects; safeguard records by copying to film, videotape, disk, or digital formats.

- Authenticate and appraise documents and materials

- Organize and classify archival records for ease of access; create and maintain accessible computer archives and databases.

- Direct workers who arrange, exhibit and maintain collections.

- Provide reference services and help for users; administer policy guidelines concerning public access to materials.

- Locate new materials and direct their acquisition and display.

The hours: Part-time or full-time.

Median pay: $21.73 an hour.

Qualifications: Although archivists may enter the profession with a variety of undergraduate degrees, most employers prefer a graduate degree in history, library science, archival science, or records management. Many colleges and universities offer courses or practical training.

Thinker Job #3: Curator/Museum Technician

As a *Curator*, you will oversee collections, such as artwork and historic items, and prepare and restore objects and documents in museum collections and exhibits. Working as a *Museum Technician*, you will assist the *Curator* with preparing and caring for museum items. You also will interface with the public, responding to their questions, as well as with outside scholars, helping them to make use of the collections.

Curators and *Museum Technicians* work at museums, zoos, aquariums, botanical gardens, and historical sites. *Curators* in large institutions may travel extensively to evaluate potential additions to the collection, organize exhibits, and conduct research.

The hours: Part-time or full-time.

Median pay: $20.34 an hour

Qualifications: Most museums require curators to have master's degrees in a discipline appropriate to the museum's specialty, or in museum studies. Museum technicians usually need a bachelor's degree related to the museum's specialty, as well as training in museum studies, or previous experience working in museums and designing exhibits.

Other important skills include: *Analytical and critical-thinking skills*—to determine the origin, history, importance, and authenticity of the objects with which they work. *Customer-service skills*—to work directly with the public, describing the collections to nontechnical visitors. *Organizational skills*—to organize collections logically for display. *Technical skills*—to use chemicals and techniques for preserving documents, paintings, fabrics, and pottery, in order to prevent further deterioration.

Thinker Job #4: Map/Survey Technician

As a *Map Technician,* you will collect and use geographic data to assist surveyors and cartographers in making maps of the earth's surface. As a *Survey Technician* you will make site visits to take measurements of the land, working outside in all types of weather, walking and sometimes climbing hills, with heavy packs of instruments and other equipment.

Map Technicians work primarily indoors on computers. *Survey Technicians* travel as a part of the job, sometimes staying overnight, or even relocating temporarily, to be closer to a survey site.

The hours: Typically, full time, possibly with longer hours in summer, when weather and light conditions are most suitable for fieldwork.

Median pay: $18.22 an hour

Qualifications: For *Map Technicians,* postsecondary training is more common. *Survey Technicians* generally need a high school diploma, although some have postsecondary training. An associate's or bachelor's degree in a relevant field, such as geomatics, is beneficial.

Other useful background includes: algebra, geometry, trigonometry, drafting, mechanical drawing, and computer science. Also needed are well-developed skills at decision-making, listening, teamwork, technology and troubleshooting.

View #4: Work that Balances Well with Our Lives

So, you say, "I see so many job opportunities that do sound interesting and could be fun. And I know I have the *experience* and the *wisdom* prized by employers. But ... I'm not so sure about my level of *commitment!* Yes, I *do* want to work. But I *don't* want to work...

...during January, because we live in the north... and I hate the winters... so I need to get away...

... in the summer... because we have a boat... and nothing interferes with our nautical trips...

...early in the morning... it would interfere with my early golf game, because we tee off at 7 AM...

...late at night... I don't drive in the dark... too many intoxicated people on the road...

...on or near the Christmas holidays... it's my favorite time with my extended family...

...full-time... I did that for too many years... putting in 10 to 12 hour days... I'm done with that...

...too far from my home... due to the high price of gas, and how much I value my time...

In other words, I want to be in the driver's seat. I want to work when it is convenient for me to work, doing something that is interesting and fun, on a schedule that fits into my new lifestyle. Am I living in Xanadu? Am I out of touch with reality? Do I really believe that such ideal opportunities exist for someone 55+?

In fact, all of this is, indeed, possible. Starting with the jobs we have already discussed, and adding a few more, here is a smattering of the types of part-time work available to those of us who want to work when we want to work, or who otherwise do not want our next work to interfere with our play.

Jobs with Summers Free

Good plan! You want your summers free—so that you can travel...take care of the grandkids...work in your garden...sail. There are options workwise, especially if you plan to work with your local school system in in some capacity. Some job options include:

- tutor
- teacher's aide
- adult education teacher
- substitute teacher
- athletic coach
- referee
- adjunct professor

- school secretary
- school photographer

Winter-Only Jobs

Winter-only jobs leave you lots of options during the rest of the year. These work out especially well if you have a migration pattern of living in different places based on the season and the weather. If you want to work only in the winter, some options would include:

- ski lodge employee
- seasonal employee in mountainous regions people seek out during the winter months
- holiday decorator
- holiday party organizer
- supplemental gift store staff
- trip or expedition guide to warm destinations closer to, or South of, the equator
- Santa Claus

Summer-Only Jobs

Perhaps you want to work only in the summer. Or maybe you are migrating from one place to another and hope to combine a winter job in one place with a summer job in another. If this work pattern sounds ideal to you, some options could include:

- camp counselor or camp bookkeeper
- lifeguard
- swimming teacher
- child care provider
- art, drama, science children's summer program leader
- summer resort employee
- national park employee
- enrichment class teacher

- house or pet sitter
- refreshment stand operator

Spring-Only Jobs

If you are migrating hither and thither throughout the year, following optimal climates, or checking in with your family on the opposite coast, a spring-only job may be ideal for you. Sample jobs include:

- tax preparer
- landscaper
- tour guide
- graduation or wedding photographer
- graduation or wedding caterer
- home or closet organizing specialist

Confined-Duration Jobs

If you do want to work, but only for a defined period of time, and then be done with it, at least for a while, you may prefer a confined-duration job. Some examples of these jobs include:

- grants writer
- convention staff
- usher
- market survey researcher
- census worker
- event organizer

Flexible-Timeframe Jobs

Or maybe you want to work, but only when it suits you. In that case, a flexible-timeframe job may be ideal for you. Sample jobs include:

- graphic designer
- interior decorator

- handyman
- editor
- personal organizer
- survey researcher

If I Do Want to Work "Out There," Where Do I Start?

So, if you decide that you do want to work "out there" again, where do you start? The answer to this question may surprise you. Start online with these robust job search sites:

1. Monster Spend time looking through *Monster.com*, aptly named because it includes one of the largest number of job listings of any website. It also allows you to upload your resumé and offers networking boards, as well as a search alert service so you can get targeted posts delivered via email.
2. CareerBuilder Also take a close look at *CareerBuilder.com*. CareerBuilder is one of the biggest job boards, and its robust search function allows you to filter by several criteria, including location, degree required and pay range. CareerBuilder partners with news media around the country and collects job listings from them. It also provides career advice and resources for candidates.
3. Indeed A huge aggregator of postings from across the Web, *Indeed.com* consolidates listings from many job boards in one place. It also compiles information from various company career pages and allows you to search locally or globally.
4. Job.com *Job.com* offers weekly job alerts, job search advice, a resumé builder and, of course, job postings. This job search website also allows you to upload your resumé for hiring managers and recruiters to search.

5. SimplyHired

Candidates on _SimplyHired.com/_ can sort their searches to focus on companies that hire veterans, have a high rate of diversity and abide by eco-friendly practices, among other criteria. Offers an email-alert service and lets you save your job searches.

6. Google for Jobs

A product from Google that aims to help job seekers find job listings that are right for them. It compiles listings from many different sources, including other job search engines. Instead of using a specific job search site, users can simply type a job into their Google search bar. Google then pulls up related listings. Users can then narrow their search by type of job, location, company type, date posted, and more.

7. LinkUp.com

If you want to avoid spam, scams, and duplicate job listings, _LinkUp.com_ is the job site for you. LinkUp only posts jobs provided on company websites, providing applicants with often unadvertised jobs. Because the jobs come directly from company sites, you can be sure they are current openings.

8. Employment911.com

The aggregator site _Employment911.com_ allows you to post your résumé to all top 80 job sites at once, reaching over 1.5 million employers.

9. ZipRecruiter.com

The _ZipRecruiter.com_ allows users to post to more than 100 job boards with one submission. User-friendly search and links for both job seekers and employers. Features a mobile friendly interface. Employers are able to add pre-screening interview questions to ensure quality candidates.

Visit them and follow up on leads and registrations, as you see fit. Add them to your URL list and return to them regularly. But don't stop there...

More Online Sites for Job Hunting "Out There"

Some specialized Job Search Sites include:

US.Jobs The *US.Jobs* site is particularly useful for those looking for state government jobs. It collects postings from state work agencies, as well as other company websites. Job seekers have access to a database of more than a million unique, verified positions from nationwide employers. US.Jobs is derived from a partnership between the *Direct Employers Association* and the *National Association of State Workforce Agencies* (NASWA) designed to improve the labor market and directly connect employers and job seekers. There's a Veteran's Job Bank as well as a searchable schedule of upcoming in-person career events.
Dice.com *Dice.com* is the leading site for tech job seekers. You can search by company, job title, keyword, employment type, and location. Registered users can upload a résumé, get salary information, store résumés and cover letters, and track jobs. You'll also find career advice and tech news for job seekers.
CoolWorks.com Niche job websites are an excellent resource for finding job openings that aren't always listed on other sites. There are too many great niche job websites to list them all, but *CoolWorks.com* lists some favorites that are especially useful for job seekers.
TheLadders Focuses on openings for upper-level executives and professionals who are aiming for the management suite. *TheLadders.com*
Glassdoor In addition to providing job listings, *Glassdoor.com* boasts a large database of company reviews submitted by employees. The site promotes itself as giving job seekers insights into a company's work conditions, interview processes, salaries and benefits. Employers use Glassdoor to identify job candidates and market their companies to job seekers.

Additional job hunting sites that are particularly friendly and appropriate to Baby Boomers include:

WorkSearch
AARP.org/work

WorkSearch is an AARP site that offers help for seniors who want to re-enter the workforce. The *WorkSearch Assessment System* on the site allows you to:

1. Do a *job search* by key word, job category, or zip code.

2. Do a *job match* to discover what type of work best suits you.

3. Improve your skills using their free *Tutorials & Demos*.

Workforce50.com
Workforce50.com

This site allows job searching by job title, keyword, city, state, zip. The *Career & Education* section provides:

- salary and job growth data for a wide range of opportunities;

- information on training and education for each career listed;

- sample lists of careers in which site visitors have expressed strong interest.

USAJobs.gov
USAJobs.gov

Once you set up an account on this government jobs site, the site uses your profile information to improve your job search results. You also can use filters to narrow search results, such as location, salary, work schedule or agency.

Under the "Create a USAJOBS Profile" tab, explore the government "Hiring Paths" for possible preference categories for which you may be eligible. Check out the tab for "Explore Opportunities" to see urgent hiring needs of the US government.

NowWhatJobs.net
NowWhatJobs.net

Geared to Baby Boomers and active seniors, this site provides job opportunities, timely advice, corporate profiles, and continuing education options. Other highlights of the site include:
- **The Law**: actual content of applicable laws protecting against age discrimination: *Age Discrimination in Employment Act of 1967*
- **Radio Segments**: live streams from "Careers from the Kitchen Table" and "The Dr. Anne Marie Evers Show"

Retired Brains

www.RetiredBrains.com/search-jobs.html

This free service site offers search areas for: 1) Job Seekers, 2) Work at home, 3) Employment Assistance, and 4) Volunteering. Site search uses the ZipRecruiter Search engine posting thousands of full-time, part-time, temporary and seasonal jobs. Sign up for Job Alerts by setting your criteria.

RetirementJobs.com
RetirementJobs.com

To use this site, you will need to create an account. Once you have joined the site, you will be able to search for jobs by zip code.

Senior Job Bank
http://www.SeniorJobBank.com/

The mission of this site is to bring together employers with qualified older job seekers. From this site, you can job search by keyword, company, city, state or zip code.

> *Retire &Consult*
>
> *https://ConsultantJournal.com/blog/Retire-and-Consult*
>
> Using the site links, you will be able to: design your consulting business, develop your expert status, set consulting fees, build credibility and enlist a one-on-one coaching.

Where Else Do I Look?

In addition to *Online Sources*, the more traditional strategies for job hunting also apply to finding your next job "out there." Four powerful approaches to finding work that can be adjusted to fit your own design, include:

Networking: Communicate with your network of associates, providing specifics about your plans, including the type of work you are interested in pursuing.

Community and Local Leads: Keep an eye out for possibilities in publications and postings in your community.

Spot a Need to Fill: Look for what does not exist as well as what does. What needs to be done that isn't getting done? Who may need help? Could you fill one of these needs?

Volunteer and Transition to Paid Employment: Watch for opportunities to volunteer for projects that could develop into paid employment. This will give you a trial run before committing to work long-term.

My Personal Trifecta

My own search for work after I retired provides a potentially useful model. In sum, my post-retirement jobs—a drama in three acts— came through three sources: *Networking, Community/Local Leads*, and *Online Searching*.

Act I: Networking Nets Surprising Results

To paraphrase a line from a song— "Everybody knows somebody sometime." Put another way, never underestimate the potential of networking, and where it will lead. And don't be shy about tapping into the positions and connections of former and current friends and colleagues. After all, remember that, at some point, you, too, will be in a position to return the favor of making connections for them.

After retiring from a demanding career as a public-school district administrator, I initially experienced the typical "nowhere to go and nothing to do" syndrome. It seemed that all my other retired colleagues had a niche of some type. They all seemed settled and content in pursuing meaningful activities—whether for pay or pleasure—or both. I, on the other hand, felt lost at sea in terms of filling the 12-hour work day void in which I found myself.

All this changed quickly when I began to talk honestly about my sense of being lost, with nothing to do and all day to do it. Two of my former colleagues, who were now supervising teacher interns and student teachers at one or more local universities and colleges, suggested that I call Mr. X at University Y to ascertain whether there were any needs or openings for more supervisors. And, yes, I could use their names as a reference. When I made the call, referencing these colleagues, I soon found myself scheduled for an interview, and the rest is happy history.

I absolutely relished my part-time work as a university supervisor of teacher interns and student teachers, working with talented, dynamic, promising young people, while simultaneously remaining current on national and state initiatives related to my former full-time career as an educator. I made this happen by taking the initiative to *network* with colleagues. Oh, and yes, I'm earning my monthly allotment of "mad money," too!

Act II: Filling the Need Next Door

Each quarter, I looked forward to reading the various booklets, brochures, and flyers that local community organizations published describing workshops, mini-courses, and learning activities where, for a reasonable fee, adults, both young and old, can explore and learn a technical skill, an academic subject, a sports related activity, an arts and crafts technique. These classes are often offered in the evenings, at times that are convenient to students and workers, for a duration of just a few weeks.

I am always in the market to improve my skills in current technologies and to learn new skills as additional technologies emerge. There's so much to know! How to reign in digital pictures! How to master the social networks such as FaceBook and Twitter. How to develop a "marketable skill," such as *QuickBooks* or the latest version of *MS Office* or *Adobe InDesign*. Expert strategies for searching the Internet.

I fully expected to see a menu of choices and offerings to satisfy my technology needs and interests and was eager to sign myself up! Wrong! Not so! There was not one single technology offering by either of the two major organizations near me. How could that be? Was it a lack of interest on the part of the public? Unavailability of knowledgeable staff? Were these technology needs being filled by more extensive, credit-earning courses at local 2-year community and 4-year colleges?

One phone call to both community organizations indicated that, for a combination of reasons it was true that, no, these two groups had nothing to offer would-be technophiles, although, yes, there was a clear demand and need for such programs. Carpe diem! I seized the day! "If I were willing to design and present some workshops that I thought might grab the general public's attention," I said, "would you include them in your next quarterly offerings?" "Yes!" was the enthusiastic response. "And when can you come in for an interview to discuss further your ideas about what you could offer and when? Oh, and would you please just bring along descriptions of the workshops you think might be marketable and attractive to our community audience, so we can get started immediately?"

The end (or should I say, the *beginning*!) of this story—I designed and taught six different technology-related mini-courses, sharing with others two of my passions—teaching and technology—while augmenting my "mad money" fund!

Act III: Online Is Where It's At!

So many of us are "poster people" for the maxim "Luck is when preparation and opportunity meet." In fact, throughout my career, in mentoring younger professionals, I've often used this adage not only to impress upon them the importance of lifetime learning, but also to congratulate them when they secured that perfect job or career opportunity as a result of their hard work and preparation.

And I'd like to think that I've applied this same belief throughout my life as I pursued multiple degrees to prepare myself for that next potential career challenge. But the corollary to my constant drive to learn more about more is that I'm always looking for opportunities to teach—to share what I know with others—to watch for that priceless "aha" moment, when I know my students "get it"!

In my "search to share," I often spend time surfing the online employment opportunities links on local college websites. In our state, we have regional consortiums that offer supplementary academic and training support to our state's public-school districts. Services extend to professional development for teachers, consulting, curriculum design and development, and policy writing services.

While surfing one such job board, when lo and behold, I spotted an opening for a part-time technology trainer. A local nursing home needed someone to teach "basic computer skills" to a group of 100 nurses. And a small public library had received a similar grant to teach local business people.

Without missing a beat, I submitted a résumé, made a follow-up phone call, then designed and submitted eight different mini-courses, ranging from web usage and strategies to MSOffice skills to organizing and presenting digital photos. These workshops were offered in 2–3-hour increments, with morning, afternoon, and evening choices, to accommodate the nurses, who work a variety of shifts, as well as the 9-5ers.

It would be a toss-up to determine who enjoyed these sessions most—who learned the most—the instructor or the participants. And adding to my "mad money" fund was a plus!

Could YOU Be Santa Claus?

To return to a winter-only employment option mentioned earlier in this chapter... What qualifies you to be a professional Santa Claus? How *do* you get a job as Santa Claus? And if you do land such a job, what will you be doing, exactly?

First, you need to look the part. It is best if you are over 50, with a belly, and able to grow a beard. As Santa Claus, you will sit for hours, smiling in a bulky red Santa suit. Wriggling children of all ages will climb up on your lap to whisper their Christmas wishes into your ear. If you are ready and rested, and armed with breath mints, tissues, hand sanitizer and a kind disposition, this work can be pure magic.

If you are hired by an outside Santa Distributor, a firm that places Santas at the 1000+ enclosed shopping malls around the country, the mall to which you are assigned may be at a distance, requiring you to commute, or to spend 40 or more days camped out in a nearby motel room, equipped with a small refrigerator and a microwave.

The Hours: Contract Santas at shopping malls typically work six weeks, starting at Thanksgiving—10 hours a day, with meal breaks. For other Santa jobs—private parties, events, independent stores—hours vary.

Median Pay Range: From $10 an hour to thousands per season. Contract pay for the 40-day season can range from around $10,000 for a rookie to more than $50,000 for a more experienced player, depending on the mall and location.

Qualifications: It helps if you look the part —older, plump, a white beard and a jovial laugh. Santas can be of any race —depending on the venue —but they must be male, although there are some openings for Mrs. Santas and Santa's helpers, too. Having a natural beard is often a prerequisite. You can dye it if necessary—and tuck in padding to get that jelly belly.

Contact smaller malls, department stores, photo shops and special event party planners directly for openings. Also check Craigslist and local classified ads. National staffing services typically provide Santas to the larger malls. Three of the larger staffing services are: *Cherry Hill Photo Enterprises Inc., Worldwide Photography*, and *Noerr Programs Corp.*

You will need to apply to these online agencies and appear for an in-person interview. If they like your look and personality, you will be asked to slip into costume and make-up for them to shoot the headshots that will be sent to mall reps for selection. If you are selected, the service will negotiate your contract and send you to *Santa School* for tips on appropriate behavior and dialog, how to draw out the shy children and calm down the overexcited ones, and even tips about make-up. There will be a criminal background check and drug screening. And be sure not to forget your flu shot. Ho, Ho, Ho!!

Now What About You?

Select three specific actionable ideas for working "out there." to add to what you will consider later when you "make your match and move." Record your three top choices.

And So...

You know now what is "new" and appealing to you about working "out there." You know that employers do want you and that there are many interesting job areas available and growing. You know what work appeals to Boomers as a group, and what work is most likely to engage you, according to your temperament. And you know how to balance work with the rest of your life by deliberately selecting jobs that leave you free during your season of choice... Or with a defined duration ... Or where the work schedule will be flexible.

All of these possibilities involve working FOR someone else. And this may be just what you want to do next.

But before you decide to work FOR someone again, read on. In the next chapter we will look at the option of "Hiring" Yourself or Partnering Up." After all, there's no business like YOUR business...

CHAPTER 10:
Option #3: "Hire" Yourself or "Partner Up"

Some things in life are for certain after all. If you do not EVER AGAIN want to work for someone else… Or if you have the notion that no-one will appreciate what you have to offer… Or if you think the economy is such that even if you did manage to find employment, it would not reward you adequately, either in terms of fun or profit, or both… In any of these cases, there is good news.

There is one employer you WILL want to work for, who WILL appreciate what you have to offer, who WILL want to hire you, and who WILL offer you employment that will reward you.

"And who would that employer be?" you ask. That employer would be YOU. YOU could well be your own best possible future employer.

"But what kind of business would I start?" you ask next. In short, plan to start a business that meets a *need*. Needs can come in three main forms, with various combinations thereof:

1. **Needs for Goods:** What goods do people need (or want) to buy.

2. **Needs for Services:** What services do people need (or want) to have provided for them?

3. **Needs for Creativity:** What do people need (or want) to have created for them?

When you have determined which of these types of needs you could meet, either for goods, services or creativity… And once you determine specifically how you would meet them… And after you have thought about the degree to which filling these particular needs would bring you enjoyment and fulfillment… Then you are ready to design a business that meets those needs, making full use of your own unique twist or advantage. Then you would launch, market, and promote your business, making connections between what you are offering and the people who may need or want it.

Consider Mark Twain as a role model. What was the need he set out to meet—beyond the obvious one of his audience's need and desire to read his humorous stories? Well, apparently one thing Twain determined that people needed was a replacement for suspenders!

Mark Twain Granted His First Patent

December 19, 1871 *[PRESS RELEASE]*

Samuel L. Clemens received patent #121,992 on December 19, 1871 for an Improvement in Adjustable and Detachable Straps for Garments.

Clemens, better known as Mark Twain, and famous for stories such as *Huckleberry Finn* and *Tom Sawyer*, also was an inventor and received a total of three patents. While living in Hartford, Connecticut, Twain received his first patent for an adjustable strap that could be used to tighten shirts at the waist. This strap attached to the back of a shirt, fastened with buttons to keep it in place and was easy to remove. Twain's invention was used not only for shirts, but for underpants and women's corsets as well. His purpose was to do away with suspenders, which he considered uncomfortable.

In 1873, Twain received a patent for a self-pasting scrapbook that was very popular and sold over 25,000 copies. In 1885 he received a patent for a history trivia game.

If the idea of starting a business that meets a need sounds like too much work, think again. Why would you want or need to do all the work yourself? Instead, consider teaming up. Are there people you have known in the past who might, like you, be immersed in their own search for a meaningful pursuit for their next phase of life? Who among these might best complement you and your own talents? Who would you most enjoy working with?

One of these past friends or associates could become your perfect business partner. Or your top choice may even be your life partner. We will talk more about "partnering up" later in this chapter.

There are many ways to get the work done, while at the same time limiting the amount of work that you do yourself. Of course, you always have the option of starting a business that creates jobs for others. You could "hire" yourself as the manager and employ others to carry out all or part of the work under your guidance. You could even hire someone else to function as the acting manager to take charge of ongoing operations and make yourself the "manager in chief." These are essential considerations if you decide to "hire yourself" and start a business, large or small. Your work does, after all, need to balance with your emerging retirement lifestyle.

Businesses that Meet Needs for Goods

Looking around my own small rural locale for ideas about unmet needs for goods, my first thought is that we need a new source for pie! In past years, the Terrell Country Store, at the main (and only) crossroad in our tiny town, has been our primo pie supplier. Demand for pie is so great in our town that the Country Store has been able to run a tight ship, pie-wise, over the years. Locals learned early on that they would have little or no hope of purchasing a pie if they just dropped by the store. If we wanted to be "allowed" to purchase the pie of our choice, we knew we had to follow a strict set of "pie rules." And we knew we were going pay a premium for our pies, around $15 each.

The "rules" ... All pie orders for the week ahead had to be submitted and paid for by Sunday, then picked up the following Wednesday. Pie deadlines were even more stringent before Thanksgiving and Christmas, when orders had to be submitted and prepaid two weeks in advance. And, due to the crush of orders to be filled during the holidays, cream pie orders are NOT allowed at those times! Were these pies worth the trouble, not to mention the cost? Absolutely! And, no, a frozen or supermarket substitute would never suffice!

But then a crisis was upon us! The Country Store went out of business. After that—no more pie! Voila! A golden opportunity for a potential business to meet a pressing need. And this could be a business with *sweet* benefits!

There are hundreds of other ideas for businesses to supply needed (or wanted) goods. We start with pie, then add other items to the list to stimulate your thinking:

- Great pie!
- Specialized parts for classic cars
- Pet treats, toys and holiday costumes (yes, really!)
- Toddler toys and puzzles made from wood, not plastic
- Woven table mats, scarves and garments
- Comfortable walking shoes; shoes that come in WIDE
- Yard and patio furniture that lasts

You have your own ideas to add to this list. And if something is on *your* list as a need or a want, it is likely on other people's lists as well.

Businesses that Meet Needs for Services

Who needs the services you have to offer? So many choices—so many opportunities—so many roads to Oz! Let's start by considering some major groups of people who are ripe for services, beginning with:
- children of all ages
- teen through college students
- working adults
- retired people

When you consider the variety, breadth, and depth of services that each of these groups uses, demands, and needs, just think of all the services you possibly could offer. Again, base your services concept on your own newly designed lifestyle, considering your reinvented and unique SELF—personality, skills, talents, and interests.

Services Children and Their Parents Need

Think about how the society of the family has changed within the last 60 years! When we were young children, working mothers were the exception, not the rule. The" ideal" wife and mother was one who consciously chose to be a stay-at-home mom, dedicating her time and energy to raising her children, tending to household duties, and supporting her husband emotionally and domestically. Conventional wisdom dictated that, ideally, children needed to remain home with mom for as long as possible, to be nurtured and raised under her watchful eye, absorbing her moral values within a stable environment. The terms "pre-school" and "pre-K" were nowhere to be found on society's radar screen.

Dad was the sole bread winner. His role was that of CFO—Chief Financial Officer—who earned enough money to tend to the family's material needs, paying a high price by working long hours, and being subjected to the work world's pressures and stresses. His work sometimes required extensive travel that sometimes kept him from being a part of family activities and occasions.

Now fast-forward to the 21st century. Mom and Dad both work, often both in demanding professions that require long days, frequent business travel, and a myriad of human, work related pressures. Consequently, many couples today have chosen to have smaller, and often delayed, families.

WOW FACTOR

In 1957, the average number of children per family peaked at 3.7. Currently, the average number of children per family household in the United States is .94—less than ONE. In 1957, children ages 0-17 comprised 35% of the total population. In 2012, this same demographic group makes up only 24% (*www.ChildStats.gov/*).

We all are aware of the many reasons for this decline in the number of children being born in the USA—costs of raising a child, priorities that professional couples place on their careers, trends towards starting a family later in life. However, while the number of children per household has substantially decreased, for those couples and single parents who do choose to have a family, the importance they place on how they raise their children has become all-consuming. Average expenditures per year, per child, have risen 40% in the past decade, from around $10,000 to around $14,000. Based on findings from the "Cost of a Child" survey, today's parents spend between $170,000 and $390,000 to raise each child from birth to age 18, *not* including their college education (Jessica Dickler's *The Rising Cost of Raising a Child*. September 2011; CNN Money; *https://CNN.com*)

Increasingly demanding dual careers, combined with escalating parental concerns about children's physical safety, material, social and academic needs—all these factors translate into an extensive list of needs for services targeted to children. This, in turn, suggests business opportunities that serve this population.

Parents with children age 0–12 have urgent needs to find:

- a satisfactory sitter
- a suitable nanny
- the ideal day care center
- the best possible pre-school, pre-K, and K programs
- a safe carpool
- the perfect music, art, dance, athletic program
- an after-school tutoring program
- a reliable after-school care service

If you enjoy working with children, think about each of these categories in terms of your own interests, skills, and talents. Whether you prefer a primary or secondary role, as the one who is in direct contact with children, or as the manager who keeps the enterprise afloat, you have an almost limitless number of opportunities to work meeting one of the above needs, or any number of others.

Services Teen through College Students Need

We are all aware of the social pressure brought to bear on pre-teens, teens, and college students. Their needs loom large—academically, socially, and emotionally. Parents acknowledge the fragility and urgency that characterize these age groups. Pre-teens are plagued with all the frustrations and trauma that come with puberty—their bodily changes, their need for social bonding, their process of self-discovery.

High school kids find themselves dealing with the pressures of alcohol, drugs, dating, developing maturity, peer pressure, and academic achievement. They need to come to terms with their passage to adulthood—the "what do I do next?" question emerges all too soon. College? Military service? Vocational training? The work world?

If college is their choice, many young people find they are not ready to handle the freedom and independence college life brings. Many also face financial hardships in the form of student loans and possibly the need to work while in school. The ambiguity of choosing a future career, and the necessity of maintaining a respectable GPA, add stress to the balance, especially when combined with a need to be employed.

What can you, as a self-hiring retired person, offer this group? To start your thinking, some of their needs include:

- after-school supervision
- homework help or tutoring
- after-school music or art activities
- exercise, aerobics, sports or other physical activities
- social networking supervision
- reliable transportation to work, social, school, activities
- assistance with academic research and projects
- counseling or mentoring
- summer programs
- part-time employment opportunities

Can you, as a self-hiring retiree, see yourself assuming one of the above roles, providing these services to young people, through either direct or indirect involvement? There are so many ways to be in the company of young people, to give them the opportunity to interact with an experienced member of an older generation, while providing a needed service that you enjoy doing, and that supplements your retirement income! It doesn't get any better than that.

Services Working Adults Need

The entire population of working adults has needs, whether they have children or not. And this is our largest group, comprising more than 63.7% of the total population in 2012, according to the *Bureau of Labor Statistics.*

The opportunities that self-hiring retirees must work for and with this demographic group are endless—ranging from the mundane to the exotic—from housekeeping to horticulture—from accounting to adventure travel—from home baking to grooming poodles. Whatever you offer to do for this time-challenged group, you can be sure that someone out there, fighting the good fight, climbing the corporate ladder, needs to have it done. All that is needed is for you to find each other and make a match!

Remember what your life was like when you were working full time? All non-work-related chores, tasks and appointments had to be squeezed into your so-called "free time"—those too short lunch breaks, after work and weekend timeslots. There never seemed to be enough hours in the day to do everything you needed to get done. With your constant juggling and multi-tasking, admit it—sometimes you dropped the ball, threw your hands up in frustration, and ceded defeat! A true confession—I once had to retrace 20 miles and drive back into Charleston because, after leaving my after-hours job, to my shame and amazement, I was half way home before I realized that I had forgotten to pick up my children!

During your working years, you were the one who needed any help you could get! Now your role is reversed. You find yourself in a position where you can be the one to alleviate some of the pressure that the working majority faces on a daily basis. *You* can become their hands, feet, brains—their full-service concierge—the very person *you* so desperately needed before you retired—the one whose services you would have been thankful to use, if only you could have found someone reliable, energetic and capable like YOU to help you out.

Tasks that working adults need to have done, include:

- **Mundane tasks—**
  Watering plants; picking up dry-cleaning, mail, drugstore or department store items; maintaining calendars for appointments, children's activities, family functions.
- **Pampering tasks—**
  Providing fresh flowers, candle scents, gift shopping.
- **Domestic tasks—**
  Organizing cupboards, closets, drawers; taking care of gardens, lawns, yards; redecorating; house sitting; home maintenance; home cleaning; shopping and stocking household items; routine tasks like laundry, ironing, mending; organizing and displaying family and travel photos.
- **Social tasks—**
  Planning, organizing and orchestrating parties (birthday, holiday, wedding, anniversary, family celebrations, graduations); designing and sending invitations; purchasing and setting up

decorations; planning menus; providing food; arranging music and entertainment; procuring photographer, favors/gifts.

- **Travel tasks—**
Making complete reservations, including transportation, lodging, sightseeing, adventure activities, shopping; planning suitcase contents; child-sitting, pet-sitting, plant-sitting, house-sitting, business-sitting, elder-sitting.

- **Food-related tasks—**
Food shopping; menu design; planning and executing formal dinner parties or informal gatherings; high-quality home-cooked entrées and prepared meals; home baking.

- **Fashion tasks—**
Shopping for clothes, utilizing the best online clothing sites, including specialty and discount shops and department stores.

- **Petcare tasks—**
Feeding, walking, cleaning animals and their living environments; arranging for and taking pets to vet appointments.

- **Body-related tasks—**
Providing massages, personal training, hair, nails, cosmetics products and services. Pedicures.

- **Money and business tasks—**
Personal accounting, tax preparation, checkbook monitoring, bill paying services; filing and organizing personal documents; travel reimbursement paperwork; business correspondence.

- **Large project tasks—**
Cleaning/organizing attics, basements, garages, file cabinets, closets. Repurposing space for master suites, home offices, home theaters, playrooms, art studios, workshops, home gyms.

- **Maintaining entertainment and technology systems—**
Ensuring that all video, voice, network, data systems, computers, phones, TVs are in perfect working order. Teaching personal technology use, one-on-one.

Services for *Us*–What Retired People Need

Another group with needs for services is *us*—the ever-growing senior population, ranging from those of us who are newly retired to those who have been retired for a decade or more.

With 77 million Boomers, our demands for services are growing at exponential rates, creating a current and emerging target market that holds many exciting and potentially lucrative possibilities. In fact, we have dedicated the entire next chapter to this group.

Again, the focus of our discussion, both now and later, is "What does this group need?" What kinds of services do people like *you* need that *you* may want to be the one to offer? Services that retired people need, and will gladly pay for, include:

- Recreational and activity needs
- Intellectual and mental stimulation needs
- Physical and health needs
- Financial and money management needs
- Home maintenance and remodeling needs
- Travel needs
- Transportation needs

SNAPSHOT: Ralph

Ralph was the town dentist, with his offices on Main Street of his small Virginia town. So, what does a dentist do next after he retires? And what does he do with the Victorian-style home that had housed his dental offices? The answer to this question is that he, along with his wife Betty, found a need and met it. They transformed the office into Zazzy'z, a popular and comfortable local hang-out, serving breakfast, coffees, and lunch. And, for those who prefer not to cook at all, Zazzy'z also offers frozen home-cooked entrées to take home for dinner, with delectable options that include: Tidewater Crab Cakes with spicy mustard sauce, rolled in hand-crumbled crackers and lightly sautéed, served with fresh steamed asparagus and white rice. Or Champagne Chicken with artichoke hearts, baked in a champagne cream and served with steamed rice.

Zazzy'z quickly became a local favorite. Small groups gathered in lounge chairs around a large round coffee table in the bookshop bay window. Repeat customers snagged their favorite tables, and settled in. Local artists displayed their work on a rotating basis, gaining both exposure and sales.

> *Ralph and Betty started Zazzy'z with the idea of ultimately turning the business over to their daughter and son-in-law. But they drifted in and out all day. Betty also writes books about antiques, her area of expertise. And Ralph became Director of the College for Older Adults, operated through the SWVA (SW Virginia) Higher Education Center. He also has his own radio show on WEHC FM (an NPR affiliate) called "Minding Your Brain," where he interviews experts, adding his own research-based commentary, on Brain Health.*

You surely can expand on these various categories and lists of services. Where could the reenergized and reinvented YOU and the diversity of needs for services match up? What could you offer to:

1. Capitalize on the talents, skills, experiences and interests that you personally and professionally could bring to bear, and
2. Meet the needs of one or more of the above categories—children, teens through college, working adults and retired people?

Businesses that Meet Needs for Creativity

Returning to Richard Florida's research introduced in Chapter 4, a growing role of creativity in our economy is the fundamental theme that runs through a host of seemingly unrelated changes in American society. The ongoing increase in the options for creative work suggest some excellent opportunities for retirement work that would engage you, and through which you could express your special gifts.

"Creative class" workers are found in a variety of fields, from engineering to theater, biotech to education, architecture to small business. Creativity workers constitute an estimated 40 million individuals who fall into two broad categories (based on the *Standard Occupational Classification System* codes): 1) the *Super-Creative Core*, and 2) *Creative Professionals*.

The *Super-Creative Core* is a group that comprises about 12% of all U.S. workers. This group includes a wide range of occupations (science, engineering, education, computer programming, research), with arts, design, and media workers forming a small subset. Their primary job function is to create and innovate, contributing commercial products, consumer goods, problem solving and "problem find-ing" (Florida, 2002). The *Creative Professionals* are classic knowledge-based workers, including those working in healthcare, business and finance, the legal sector, and education. They "draw on complex bodies of knowledge to solve specific problems."

WOW FACTOR

Although creative work makes up roughly 1/3 of total em-ployment, it accounts for more than 1/2 of all wages and sal-aries in America. Creative employment has seen relatively low rates of unemployment during the course of the eco-nomic crisis and is expected to account for roughly HALF of all projected U.S. employment growth - adding 6.8 million new jobs by 2018.

How to "Go Creative"

So... What does the "creative class" have to do with you? It has eve-rything to do with you! The whole purpose and thrust of this book is to address your "specialness"—to determine a match between your uniqueness, your passion, and what needs to be done. This journey of personal discovery may well take you down a new path that culmi-nates in you launching yourself into creative work of some type.

What would your own creativity work be? You may engage in work that is typical of the *Creative Core*—writing, painting, photography, sculpture, woodwork. Or you may take off in the entirely different creative direction of a *Creative Professional*, engaging in problem solving or even problem finding. You may invent all new products... Or create solutions... Or design better systems... Or otherwise make the world safer, more comfortable, more accessible, more engaging...

How About Creative Consulting?

Think about it—for x number of years, you worked within a field—as a plumber, a nurse, a truck driver, a financial analyst, a teacher, a chef. Think about the unique experiences you had and what you learned along the way—experiences and knowledge to which only those in your type of work have been privy.

You can most certainly parlay that knowledge into offering valuable, revenue-generating advice to others. Consulting is an ideal way to earn a supplemental income. You can work part time, set your own schedule, choose which clients and types of work you want to engage in, and even determine your own salary.

Businesses that Meet Needs Abroad

Since it will be you who decides what business you start, whether it offers goods, services or creativity, it also will be your decision to determine where it will be located. Here's where it pays to dream big.

International Living Magazine (*InternationalLiving.com*) claims that there are appealing places in the world where you can live comfortably on less than $700 a month. Or you could retire like royalty on a $1,600-a-month budget (for a couple) that will "buy you a comfortable home in a beautiful setting, pay for your food, utilities, housekeeper, gardener…and even leave you with money left over for entertainment and travel!" *International Living* has been helping readers for over 31 years to "live better lives for less, retire earlier, travel further, have a lot of fun, and even make money—overseas." Many people, including many retired people, are doing just this.

What Business to Start

It's not surprising that many of us, at one time or another, have given at least a cursory nod to the idea of starting our own business. Possibly the thought came from reading about someone who had achieved phenomenal success following their passion. Or maybe some specific life experience sparked the thought "I have a great idea that I think could make money, and I would love to try it!" Perhaps now is the time to take that leap of faith into the entrepreneurial pool!

Of course, there is no guarantee that if you decide to launch your own business, you'll soon be featured on the cover of Forbes. But, like many of us, you may have a latent money-making idea that has remained dormant all these years as you carried out the important business of making a living, raising a family, and saving for retirement—an idea that has stubbornly persisted to this day, creating a spring to your step, a sparkle in your eye, and a fire in your belly when you think of the possibility of following through on your dream. The question is, what do you do with it now? And if not now, when?

To move ahead towards a plan, or to at least think through the possibilities, here are the three keys:

1. Identify matches between what people need and what you most enjoy doing.
2. Select work that would engage your essential self, including your type, temperament, interests, values, skills, and traits.
3. Consider if you may want to partner up.

Identify Matches Between What People Need and What You Enjoy

In our previous lives, we worked and worked, then tried to "fit in" a small packet of fun. Now we find that our whole formula for living has been reversed! We can play and play, then intersperse our leisure with some form of work, if we so choose. How delicious and delightful!

Of course, the question is, "Now that I have all this latitude, precisely what is it that I want to do? What is it that I always look forward to doing—that so consumes me that I lose track of time?

And what if there was a way my natural drive, my creativity, my love for horseback riding or sailing or travel, could become a source of limited, but adequate, discretionary cash? Imagine doing something that I am passionate about, that I would want to be doing anyway, for the fun of it, and getting paid for it! What might that be like?

Clearly, as part of embarking on this "what if I could get paid to do what I already love doing and would do anyway" journey, it is also necessary to ask yourself if anyone needs to have done whatever it is you love to do. Return now to some of the ideas about what people need, and look for items that you do well, and possibly even do for fun.

Read through these areas of need and check those that you enjoy and do well. Then from those you checked, circle the checkmarks of the ones you might consider doing for others—for pay, of course.

What Do You Like to Do?	
☐ **Organizing**: cupboards, file cabinets, drawers, clothes closets, offices, garages, basements	☐ **Yard and Garden**: planting, mulching, weeding, lawn care, hedging, pruning
☐ **Redecorating**: painting, wallpapering, furnishings, functional design, decorating	☐ **Party Planning**: birthday, holiday, wedding, anniversary, graduation, family celebrations
☐ **Sitting Services**: child-sitting, pet-sitting, plant-sitting, house-sitting, business-sitting, elder-sitting	☐ **Food Planning Service**s: shopping, menu designing; meal preparation
☐ **Pet Services**: feeding, walking, cleaning animals and their living environment	☐ **Photo Services**: organizing, enhancing, and displaying family and travel photos
☐ **Tutoring**: assisting children who have difficulty learning in the school setting	☐ **Writing Services**: business correspondence, memoires, family histories and stories
☐ **Catering**: formal dinner parties, meal-centered family gatherings, celebrations, receptions.	☐ **Home Maintenance**: painting, repairs, sprinkler systems, AC systems, repairs, shelving
☐ **Travel Planning**: reservations, for transportation, lodging, sightseeing, adventure activities, shopping	☐ **Financial Services**: personal accounting, tax preparation, checkbook monitoring, bill paying
☐ **Major Home Projects**: patios, porches, sunrooms, outdoor living spaces; basements, home offices, art studios, workshops	☐ **Technology Services**: ensuring that video, network, computers, phones, TVs are in perfect working order; teaching personal technology use

Select Work that Engages Your Temperament

Returning to the four temperaments (from Chapter 5), one of which defines you—*Guardian, Artisan, Giver* or *Thinker*—whatever business you develop needs to be one where the work you will be doing is work that will engage you over time, given your temperament.

Think through what the actual tasks will be. Then evaluate that option based on the degree to which you will gain satisfaction by completing those tasks over the months and years ahead.

If the major tasks of a goods, services or creativity business do not suit you, and will not engage you long term, that may not be the right type of business or enterprise for you. On the other hand, if some of the tasks of a business do excite you but others do not, this venture may still be a good possibility for you IF you find a partner whose interests and unique abilities balance and complement yours.

If you are a **Guardian** (SJ), with a drive to be useful, your temperament may fit well, and be well engaged, by service business possibilities. Your inclination to seek stability and orderliness, and your underlying capacity to be practical, organized, thorough and systematic, make you a natural for providing many of the types of services that are particularly in demand.

If you are an **Artisan/Experiencer** (SP), with a need to act freely, you may find your best match with either a service or a creativity business that involves action, challenge and resourcefulness. To add to the excitement and adventure of an opportunity, consider shifting the location of your business abroad.

If you are a **Giver** (NF), for whom purpose, and personal growth are essential, your best options may be providing services or creating products or solutions that focus on human potential and that bring out the best in others.

If you are a **Thinker** (NT), with a drive to improve, your best selections of possible goods, service or creativity businesses may be ones where you will be adequately challenged. Your ability to see possibilities, understand complexities and design solutions are of considerable value, and will need to be engaged in order that an enterprise holds your interest over time.

Consider Partnering Up: Joint Employment

If the scope of work goes beyond what you can hope to accomplish by yourself, it may make sense to think bigger and consider enlisting a partner. Think about what your full list of collective capabilities would be if you combined what you can do with what your spouse can do. What if you added your son into the mix? And his wife? And your daughter? And her husband? Or what if you went beyond your family and added in your best friend? Or a former colleague?

Pick Your PARDNAH!

If you do decide you would like to partner up with someone, the question arises, "Who?" Start by looking nearby, possibly your spouse. After all, for all these years, you have shared your hopes and dreams with this person. Who better knows your Achilles' heel, your "ups and downs," your "highs and lows"? Or maybe your best option is your longtime friend and college roommate. You know—the one who was best man or maid of honor at your wedding; the one after whom you named your first-born; the person you always seem to call first in good times and bad. It might be someone you met recently, brought together by the very business idea you are planning to bring to fruition. You may have met online, or at a conference or expo, or any similar type of venue where people with similar interests, talents, and skills gather to see what's new, to glean ideas for their own projects, and to meet and network with colleagues.

In any of these scenarios, before you even consider the possibility of venturing into a professional working partnership, be sure that:

- there exists a high level of mutual confidence, trust, and respect;

- each partner has a clear understanding of his/her role and is well qualified to perform it;

- the individual skills, talents and strengths of each partner are clearly defined and understood by both parties;

- you have had at least some practical, long-term experience working together on defined projects or activities;

- you share the same vision for your venture and agree upon the strategic direction your endeavor should take;

- you both have clear expectations (financial and professional) of what each person hopes to derive from the partnership; and
- you have a balance of skills, talents, strengths and expertise that complement and supplement each other.

Communication Is Key

As with any partnership, including marriage, the importance of communication between business partners cannot be overestimated. A regular "coming together" for reality/progress checks, whether remotely or in person, is essential and critical to the success of any partnership.

Think about how many personal relationships have disintegrated because of a lack of communication on the part of one partner or both. In advance, agree upon a means of communicating both formally and informally on a regular and frequent basis, whether these connections are made through:

- scheduled meetings
- informal breakfast/lunch/ sessions
- phone conversations
- e-mails
- annual shared trips or conference attendance
- Skype sessions or texts

In these times of virtual commuting, it is easier, but even more important, to work "side by side" even when you live 500 miles apart.

Partnership Pros, Cons & Potential Minefields

Pause to consider the pros, cons and potential minefields of partnering up before you make the leap. Determine if the *Pros*, in your case, outweigh the *Cons*. And make every effort to avoid the *Minefields*.

Pros

By partnering up, you will:

- Enjoy a partner who complements and supplements your personality, skill set, talents and areas of expertise.
- Get to share the workload. This allows both members to enjoy vacations without worrying about "who's minding the store."

- Gain another perspective on your ideas by listening to your partner's point of view.
- Share the financial burden of start-up and maintenance costs.
- Share the risks of failure as well as the joys of success.
- Have someone with whom to commiserate and problem solve when setbacks and unexpected roadblocks appear.
- Share the burden of responsible decision-making.
- Have a partner with whom to discuss current steps and future directions in your business plan.
- Expand your circle of colleagues with two sets of business and social contacts.

Cons

Are you willing and able to work collaboratively, as a member of a team, knowing that sometimes your ideas may need to be adapted to accommodate your partner's perspective? Highly inflated egos can easily jeopardize a potentially healthy partnership. Intelligent compromise, based on objective data, needs to rule the day, rather than emotional attachment to an idea that flies in the face of current conventional wisdom.

Are you ready to take the risk of jeopardizing the permanency and health of the relationship you had with this person before you entered into the partnership? Many a marriage, friendship, and business relationship has bitten the dust because of the partners' failure to resolve conflicts and come to a meeting of the minds. What happens when you and your partner cannot agree on a major business decision that needs to be made? "Irreconcilable differences" apply in business as well as in marriage!

The element of trust must be paramount when it comes to sharing the financial burdens and ramifications of operating your business. You or your partner always runs the risk of withstanding the worst of the other's financial incompetence or possibly even dishonesty.

Don't underestimate the role that money plays in a successful partnership. Having enough money, agreeing on expenditures, determining how much each party will contribute—agreement on all these factors can make or break a successful partnership.

Potential Minefields

If you decide to partner with your spouse, pause to anticipate what this will mean. You already share your bed and breakfast, your mornings and evenings, and all other things domestic, social, and familial, with this person. Think long and hard. Do you really want to add to all this time together working with him/her all day, every day? Similar issues apply when considering a business partnership with a friend. If you value your friendship as a haven from the stresses and challenges of your life, do you really want to load down your relationship with a shared enterprise?

Before you embark on such an expanded commitment, consider, too, your personality similarities and differences. Think about the professional assets and liabilities that each of you would bring to the partnership. Setting emotions aside, do the two of you, combined, possess all the skills, talents, knowledge, and connections that are essential to ensure the success of your proposed business?

A friend of mine jokingly refers to his female business partner as his "work wife." The analogy refers to the proximity that business partners experience, and the potential fragility of such relationships. Just as seemingly perfect marriages can end in bitter divorce, so too can a business partnership between spouses or best friends end in disaster. At the outset, potential partners need to confront the possibility that joining forces in a business partnership may change forever what is now a special relationship.

And although that person you met at that fabulous weekend expo in Vegas may seem to be the one, how much do you truly know about this person? In a few days, how much could you possibly have learned about his/her value system, character, work ethic, personality, and actual expertise as it relates to the business you plan to start?

Kahlil Gibran's famous observation that "your joy and your sorrow spring from the selfsame source" aptly applies to the entire gamut of issues to be considered when seeking out that ideal complementary business partner. First, consider personality styles and differences. Should both parties be different or the same when it comes to being—

- laid back versus regimented

- gregarious versus introverted
- task-oriented versus idea-generating
- impulsive (works in spurts) versus structured (adheres to a schedule)
- Concrete/Sequential versus Random/Abstract

Second, examine the importance of *complementary talents and skills*. Who has the greatest strength when it comes to—

- business acumen
- effective money management
- task focus
- technical skill
- interpersonal skill
- marketing/sales experience
- community/social/political connections
- content expertise

Third, consider the *different lifestyles* within the partnership. Is the business relationship jeopardized or enhanced if—

- one member works full time while the other is semi-retired
- one is self-employed, while the other is employed by an organization that makes demands
- one has major family involvements, while the other is free-wheeling and independent
- one has more of a commitment to a hobby or leisure time activity than the other
- one has more volunteer or travel priorities than the other

Hire a Good Lawyer!

So ... now that you have waded through the labyrinth of potential partnership pros, cons and minefields, you are surer than ever that you have the right idea, the perfect partner, and all the stars are aligned in your favor. This is good, but you are not done yet. Next on your list is to get yourself a good lawyer!

Yes, you will need to secure professional help to draw up a legal partnership agreement, *regardless* of who that partner is—faithful spouse, eternal friend, close relative, or newly-found business colleague. In fact, the closer the personal relationship, the more important it is to crystallize any business plan in writing, from startup requirements to exit strategy. It is in the best interest of both parties to realize that such a strategy provides protection for you both.

Get it in Writing!

Darrell Zahorsky, small business expert and consultant, says that, according to the Small Business Administration (SBA), a good business partnership agreement should include:

- type of business
- amount of equity invested by each partner
- partners' pay and compensation
- how profits and losses will be shared
- restrictions of authority and expenditures
- dispute settlement clause
- length of partnership
- settlement plan in case of death or incapacitation of one partner
- provisions for changing or dissolving the partnership
- distribution of assets on dissolution, including cases in which one partner is obliged to buy out the other's interest —for instance, if one wants to quit the business
- how to assess the total value of the business at dissolution, including who will do the appraisal, using what methodology

How to Start Your Own Business

Once you have identified your business concept and feel certain that what you will be doing meets your own needs as well as the needs of one or more target groups, move through this six-step process, first mentally (and on paper), then for real.

1. Consult resources
2. Design your business
3. Design your promotional materials
4. Create your business
5. Prepare to launch
6. Launch, market and promote

Now let's discuss each of these in turn, in very general terms, for now. Clearly, it will be necessary to consult resources beyond this book if you do plan to start a business. But this will get you started.

Consult Business Startup Resources

Let's get real! you say. There are so many skills to hone, so many landmines to navigate, so many non-believers to avoid, so many dollars to raise, so many details waiting to sabotage my ambition.

Fear not. Don't lose heart. Help is on the way in terms of specific resources designed to help you launch your dream. For starters, explore the links on these five websites:

USA.Gov: *USA.gov/Start-Business*   Provides resources for the self-employed, including financial assistance, hiring, laws, scams and fraud, and taxes.
Business USA: *www.BUSA.org*   Describes itself as "A product of collective thoughts and inputs from agencies... committed to making this site a one-stop shop for everything related to business in the USA.
Small Business Administration: *www.SBA.gov*   A wealth of information on starting and managing a small business.
Entrepreneur: *www.Entrepreneur.com*   Features "How-To" Guides for starting your own business.
BizFilings: *www.BizFilings.com*   Covers all aspects of starting, running, and growing a business. Offers a *Learning Center* to get you up to speed as a business owner, and an easy online incorporation process.

Design Your Business

If you are establishing your own business, take a few weeks to contemplate the "What? Who? Where? When? and How?"

- WHAT will your business be called? WHAT will it offer?

  Create a name for your business that clearly describes the services you provide.

- WHO will your business serve?

- WHERE will your business be located?

  Is it your plan to base your business from home? Online? Abroad? All three? A good means for deciding the *where* is to decide where *you* would like to live as your business evolves.

- WHEN will your business be open?

  Will your business be available full-time? More importantly, how much of the time will you need to be there? Only certain hours of the day? Certain days of the week? Certain weeks of the month? Certain months of the year? If you want your own on-site time to be limited, consider who will serve as Manager-in-Chief in your absence.

- HOW will your business operate?

  Will you operate your business on your own? With a partner? By hiring staff? By hiring a manager plus staff? Consider what you want as a lifestyle, as well as financial limitations and ramifications, then work backwards from these criteria.

Design Your Logo, Promotional Materials & Website

Next create your promotional materials and website.

- Select a URL for your business website that aligns with the terms your potential clients will use when they do web searches for the goods, services, or creativity you will provide.

- Set up a simple website for your business or hire someone to do this for you.

- Create a brochure and business cards for your business, with your Website address and other critical contact and descriptive information clearly displayed.

For a simple business, these tasks will take much less time and will be much less daunting than you may expect, because there are so many productivity tools available to help you get started. To locate a great URL for your business, go to *GoDaddy.com* and do searches using various combinations of words, phrases, and titles you would consider to be suitable until you locate one that is still available. Then click on "Register" and GoDaddy will take care of the rest for you, charging your credit card about $15.

To design your website quickly, you may consider using other products available through GoDaddy.com that allow you to "create your website tonight." This will get you up and running quickly. You can always return later with a more complex website that you design using more powerful tools and templates like DIVI. Or, for a price, elicit the services of a professional to design your site for you. You may even consider hiring one of your children (or grandchildren) to accomplish the task.

To prepare your brochures, business cards, and announcement cards, go to *VistaPrint.com* and start playing with the various design tools. For each of these items, type in some appropriate, relevant words, select various images and colors, and experiment with different fonts. When you arrive at a draft that satisfies you, click it into your shopping cart. If you need professional graphics to add to your design, purchase them through *Dreamstime.com*. Your brochures, business cards, and announcements will be on their way to you within an hour or so, and without a major outlay of cash.

Later you may come back to VistaPrint for additional products and services, such as:

- mailing lists tailored to your market demographics and locale
- postcards for direct mail campaigns
- services to print, address, and mail postcards to your lists of potential and/or current clients

- T-shirts, pens, ball caps, car door magnets and other promotional items carrying your business logo

Prepare to Launch

Next, set a date for launching your business. Let the world know what you will be offering, and otherwise get the word out.

Begin by completing these tasks:

- Announce your business to family, friends, and community;

- Set up Google ads and post on Craigslist and Facebook to advertise the services you offer;

- Incorporate your business using the business type most appropriate for what you are doing;

- Open a business bank account;

- If you will be accepting credit card payment, select a payment processing service such as Intuit, or plan to use PayPal.

To select what type of business "entity" you want to be, and to carry out your incorporation, begin in the *Learning Center* on the *Bizfilings.com* website, where you can learn about your choices, and the advantages and disadvantages of each. It is relatively easy to gather enough information about your incorporation options to then move forward with confidence, undaunted by the alphabet soup of types and terms—C Corp, S Corp, LLC, LP, LLP, or PLLC. Once you have made your decision, you can even use the website to guide you through your incorporation process. Or you can have your lawyer set your business up for you.

Once you have established yourself as a business entity, you will be able to use your business EIN number to open a business bank account, and even to arrange for a payment processing company (like Intuit) to accept credit card payments on your behalf and deposit the money you earn into your account.

Launch, Market and Promote

Once the date of your launch has come and gone, establish marketing and promotion as ongoing tasks. Follow these and other plans to keep your business in the forefront of the minds of all those potential clients who may need and want your goods, services, or creativity.

- Continue your Google and Facebook ads;

- Continue posting via Craigslist to advertise your services;

- Make presentations to groups whose membership includes, or has contact with, your potential clients;

- Promote your Website using SEO (Search Engine Optimization) techniques, or hire someone to do this for you;

- Circulate your marketing materials until you have all the business you want or need.

Even your business bookkeeping becomes surprisingly manageable using a combination of Quicken or *QuickBooks* and a payment processing service such as Intuit. Go to *Intuit.com* to watch videos and learn how client payments will be processed and how your business accounting tasks will be accomplished. Your role will be to set up your list of clients, oversee the invoice and payment processes, then monitor the deposits made to your business bank account.

The short version of this process using QuickBooks is:

1. Set up your client information in *QuickBooks*;
2. Invoice your clients for payment;
3. Client pays by credit card;
4. Accept the payment, and;
5. Money shows up in your bank account.

What once would have required a staff to accomplish, now can be done by you weekly (or biweekly or monthly), in an hour or less. And it can be done at any time, day or night, and from anywhere you happen to be living or visiting at the time.

15 Sample Goods, Services or Creativity Businesses

Consider these sample business ideas to get you started. There are many others you could add. Do not allow these suggestions to limit your creativity, imagination or options.

Scrapbooking

The latest trend among families is to preserve their memories in fancy albums. These memoires make great gifts for any occasion—birthdays, anniversaries, weddings, religious events, and holidays. An entire industry has arisen around buttons, bows and gizmos to adorn the pages of scrapbooks. For someone who is artistically inclined, scrapbooking is a dream hobby that can turn part-time job if you offer these services to others.

Preparing Home-Cooked Meals

If you like to cook, the armies of working parents who want to feed their families home-cooked meals, but lack the time or energy to do so, would love to meet you. When both Mom and Dad work all day, who is left to prepare a daily feast in time for the family to sit down to dinner together at six o'clock—before or after shuttling the kids around to scouts, gymnastics, karate, band and dance lessons? Enter *you*, who will do just that, and deliver it ready-to-serve. Move over fattening fast food. Make way for balanced, healthy, nutritious, delicious, freshly home cooked meals, served piping hot and with a smile. Clean-up services included, on request!

Sewing & Mending

You truly enjoy TV and have a long list of programs that claim you as an avid fan. In fact, you usually schedule your daily tasks and errands around your favorite TV shows. However, you can't just sit idle as you watch the latest edition of *Dancing with the Stars* or *American Idol*. Your hands need to be busy... and you just happen to derive a great deal of satisfaction from sewing. Enter the need for hems—on skirts, on pants, on slacks, on sleeves! No need for a fancy sewing machine—all you need is a small sewing kit and a few extra-busy clients with fancy wardrobes!

From Whence Did I Come?

You have spent hours on the computer researching your family's lineage, developing trees and charts tracing your genealogical heritage. And your research finds you ever more fascinated with the past. Why not parlay your experience into a for-profit endeavor? In our age of multi-culturalism, families have developed an ever-growing obsession in knowing about their ancestral roots. This is an interest you can satisfy by conducting authentic research, then writing up the findings and presenting them in an appealing graphic format.

Honey-Do List Doer (AKA: "Domestic Peace Keeper")

How often have you been the recipient (or the perpetrator) of your spouse's frustration, disappointment, even sometimes anger, over household chores that have remained undone, and broken things that have remained unfixed? And none of your various excuses (no time, no tools, no skills) have succeeded in mollifying the annoyed, harried, harassed requestor. Rest assured, you have many fellow "fixers"—some capable, some not—all buried beneath their own "Honey Do" lists that only get longer.

Mr. Handyman you to the rescue—the hero who gets a high fixing the unfixable. You might as well get paid for the fun you have solving problems. Hearing the sighs of relief and seeing the smiles on your clients' faces is almost worth as much as the money you earn. If you tackle this as a self-employed fix-it-up service, count on a smorgasbord of odd jobs that range from repairing running toilets to tightening loose door handles. It can be a toss-up of woodworking, plumbing, and even painting projects. There are more structured opportunities in this arena with building owners who hire part-time workers to perform basic maintenance. Pay ranges from $15 to $25 an hour, and up to $50 an hour for certain custom work.

If you are competent in various aspects of home improvement, have your own tools, are self-motivated and have good customer-service skills, this business may be for you. Be sure to achieve a first-name basis with the manager of your local hardware store.

National Geographic, Here I Come

Do you have a photographer's eye, and a passion for photography? While others never leave home without their iPhones and Kindle Fires, is it your camera that has become the extension of your hands? Have old country barns, unusually shaped trees, modern "Madonna with child" images, reflections in still waters become your specialties? Why not matt your best work inexpensively, and show off your wares at spring, fall, and holiday craft fairs? Or you could sell your best images online.

Lori Allen, in her article about the "math" of stock photography calculates that if you upload your photos to four agencies at the rate of 20 photos per week and assume that you will earn around $1 per image per month, your photography income will reach over $23,000 within one year, $69,120 by year two, and $115,200 by your third year. Of course, for this to work, you will need to consistently take good photos that sell. And you will need to learn to edit your images in a program like *Adobe Photoshop* or *Lightroom* before you submit them to agencies.

Animal Lovers Delight

It seems as though animal owners and animal lovers have taken their relationship with animals to an all new level. We now take our pets to the dentist. Vets administer MRI's. Hotel and motel chains offer "pet-friendly" rooms. Owners arrange for "play-dates" with "compatible" animal friends. Today's pet owners will go to any length and will spare no expense to assure adequate care and comfort for their beloved pets and animals. Average expenditures are around $11,000 over the lifetime of an indoor cat and $13,000 for a small to medium-sized dog (*PetPlace.com*).

So, you are someone who prefers animals to people. You are happiest when these small or large furry creatures surround you. Here's your chance to pet sit, walk, groom, or otherwise cater to, your friends', families', neighbors', community's animal needs. Pet grooming a pooch or kitty runs the gamut from bathing to nail-trimming to brushing to cleaning ears and clipping coats. Pay ranges are from $7.76 to $17.80 an hour, up to $25 to $30 an hour for an experienced groomer.

Pet sitters handle daily exercising, prepare meals and fill water bowls, feed fish, hamsters and gerbils, and scoop out litter boxes—along with spreading around that all-essential dose of special love and attention. The main requirements for this kind of work are a rapport with animals and a reputation for being dependable. The charge for a single visit to a pet can range from $10 to $22 and up, depending on the location, and $45 or more for overnight care. *Dog walkers* often walk more than one dog at a time, in all kinds of weather, at least twice a day. Median hourly pay is $8 per dog, up to $37.50 with experience (according to *PayScale.com*).

Calling All Fitness Freaks

Now that you are retired, you still want to retain those firm thighs, that flexibility. In the warm months you are happiest when you are biking, hiking, or swimming. You are familiar with all the best biking and hiking trails within a 100-mile radius. You know their lengths, degrees of difficulty, and how to spot and identify wildlife along the way. In the cold months, you are adept at cross-country skiing, snow shoeing and even sledding. You know which trails are best groomed, how to dress appropriately, how to pace yourself.

Why not become a fitness guide who caters specifically to those in the over-55 crowd who want to stay in shape? Members would pay an annual fee for your "club" membership that features a monthly newsletter of fitness tips and includes yourself as guide on a range of trips and adventures. Imagine doing what you love, staying fit, sharing your passion with other Boomers, and getting paid in the process.

Flea Market Maniac

Flea markets are "your thing." You truly believe that one man's trash is another man's treasure. In fact, you have finally admitted that your garage is now maxed out housing the goodies you have managed to amass in the short time since you retired, and you are seriously contemplating investing in an outdoor shed to house future acquisitions.

Enter *E-Bay*—the answer to every collector's dream. Wouldn't it be fun to see whether others share your taste in collectables by posting some of your items for sale—that is, if you are emotionally ready and able to "let go" of your flea market finds. Consider this. Every time you make a sale, this will generate a "need" for you to do more shopping!

But let's take this eBay frenzy one step further. Why not become a broker for those hoarders who seek a vending outlet for their treasures, but have neither time nor talent nor inclination to master the E-Bay process? For a percentage fee, you can be the "connector" between buyer and seller. Your task—to photograph, describe, and post product descriptions, photos, selling conditions and prices for your clients' goods. Imagine... Then you will feel perfectly guilt-free when you spend more time surfing E-Bay goodies!

Bartending/Waitressing/Catering

If you are an amiable person, with charm and an uncanny ability to smooth ruffled feathers of disgruntled customers... And if you have patience, a good memory and organizational skills, and can smile though your feet are aching... You may be the perfect candidate for starting a food and beverage service business. These services are in high demand, especially during the end-of-year holiday party season, and for all those special family and social occasions. Schedules will fluctuate. Nights, weekend, and lunch times can peak during the weeks before and during holidays. Median pay for bartending and wait staff services ranges from $7 to $15 an hour, plus tips. Caterers should expect an hourly range between $10 and $20 an hour.

Running a Cleaning Business

Are you kidding?! I *hate* house cleaning! In fact, I'll do anything to avoid it, using every real or imagined excuse to postpone pulling out that vac, managing that mop, dusting those knick-knacks. But, then again, you might be one of those persons who derive a great deal of satisfaction from all that scrubbing, scouring, and shining, and seeing the immediate and tangible results of your efforts.

The good news—you won't need a great deal of start-up money, nor will you need an advanced degree in Housekeeping 101. Other benefits—because it's a cash only business, you will not need to get involved in billing procedures, or otherwise wait to get paid. And you will be able to work at your own pace, part time or full time.

You may want to specialize—such as vacation rental homes or small local businesses or a specific type of cleaning such as organizing closets and drawers, shampooing rugs, pressure washing patios and decks, or even being the rare individual who *does* do windows.

And if you don't want to dirty your own hands, or you don't have the energy for all that "bend and stretch," you can always hire someone else to do the actual cleaning and pay them an agreed-upon amount, while you spend your time supervising and marketing your business.

Operating a Bed & Breakfast

If, as a couple, your favorite place is your own home and you are happiest when you are there… If you spend most of your financial resources on home improvements, inside and out… Opening a Bed-and-Breakfast might be the ideal way for you to earn extra cash—especially if, as empty-nesters, you have surplus rooms standing empty.

There are a few realities you will need to anticipate and plan for. First, you had better love to cook, because you will need to commit to preparing irresistible meals every morning. Or, of course, you could hire a local to come in to prepare gourmet meals for your guests. If so, be sure to have them prepare enough extra for you and your spouse, and thus enjoy the side-benefit of a personal breakfast chef. Then there's the "spotless sunshine" factor. Do you think you'll really enjoy cleaning up after strangers...day after day? Of course, these tasks, too, could be "outsourced," possibly relieving you of many of your own household duties. Oh well…

Most importantly, would you welcome the "adventurous" opportunity to meet all types of people from every walk of life? Travelers who choose to stay at B & B's tend to be friendly, gregarious, well-travelled, and laid back. A morning breakfast can easily turn into a two-hour social gathering, with conversation covering a range of topics. As a host, you will need to be interesting and interested, not only in the world around you, but also in your guests.

An ideal location for your enterprise would need to be remote enough to provide peace, quiet and bucolic beauty, but also close enough to one or more cultural, tourist, resort attractions to be an interesting vacation destination. This may require that you move to a more appealing spot, which is not much of a problem, since you will be able to enjoy your new, improved location along with your guests.

Gardening, Lawn Care, & Landscaping

I have a brother who refuses to purchase a power lawn mower. He just loves "the feel" of controlling the hand mower, and the satisfaction he derives from forming his own mowing patterns crisscrossing his lawn. But mostly, he finds mowing to be an effective way to stay in incredible shape! Luckily, his yard, although quite large, is relatively flat! No one is suggesting that you would want to go to these extremes to stay in shape. But you may be a person who gains a sense of pleasure and accomplishment when you transform a bland yard, or a wild tangle, into a tidy, aesthetically-pleasing vista.

For this type of business, you will need basic yard equipment like what you use on your own property. The difference—you also will need to invest in more and better tools, as well as a means for transporting them. So, you will have the perfect excuse to purchase that edger or pruner or small cultivator that you secretly would love to own and use on your own property. And what about that small (or large) pick-up truck, with trailer-hitch and flatbed trailer? All these may come in handy for your own yard tasks as well as for carting around your equipment to your clients' properties. All this equipment and transport will be tax deductible, of course, since these purchases are needed to support your business. Being able to purchase plants at wholesale prices will be yet another nice perk!

One caveat... In the summer months, it will be important to avoid the high-noon heat. So, you will need to plan your work for early mornings and late afternoons. Of course, you could always designate the high heat part of the day as siesta time! What a hardship...

Online Store

The idea of launching an Internet business sounds intriguing, you say, but where would we start and what would we sell? Start by taking a minute to think about how you currently spend your time when shopping on the Internet yourself. What could you sell that would appeal to a shopper like you? Do you spend hours searching fishing-supplies websites to find the latest, greatest lures? Do you surf from one site to another looking for unusual baby nursery items for your recently-born twin grandchildren? Do you have a passion for collecting vintage dolls? Are you involved in a serious hobby, like crafting or handiwork or restoring classic cars or welding yard art from metal scraps?

If so, your first product may be waiting to be discovered in your garage, attic, workroom, or basement. The sky is the limit in terms of what you may want to sell, how you would present your product, how many hours you would invest in your new venture. A few caveats... There will be expenses involved to launch your online business. Also, it will help if you have at least some background in sales and marketing. And you will need to be computer savvy.

Teaching Abroad

The advantage of teaching abroad lies in the fact that to teach abroad, you will need to live abroad. This is an ideal way to experience the true ambience and flavor of a foreign culture. Teaching abroad can take many different forms. Most American military bases employ U.S. educators to teach children of military families. Many American parents living abroad for business or job obligations, prefer to employ the services of an American educator. Even some foreign families with the financial means, seek to hire American teachers to teach their children in English, rather than in their native tongue. Or you (and possibly your partner as well) may be fortunate enough to secure teaching positions in your content areas in foreign schools.

This type of venture will require unique personalities who are able to adjust to living in a foreign country and immerse themselves in a culture that is very different from their own. As a couple, you will need to be mature, broadminded, and flexible, with a sense of humor, and the ability to adjust to unexpected, even unusual, circumstances. You may consider offering specialized services such as preparing students attending high school overseas to return to the USA for college.

A Cautionary Note

First, let's not forget where and why you decided to start your newly established "fun and funds" project. Your primary objective is to have fun doing what you love to do—what you would be almost willing to do for free—for the sheer joy of doing it. Do not become so obsessed with your passion that it ceases to be play and instead becomes drudgery. Secondly, keep the financial rewards in perspective. You may never make a full living "working" at your hobby, on your own schedule, in tandem with your other retirement activities. But at this point in your life, this hopefully is not your sole source of income. And it's not only about the money anyway. If your goal is to earn supplemental retirement income—enough, perhaps to travel regularly or to indulge some other passion—you are on the right course. You may even make enough to sustain your fun, so you won't need to tap into your basic retirement savings—yet.

Now What About You?

Select three specific actionable ideas for hiring yourself or partnering up." Record your three top choices.

And So...

You might have found the content of this chapter the most personally attractive, the most relevant of all. This idea of "hiring yourself," and possibly "partnering up," can be very appealing, especially if the business you pursue is something you love anyway. So, if you catch yourself shouting "Yes, I can do this!" then what are you waiting for? After all, you are at that point in your life where you want to do what you want to do. This could mean that the time has come. The stars may now be aligned for you to go forth and tackle, on your own or in collaboration, your new venture.

But first, before your business concept is locked in, read ahead to consider whether you may want to expand or adjust your plans to include us, the 77 million retiring Boomers as your potential clients. Who better to benefit by serving the needs of this exploding population than someone who is one of us?

CHAPTER 11:
Option #4: Work For "Us"– Seniors Serving Seniors

"Why would I want to work for or with Seniors as my retirement business?" you ask. After all, I *am* one myself. Whatever I might have to offer older adults by way of goods, services, or creativity, may be something that I need, too.

You've just identified one of the whys to consider working for "us" as a retirement option. Who better than *you* to know what goods and services Seniors will need and want, since these are things you may need or want yourself, either now or in the future. You will be brilliantly capable of anticipating what other Seniors will seek out, and understanding the relevance, even the urgency, of obtaining it.

Boomers Are a Very Large Group

A second "why" for choosing the option of working for "us" is that the retiring Boomer population is a *very large* group, as you have learned throughout this book. Starting with the first wave of Boomers who reached full retirement age in 2011 and continuing over the next 20 years at the rate of around *10,000 each day*, over 77 million Boomers will retire. According to the *UN Population Division, by 2035 one out of every five people will be 65 or older.*

The Boomer group is not only prolific in number, but also unprecedented in longevity. Adding in retirees from the Silent Generation and dividing ourselves into subgroups based on common market needs and demands, clarifies some of the emerging entrepreneurial potential. With the "Young Old" (ages 65-74), "Middle Old" (ages 75-84) and "Older Old" (ages 85 and above), we can anticipate that the growth of each of these subgroups over the next 20 years will be startling, due to significant increases in life expectancy. The "Older Old" subgroup will show the most stunning growth rate of all.

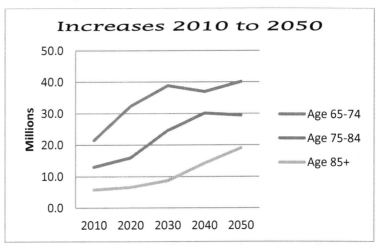

The Young Old age group will increase from 21.4 million to over 40 million between 2010 and 2050, according to the U.S. Bureau of the Census. This represents a growth rate of 87%. The Middle Old age group will show a steady rise from 13 million to over 29 million between 2010 and 2050— enlarged by 126%.

By far the fastest-growing segment of the total population will be the Older Old—those 85 and over. This subgroup will more than triple, from 5.8 million in 2010 to over 19 million, by 2050, representing a stunning surge of 228%. This rate of increase is twice that of the Young Old (65-74), and almost four times that of the total population.

Growth Rates by Subgroup			
	Young Old Age 65-74	Middle Old Age 75-84	Older Old Age 85+
2010	21.4 million	13.0 million	5.8 million
2020	32.3 million	15.9 million	6.6 million
2030	38.8 million	24.6 million	8.7 million
2040	36.9 million	30.1 million	14.2 million
2050	40.1 million	29.4 million	19.0 million

Boomers Have Resources to Spend

A third "why" for looking closely at the needs and priorities of aging Boomers as an option for your retirement business is that as a group Boomers control a major part of all material resources. They have the greatest buying power in the history of our country, with more discretionary income than any other age group. And they spend more money in proportion to their numbers.

WOW FACTOR
Boomers hold 70% of the total net worth of all American households—$7 trillion of wealth. They own 80% of all money in savings and loan associations.

Even during the recession, *Baby Boomer Magazine* (*Babyboomer-Magazine.com*) reported that Boomers were still the largest consumer group in America, accounting for a dramatic 40% of total consumer demand.

As empty nesters, Boomers spend their money on goods and services for themselves. They are Internet-savvy, and use technology for business and pleasure, shopping, communicating, and reading online. They own and use the latest technology tools and toys, including smartphones, high-end TV's, and high-tech cars.

WOW FACTOR
While the 50+ population represents 32% of the country's population, they currently earn almost $2 trillion annually, and control 77% of the total net worth, almost $46 trillion. This group generates 50% of discretionary spending, 2.5 times the average of younger households. (Ken Dychtwald, CEO of Age Wave: *www.Marketwatch.com*).

Boomers Are Creating New Markets

A fourth "why" supporting the idea that aging Boomers are a market that is ripe with possibility for all manner of goods and services, is that, according to most predictions, Boomers will predominantly choose to live independent lifestyles until late in, if not throughout, their lifetimes. Whole industries are emerging to offer the products and services that will make this prolonged independence possible.

This trend translates into many potential opportunities for you to generate an income stream that supports your own lengthened and more expansive lifestyle, and that also keeps you fully engaged well into the future.

SNAPSHOT: DJ Wika Szmyt

DJ Wika Szmyt, 73, spends her retirement days behind a DJ console, playing music at a club in Warsaw three days a week, and watching people dance to her rhythms. She plays disco, rumba, or samba for a mostly older audience, because she feels she is giving them a new take on life. As well as working at the club, DJ Wika has also been involved in other musical projects, including parties where she plays for younger audiences.

Transgenerational Design

The terms "transgenerational design," "universal design," "design for all" and "human-centered design" have entered the lexicon specifically to address the emerging "practice of making products and environments compatible with those physical and sensory impairments [that are] associated with human aging and that limit major life activities" (*Transgenerational.org*).

As the world's population rapidly grows older, businesses are recognizing that it is important to create new products that are easily used by people throughout their lifetimes—whatever their current capabilities or limitations. The Transgenerational Design initiative dictates that intelligent decisions be made during a product's design, production, marketing, promotion, and sales processes in order that these products and services may be used comfortably by an aging population with a wide range of abilities.

When applied effectively, Transgenerational Design addresses the need for products that enhance the quality of life for users of all ages. When considering common functional limitations and how they could inhibit independence—such as sensory changes, balance and falling, dysmobility, and memory and confusion—the intent and the challenge is to develop products that support and extend independence by accommodating human limitations in vision, hearing, touch, dexterity, and mobility. These types of product microenvironments will "enhance the overall quality of life for people of all ages and abilities," according to James Pirkl, author of Transgenerational Design: Products for an Aging Population.

One major trend, according to Ford Motor's Pete Hardigan, is to design cars with features that make them safer for aging drivers, including blind spot monitoring and lane departure prevention systems that use cameras and radars to monitor the area around the car. These new systems offer visual and auditory warnings and intervene if the vehicle starts to drift out of its lane or turns towards a passing car. Ford and Nissan have developed "old age" suits to be worn by their engineers, using a system of straps and braces to restrict movement and simulate a decreased mobility condition like arthritis. Sight-limiting goggles do the same to simulate reduced vision.

As positive as these design innovations have been, the rapid development in the production and actual emergence and implementation of self-driving cars carries with it the promise that physical limitations and handicaps vis a vis driving may soon be a non-issue.

Architects and homebuilders, too, are increasingly attentive to Transgenerational Design. As applied to housing, these concepts stress accessibility and comfort for all people, whether young, old, in peak physical shape, or physically challenged.

According to a presentation at the American Institute of Architects' 2012 National Convention and Design Exposition, entitled "Welcome Home," the aging population in the 21st century will demand design concepts such as:

- main-floor living
- step-free entries and access between rooms
- non-slip flooring
- five-foot turning radii in rooms
- increased daylight or special lighting

Meanwhile, there will be an increasing demand for plaza-style communities that combine housing, shopping, dining, and services to accommodate a lifestyle that does not require a car (Taryn Plumb, 2012, in Worcester Business Journal Online; www.wbjournal.com).

The priority that Boomers place on independent living impacts existing housing as well as new. Dozens of thriving businesses offer various home renovation products to support the continued ability of older people to live in their own homes. Some highly-affordable examples include:

- *Shower roll-in* conversions. Cost: $1200, installed;
- *Bathtub walk-in* conversions. Cost: $1200, installed;
- *Walk-in whirlpool* tub conversions. Cost: $1600, installed;
- *Stair lifts* that provide independence, convenience, and security, as an alternative to selling a multi-level home and moving to a single-level home. Cost: starting at $1900, installed;
- *Dumbwaiters*, to move goods and supplies up and down stairs in multi-storied homes. Cost: starting at $3700, plus installation;
- *Residential elevators*, with rigid guide rail systems that can be installed into a wood framed home. Cost: starting at $16,000, plus installation (*www.Ameriglide.com*).

Cars and homes represent just the beginning in the area of Transgenerational Design. With the goal of making independent living and mobility possible longer for more people, society's challenge will be to invent and deliver literally hundreds, if not thousands, of products and services that Boomers will increasingly demand.

Meeting Needs of the *Young, Middle & Older Old*

Some of these needed products and services to support the burgeoning population of aging Boomers are already known and available. Others have yet to be invented. And all these products and services offer income potential for you, should you so desire, at any of the key points in the Transgenerational process—from invention, to design, to production, to marketing, to advising, to promotion, to sales, to installation, to use assistance.

Boomers will be spending a great deal of discretionary income on all types of pursuits—intellectual, recreational, professional, personal, physical. And many, if not most, of these aging Boomers have every intention of retaining their independence and mobility as time goes by, and as they advance from one subgroup to the next.

So once again, as Pogo says, "We are surrounded by insurmountable opportunity." When you begin to "match" what you have to offer to those who need it, you may find that your particular talent, skill, product, or service will best serve one or more of these three aging Boomer subgroups.

What Does Each Subgroup Want and Need?

As we study each subgroup, we quickly come to realize that group's uniqueness. While there may be a great deal of overlapping in terms of serving and being served, there are also some important distinctions.

Let's begin by considering some practical scenarios. Members of the Young Old and Middle Old groups may want to satisfy their recreational and intellectual needs by becoming frequent travelers. They now may have the time and financial resources to attend more performances and to visit more cultural venues and museums. And they may have renewed interest in studying and learning.

Physically, these two subgroups may be seeking ways to maintain a regular regimen of exercise, healthy eating, and daily movement in the form of exercise or sports activities. Remember that members of this generation have been, and probably still are, avid skiers, golfers, hikers, bicyclers, kayakers, swimmers, and tennis players. If their health cooperates, they now have both the time and the financial resources to experience these pleasures more often. And they have every intention of doing so.

When it comes to managing money, members of the Young Old and Middle Old subgroups may be accustomed to managing their own financial affairs—investments, monthly bills, banking, taxes, real estate, and so forth. But now they may prefer to "outsource" these tasks to free up their calendars for more interesting pursuits.

As these members move into the Older Old subgroup, their intellectual needs might be satisfied in less vigorous ways—listening to books on tape or watching educational and cultural TV or video programs. But their needs for mental stimulation will persist, as will their needs for social relationships, personal significance, freedom and fun.

And even as Older Old find themselves slowing down physically, they still may be able to, and want to, continue some type of low impact activity such as swimming, gardening, water aerobics, walking, or yoga. But they may be more than happy now to hire someone trustworthy and competent to manage their finances, carry out correspondence tasks, make repairs and help solve problems.

Senior Schizophrenia

By now you surely have thought about the irony of your situation. You yourself probably are an actual member of one of these subgroups. Yet, if you are reading this book, you also may be considering becoming a provider of goods or services to one or all of them—*Young Old, Middle Old* and/or *Older Old.*

So, your role is both reciprocal and complementary. Given the richness of your experiences, talents, skills, and interests, you are in an excellent position to earn money by providing products or services, or even by bartering one set of products or services for another.

In fact, as you settle into this new phenomenon of extended and redesigned retirement, you might find yourself (as others have) needing to choose among several appealing ways to earn an income as a senior serving other seniors.

A New Profession to Serve Seniors: Certified Retirement Coaching

It never ceases to amaze that, for every need that arises in our society, a variety of innovative products and services appear to satisfy that need. Case in point—have you heard of a *Certified Retirement Coach*? Move over soccer coach, yoga instructor, financial planner, social secretary, and doggie trainer. Step up to learn how you can become certified to qualify as a retirement coach for every aspect of your contemporaries' lives. Think about it. Who could possibly be more qualified, empathetic, experienced, and proactive in assisting you to navigate through this, your last life adventure, than one of your very own peers?

Before looking at some possible options and opportunities that this relatively new occupation might offer to you, a senior who aspires to serve others who share your current life situation, first, let's understand and underline what a Certified Retirement Coach (CRC) is and is not. How is this position defined, and what does it do? Then, what and where are the paths I can find and follow to acquire more information about this avocation and its training opportunities?

A retirement coach is not a financial planner, a tax preparer, or an accountant who will assist you with any aspect of your finances. Instead, a CRC's purview deals with the retiree's many non-financial priorities, goals, and lifestyles.

A CRC's mission is to help retirees navigate their newfound landscape, socially, career-wise, and in chosen leisure pursuits, taking into consideration their health, values, family involvement, personal hobbies and interests, personal development aspirations, and financial limitations. As experts at assisting retirees to effectively embrace this major life change, CRCs challenge the status quo of traditional retirement by eliminating outdated beliefs and practices through innovative training, tools, and resources.

There are several online CRC certification configurations available. Some provide face-to-face learning and discussion in the form of live webinars. Others provide an independent, self-paced program, while others offer a combination of independent study and scheduled group webinars. Some feature downloadable and interactive self-assessment tools and supplemental workbooks.

Considerations such as program costs, payment plans, completion timelines, and course credits vary, depending upon the program you choose. For more detailed information, we found the following three web sites that provide authentic CRC programs worth pursuing.

- Certified Professional Retirement Coach: *CertifiedRetirementCoach.org*
- Retirement Options: *www.RetirementOptions.com*
- Financial Industry Regulatory Authority (FINRA): *www.FINRA.org/investors/professional-designations/cprc*

SNAPSHOT: Marianne Oehser

Marianne retired *twice* from her career as a senior corporate global marketing researcher. But, as she openly admits, she "didn't get it right the first time." Not only did her first retirement work out badly, but it undermined her long-term marriage, which ended in divorce. She has since remarried, this time happily.

When Marianne retired for the second time, she was clear that she needed to "retire *to* something", not just "retire *away from* something." This led her to study and qualify for a completely new career as a *Certified Relationship Coach*. Her relationship coaching business, *Between2Hearts.com*, was launched on her 65th birthday.

Through her coaching business, Marianne helped singles and couples build and maintain rewarding and connected relationships. But her extensive experience as a relationship coach showed her that some couples face particularly difficult challenges when they embark on the massive life transition to retirement.

To better address these issues and more completely serve her clients, Marianne again returned to school, this time to become a *Certified Retirement Coach*. As a retirement coach, she assists individuals, as well as couples, in building happy retirements, while continuing to enjoy healthy and mutually supportive relationships.

In order to expand her services beyond her native Naples Florida, Marianne has developed seminars and workshops, as well as private coaching, available online. She has trademarked her own original *Happiness Portfolio Assessment* and is currently writing a book: *Build Your Happiness Portfolio: Making Your Third Act a Smash Hit.*

10 More Ideas for Seniors Serving Seniors

Let's take a look at some practical, meaningful, profitable ways in which *Young Old* or *Middle Old* Seniors can serve Young, Middle or Older Seniors, while generating supplemental income, remaining engaged and purposeful, and also having fun.

1. Medical & Financial Forms Filler-Outer

How many elderly family members and friends do you know who exhibit avoidance behaviors, or even defeat, when they receive complicated, lengthy, ambiguous forms from their medical provider, their insurance company, their attorney, their financial manager, the state and local government, the registry of motor vehicles?

Here's an opportunity to provide a critical service that could prevent serious legal or financial consequences for seniors if paperwork is not completed accurately and submitted on time. Since these tasks can be on-going, it is conceivable that you could develop a cadre of clients who would need your services regularly.

2. Salon on Wheels

Think about how you feel when you walk into your favorite hair salon or barber shop, and what a transformation takes places before you emerge. I always say that I approach my salon feeling like Cruella Deville on a bad hair day and walk out with a renewed conviction that I do, in fact, have some physically redeeming qualities. Then there's the growing challenge of giving yourself your own pedicures. It seems that as you gain in maturity, either your legs get longer, or your arms get shorter. This typical conundrum provides you the opportunity to offer yet another potentially popular traveling salon service—"Fingers & Toes."

Just imagine a roving van, fully equipped as a portable "Day Spa," with all the tools to make "house calls," serving the various neighborhoods and communities where seniors live. Step inside to a menu of options—foot massage, pedicure, manicure, facial, new hairdo, or even a make-up makeover—a virtual, and actual, "Spa on Wheels."

3. Thanks for the Memories

You know you can write, and you enjoy it. Biographies have always been your favorite type of reading. When you were young, you eagerly sat at your grandparents' feet as they told the stories of their youth. And you genuinely appreciate, even relish, the ease with which seniors talk about "the good old days." Here's your chance to do something you love while providing a service to seniors and earning extra income—preserving their precious personal, family, and life stories.

Your research and interviews could culminate in a publication for the narrator to present as a family gift to be handed down from one generation to the next. This production could be in the form of a bound book, complete with photos. Or it could be a full multi-media package that combines video, prose, and photography. What a meaningful opportunity to validate the contributions of seniors, while preserving the thoughts, stories, and experiences of past generations.

4. Not-So-Fast Food Chef

You love to cook ... and to eat! In your former life you were the composite embodiment of Rachel Ray and Julia Childs. But now there is one small problem. All your off-spring have sprung the nest, and you have had trouble adjusting to "thinking smaller" and cooking less now that there are only two of you still present to partake!

What if you could parlay your culinary talents into an express delivery service of home-cooked meals for seniors who are too busy to cook—or who are temporarily or permanently unable or unwilling to deal with preparing meals for themselves anymore. You could provide your lucky clientele with a weekly menu of lunches and dinners that you will prepare and deliver daily. Or you could offer a service to restock their freezers and fridges weekly or bimonthly with a delicious assortment of home-cooked meals, ready to thaw, heat and eat.

Just think. You could cook to your heart's content, experiment with new recipes, and know that you are providing pleasure, as well as meeting an essential need, all while earning a supplemental income. You could easily provide a month's worth of meals with no repeat performances. It doesn't get much better than that!

5. Playmate, Come and Play with Me!

As seniors age, many can and do choose to remain in their own homes, even as they enter the Older Old subgroup, and even after they have become widows or widowers. These seniors can be intelligent, alert, curious, gregarious, and delightful company. Some become "stay-at-homers" by choice, preferring the comfort and security of familiar surroundings. Others have stopped driving, or have stopped driving at night, and so find themselves confined to their homes for longer periods of time.

Still, the Older Old welcome and need the companionship and friendship of others. Some would appreciate having adult "play dates" with someone whose company and presence they can look forward to sharing for a designated period each week. After all, seniors can have play dates too, just as their grandchildren do!

Imagine the camaraderie, the laughter, the fun you could share playing cards, board games, or chess—working crossword puzzles, sudokus or cryptograms—cooking or baking together—watching TV or a movie classic—woodworking, scrapbooking or working on crafts projects—reading and discussing favorite books—gardening—surfing the Web or learning how to navigate social networks—e-mailing with family, friends or even pen pals from abroad.

Going on shared outings would be additional enjoyable options— to concerts, to shops and cafes, to the movies, or even just to ride around enjoying the spring flowers, the fall foliage, or the Christmas lights in December. In fact, you could start your own "Play Date" Club. For a monthly fee you would provide transportation, refreshments and an "activity agenda" for a small group of like-minded seniors. Imagine giving and receiving so much pleasure, companionship and joy while also supplementing your retirement income!

6. "Get it Done" Agent

There is a seemingly never-ending list of to-dos and fix-it projects that some retirees never seem to find time, or have the knack, to complete. The garage needs to be cleaned out. The Christmas lights need to be put up—or taken down. The patio furniture needs to be cleaned and stored. The kitchen cabinets need to be restained. The basement needs to be converted to a home theater or an exercycle hang out, or both. The sagging pantry shelves need to be replaced. The list goes on. Murphy's Law dictates that, every mechanical or electrical device seems to conspire to take turns becoming inoperable, often at the most inconvenient times! The smoke detectors are beep, beep, beeping again! The weed eater string is used up. The bathtub drains too slowly. The attic fan has stopped working. The doorbell is broken.

However, "unhandy" or "domestically and technically challenged" or even just unwilling or unable to climb the wobbly ladder into the attic they might be, many seniors are, like me, compulsive about having everything in perfect order at home. Enter you, the reliable, honest, competent "handy person" to take charge of that daunting check list and Get It Done, performing "miracles" with a toolbox.

7. The Green Thumb

As more seniors choose to remain in their homesteads, the ongoing maintenance of their grounds and property can become increasingly overwhelming. Even for the smallest of home yards and lawns, keeping up with nature can prove daunting—a battle that older seniors sometimes prefer to cede to someone else who has more energy—someone closer to nature who enjoys playing in the dirt.

The home lawn and garden require planting, pruning, weeding, watering, nurturing, tending, mowing, and raking. Gutters, porches, patios, outdoor furniture, and roofs need cleaning. Weeds need whacking. What a great way to enjoy the outdoors while supplementing your retirement income. And as a bonus, studies show that landscapers and gardeners find their work to be therapeutic.

8. Field Trip Leader

How often have you heard active Seniors, when talking about travelling within their town, state, and region, make comments like—

"Now that I have time and money to take day trips, there are many interesting places I'd like to visit. But I hate being corralled in a big bus where we never spend enough time in any one place."

If comments like these don't sound the call for you to start your own private small-group travel service, what would? For starters, you could pinpoint your geographical location on a map and draw a set of circles 25, 50, and 100 miles from that center point. Then get online and research all the museums, AAA designated scenic routes, historical sites, gardens, lunch spots, parks, inns, entertainment venues, specialty shops, antiques, and theme-related shopping destinations (crafts, sports, glasswork, woodwork) within each of those areas.

Undoubtedly, you could offer a trip a week for a full year, and never exhaust your field trip options. Your clients could participate by membership, then pay an additional fee per trip, receiving a quarterly brochure of upcoming outings and adventures. You may consider investing in a comfortable van, or even a limo, to hold six to eight guests—a perfect number for small group travel—so you and your entourage will be able to travel in style.

You could even expand to offering trips abroad, guiding small groups on a riverboat cruise down the Danube from Germany to Hungary or along the rivers of France, or the waterways of Holland to see the tulips in spring. Your guided travel offerings could be theme-based, focusing on music or dance or history or handcrafts or theater.

Another excellent method for gaining clients is to list the "experience" you are offering through Vayable.com. Vayable.com was created with the revolutionary idea that "by exploring the world, we can better it." Its mission is to "To enable entrepreneurship, cultural exchange, community-building and exploration worldwide by empowering people to share experiences with others."

Think what a winning proposition this type of business could become. You would be motivated to become expert on a culture to provide enriching travel experiences for an appreciative audience, and earn money, too, while having fun yourself.

9. Personal "Pro"

How many times have you heard (or said to yourself) "When I retire, I'm going to learn to golf or cross-country ski or kayak or sail or play tennis or plant an English flower garden. Others are doing this too, possibly in areas where you know yourself to be something of a pro. There may be other Boomers out there who never had the time or opportunity to pursue this interest at which you excel. Why not offer your services to teach your senior colleagues how to enjoy any one of these invigorating outdoor activities?

This concept can be transferred to the world of arts and crafts, as well as to other areas of skill and expertise. There are those who don't know how, but who may be eager to learn from you. How to build furniture... How to quilt... How to speak fluent French or Italian... How to write a memoire. By offering to teach them, you will make new friends, provide companionship, use your expertise to pass on what you know, and earn money in the process!

The added benefit of any of these possibilities is that "to teach is to learn twice," as the saying goes. Through your efforts to help others learn, you will hone your own skills even further. Immersing yourself in activities that you genuinely enjoy yourself is another major plus. And don't forget, you then will be able to claim your related purchases and expenses as tax deductions.

10. Grandma & Grandpa's Closet

As a grandpa, Speedos, tie-dyes, and cut-offs, if ever they were part of your wardrobe, may no longer be in your closet or on your radar screen. But you still may have closets and drawers full of formal business suits, button down shirts, some still in their wrappings, dress shoes in their original boxes, and high-end luggage you used when it appeared you were forced to spend half your life in airports.

As a grandma, you may be nostalgically hanging on to those broom skirts, Kasper suits, and sweater sets, with your walk-in closet still filled to the max with color-coded, coordinated "tops and bottoms." When you were a career professional, you never seemed to have anything to wear! Now, after 12 or more months of retired bliss, it dawns on you that you can't remember the last time you donned even one of those previously essential wardrobe items. You are not alone! Imagine how many Boomers share your situation, with closets full of designer clothes, some hardly worn, or even never worn, with their tags still on them to bear evidence.

What about offering a "Closet to Cash" service, clearing out Grandma and Grandpa's closets, then targeting a specific audience of men and women currently in the workforce who would gladly take advantage of the professional wardrobe bargains they'd find—all offered in matched sets—from your own and your fellow Boomers' neglected wardrobe collections?

And once those closets and drawers are starkly bare, possibly for the first time in decades, you could offer to custom design and install their "closet of the future," with racks, shelves, hooks, and drawers to hold their new "uniforms"—travel clothes, golf shoes, dress clothes for attending symphony concerts…or for dancing under the stars.

And So…

Who would have thought that you would find your niche serving the very Boomers among whom you are numbered? Yet, if you think about it, who is better suited to cater to the needs of this population than someone who is one of them? Who would be more keenly aware than you of the social, cultural, and professional needs of your senior colleagues, since you share many of these same needs yourself?

For your entire working career, unbeknownst to you, you have been preparing for this, your re-invented retirement phase. All the skills, experience, and talents you have developed in the course of your past professional life now come to bear upon what, hopefully, will prove to be not only your last hurrah, but your best.

Think about the gratification you will find sharing the fruits of your younger years' experience. Each day you are realizing more and more the expertise you accumulated over your 30+ years in the traditional workforce. It may never have entered the thinking of your younger persona that you would later have so much to offer in terms of the goods and services that your own generation now needs and welcomes.

If serving the needs of the exploding population of retiring Boomers appeals to you, but not as a business venture... Or if you would thrive offering your services elsewhere, but again without the demands of creating your own business... Your future may be better served by considering work as a volunteer. Whatever of value you may have to offer, read ahead to consider whether you may want to expand or adjust your plans to include volunteering, but your way.

CHAPTER 12: Option #5:
Work for Free—But YOUR Way

"Who me, volunteer?" you ask. "I've never volunteered for anyone or any cause, and I'm not about to start now! I have no intention and no desire to volunteer for anything, anytime, for anyone—*ever*!"

There are lots of reasons why you may believe that you are not cut from the volunteerism mold. Perhaps in your former life as a member of a demanding, stressful service profession, you were forced into involuntary pseudo "volunteering" as part of the "do more with less" and "give back to the organization" mantra, and you feel exhausted and depleted by the thought of ever being drawn into doing that again.

Or perhaps you are an extremely shy introvert, who freezes up at the very thought of walking into a room of strangers or making phone calls to sometimes annoyed and hostile recipients, or otherwise meeting and greeting people you don't know. Maybe you are just now entering your "me, myself and I" phase, with an aversion to giving away any of *your* time and energy—time that you gained only recently—time that you intend to relish and protect, and to spend on *your* new endeavor, *your* recent idea, *your* current passion.

Possibly your concept of volunteering dates to an earlier age when volunteers were mainly recruited to do the mundane, unappealing tasks that none of the employed staff wanted to do themselves—tasks that required no intelligence or skill—tasks that anyone could do with their eyes closed and their brain on standby. Address these envelopes. Sit by this phone. Lick these stamps. Fill up these boxes. Peel these potatoes.

If any of these scenarios sound like you, think again. You may come to view volunteerism differently once you have had the chance to understand how volunteering has changed, and how and why it is that volunteering now can be highly fulfilling when it is personalized to your own unique capabilities, purposes and interests.

You may not be willing to volunteer to do just any old thing, at the whim of some organization. But you well may be interested, even intrigued and eager, when you consider involving yourself in some of the volunteering options now available. What if you could find a volunteer placement that is engaging, fulfilling, challenging and fun? What if you could volunteer *your* way?

Volunteerism Among Seniors is Growing

In recent years, volunteerism has increased dramatically, particularly among older Americans. Why is this? What has changed about the perceived benefits of volunteering that make it transformatively different and significantly more fulfilling?

According to 2017 data from the *Corporation for National Community Service* (NationalService.gov), 62.8 million Americans volunteer 7.9 billion hours of service each year, equating to $184 billion in value. Over a third (36%) of this volunteering is by adults 55 and over. This equates to 22.6 million older adults dedicating 2.8 billion hours to *Community Service* across the country in five focus areas: *Disaster Services, Economic Opportunity, Education, Environmental Stewardship, Healthy Futures*, as well as to *Veterans and Military Families* and through Senior Corps, with programs that include:

- RSVP

- Foster Grandparents

- Senior Companions

WOW FACTOR
Over 42% of adults 65 and over volunteer an average of 96 hours per year (Corporation for National and Community Service). Ten percent of these volunteers donate 500 hours or more annually.

RSVP engages more than 208,000 volunteers age 55 and over who serve over 46 million hours on environmental projects, mentoring and tutoring 78,000 children, and responding to natural disasters.

Foster Grandparents (FGP) engages over 25,000 loving and experienced one-on-one tutors and mentors to assist 189,000 young people with special needs. Foster Grandparents work for 15 to 40 hours a week to provide support in schools, hospitals, drug treatment centers, correctional institutions, and childcare centers. Among their other activities, Foster Grandparents review schoolwork, reinforce values, teach parenting skills to young parents, and care for premature infants and children with disabilities. In 2017, *Foster Grandparent* volunteers served a total of 21 million hours.

In 2017, 12,190 *Senior Companions* served 43,000 clients for a total of 7.5 million hours. *Senior Companions (SCP)* typically serve 15–40 hours a week each, helping between 2–4 frail seniors to maintain independence, primarily in their own homes. Volunteers assist with daily living tasks, such as grocery shopping and bill paying and provide friendship and companionship. They alert doctors and family members to potential problems and offer much-needed respite to family caregivers.

Benefits of Volunteering

Clearly communities and other causes receive major benefits from the billions of work hours contributed by volunteers. But beyond these benefits, research has shown that the volunteers themselves reap significant rewards. Most startling is the fact that individuals who meet the volunteer "threshold" of at least one or two hours a week are more likely to live longer.

Furthermore, those who engage in volunteer activities are less likely to suffer from ill health later in life, instead experiencing a positive reinforcing cycle of good health and further volunteering. States that show higher volunteer rates are more likely to have lower mortality rates and incidences of heart disease (as reported in *"The Health Benefits of Volunteering"* published by the *Corporation for National & Community Service*).

These health benefits are more pronounced for older than for younger volunteers. This is in part because, by volunteering, older individuals are provided a purposeful social role that otherwise may be missing in their lives. In addition to providing health benefits, volunteer activities can strengthen the social ties that protect individuals from isolation during difficult times. Also, the experience of helping others leads to a sense of greater self-worth.

If you need any added impetus or encouragement as to how and why *you* should strongly consider devoting some of your new-found freedom to volunteering for a cause of your choice, these research findings may be something to consider.

Oh, one last thing—did you know that you can claim your volunteer time as a tax deduction? And your expenses and gas mileage? Just another bonus for doing what you love while helping humanity in the process!

Volunteer Where, with Whom, Doing What?

But, you say, "Where would I volunteer?" and "With whom?" and "Doing what?" All valid questions.

Options for volunteering abound, some that you already may have encountered, but many others that may be entirely new to you. What will almost certainly seem new is the matchmaking process made possible by the Internet. Now you can, and will, be brought together with your optimum volunteer placement.

In the past you may have had limited volunteering options with a conventional set of organizations and agencies—political, social, medical, church-affiliated, educational. And the volunteer tasks you would have been assigned were routine ones—clerical, telephone-based, fund-raising, mail-outs, food or clothing distribution.

Now volunteering options, like the paid work and business options discussed in earlier chapters, have been transformed through the connectedness made possible by the Internet. Entire websites are devoted to matching up those who want to offer their services with those who need their unique abilities and help.

On these websites, agencies post full descriptions of what they need, as they need it. Potential volunteers can search through the countless volunteer opportunities available to identify those to which they are best suited, in terms of the:

- cause or issue that matters most to them;
- skills and abilities needed; and
- types of work activities involved.

These websites thus become powerful connecting tools that enable agencies and volunteers to find each other.

Using the Internet to Find Your Ideal Match

Discovering your own best volunteering match—whether it reflects your past work or involves branching out into something entirely different—starts, as with any meaningful search for work, with your knowing yourself well. What do you most care about? What will best engage your mind as well as your energies, your assets, and your special talents? The more you know about what you want to do, the more valuable you will be to the organization you join as a volunteer.

As a volunteer, you will have the freedom to experiment with new activities as well as to do work that calls upon skills that you developed throughout your working career. Is there something you wish you had had the opportunity to learn? Some organizations will gladly assign you to work as a "beginner" because they know you will be motivated by learning something new. Many agencies provide training to enable you to learn new skills, develop fresh talents, and otherwise be more effective as a volunteer.

Expanded Options Made Possible by the Internet

Not only does the Internet make it possible for you to locate an ideal volunteering match, it also expands the options available to you far beyond your own locale. Many volunteer tasks and projects can be done by working online or by phone, with no necessity that you travel or meet face-to-face. This means that you are no longer limited to volunteering in your own area of the country—or even in your own country. Depending on the task, it may be as easy to volunteer abroad as in your own neighborhood.

A Sample Online Volunteer Matching Service

Smart Volunteer is one example of an online service that matches needs with volunteers (*SmartVolunteer.org*). This service allows you to search for volunteer opportunities by type of agency, such as:

- Arts
- Children & youth
- Community building
- Energy conservation
- Family & parenting
- Women's issues

- Wildlife & animal welfare

You will be able to select work that interests you, then refine your list according to whether you wish to volunteer locally or "virtually." Some skill categories listed on the *Smart Volunteer* site are:

- Arts/creative
- Business development
- Child advocacy
- Board participation
- Counseling
- Writing/editing
- Videography
- Event planning
- Research

Some volunteer options on *SmartVolunteer.org* are one-time projects. Others are ongoing. Some activities are carried out locally. Others may be done online. As an example of the many types of interesting volunteer matches available through this website, browsing the *Arts & Creative* category yielded options that included:

- **Design a logo for *Green Africa***

  Green Africa (*GreenAfricaFoundation.org*) is an African organization focused on capacity development of African communities through life skill training, promotion of good health and peace within communities, and advancement towards sustainable livelihood and environmental conservation.

- **Create a T-shirt for *Voice for Earth International***

  Voice for Earth International is a non-profit organization that supports a "just, healthier and more sustainable society, irrespective of color, caste, creed or race, in any part of the human world" by meeting basic needs for food, water and shelter for all." (on *https://www.Idealist.org*).

- **Develop instructional materials for *Jumpstart***

  Jumpstart (*www.JStart.org*) is a national early education organization that helps children to develop the language and literacy skills they need for school.

- **Teach beginning crochet** at a Seniors Center.

- **Teach art** two Wednesday evenings a month.

- **Help with the silent auction** at a *Lifestyle Film Festival.*

Lists of volunteer needs on *SmartVolunteer.org* change constantly. Possibilities vary according to where you live, your preferred agency type, and what you want and can do.

Another similar matching service is *VolunteerMatch.org*. This site supplies links to a full range of opportunities for volunteers. Type in your location and review the list of opportunities near you. Some examples include:

- Become a mentor, imparting your lifelong experience to guide college students in your field;

- Refurbish donated bicycles or help with an "Earn a Bike" program, where 10 to 15-year-olds learn bike repair and maintenance while earning a bike for themselves;

- Mentor high school exchange students;

- Conduct a weekly bilingual story time to engage Spanish-speaking families in a "fun and energetic learning environment, while promoting early literacy, and strengthening the connection between parents and their young children."

Select Work that Engages Your Temperament

Considering the increased range of volunteering options, as well as the powerful means now available through the Internet, it is now possible to match yourself with an opportunity that ideally suits you. The volunteer work that you select should and can be work that will excite and engage you, considering your special gifts, interests and temperament—*Guardian, Artisan, Giver* or *Thinker*.

Consider what the actual tasks of a volunteer work opportunity will be, then evaluate that option based on the degree to which you will gain satisfaction by engaging in that work over the months and years ahead. If the major tasks of a volunteer opportunity you are considering do not suit you, and will not engage you long term, then keep looking. You may not yet have found your volunteer niche. The better you are able to define exactly what you *uniquely* want to and are able to offer, the greater the likelihood you will find your optimum volunteer placement.

Here are some examples of volunteer work that may best suit you, depending upon your innate temperament. There are many other possibilities, but these are some excellent models.

If you are a Guardian (SJ)...

If you thrive on nurturing others and being useful, your temperament may fit well, and you may be well engaged, volunteering to...

Provide Protection as a Guardian Ad Litem

A volunteer Guardian ad Litem is appointed by the court to advocate for a child who comes into the court system, primarily because of alleged abuse or neglect (*GuardianAdlitem.org*). The task of a volunteer Guardian ad Litem is to:

- Advocate for the child during court hearings.
- Protect the child's inherent right to grow up with dignity in a safe environment that meets that child's best interests.
- Ensure that the child's best interests are represented in the court at every stage of the case.

As a volunteer Guardian ad Litem, you will be required to successfully complete 30 hours certification training plus 6 hours annual recertification training. Work requires 10 hours per month on average.

If you are an Artisan/Experiencer (SP)...

Your need for action and challenge to engage your innate capacity to be resourceful may find a suitable outlet when you...

Dream Green

Consider working for an environmental or animal welfare agency committed to the protection and preservation of resources, natural areas, and wildlife in your community, nation, or world. One source of environmental volunteer projects is *The Nature Conservancy* site at *www.Nature.org,* where you can learn of opportunities in your own state or in another state where you would like to spend time.

Another example is the *Audubon Society* that organizes hundreds of Volunteer Days at Audubon Centers across the country, engaging thousands of volunteers in tens of thousands of volunteer hours of effort. Google "Audubon volunteer" in your state. As an example, Audubon volunteer opportunities in Portland Oregon include:

- Docents
- Community science
- Conservation activists
- Native plant team
- Nature store
- Sanctuary restoration, work parties and tour guides
- Wildlife care center

SNAPSHOT: Yvette

Yvette brought to her volunteering activities years of experience working in the non-profit world. So, she knew how to "do a lot with a little by reaching out to the community and its resources to get more and do more."

> *Her business background and consulting experience, combined with her passion for the environment, animals, and waterways, pointed her in the direction of focusing her efforts on environmental education.*
>
> *Groups she supports include: the Talkin' Monkeys Project (that provides a healthy, safe, lifelong home for apes and monkeys taken from private homes or released from medical labs), OneLightBulb.org, Pooches for the Planet, and the Tampa Bay & Sarasota Bay Estuary Program.*
>
> *She says: "I feel really good getting the educational message across and promoting environmental welfare and conservation... the environmental movement is trying to move in a positive direction and I'm glad to be a part of it."*

Or "Dream Green" Abroad

To increase the excitement that you need as an *Artisan/Experiencer*, you may consider volunteering abroad. Agencies like *ProWorld Volunteers* (*ProworldVolunteers.org*) match volunteers to communities that need help in Latin America, Asia and Africa, with opportunities in 14 countries, including:

- *Belize*
- *Brazil*
- *Costa Rica*
- *Ecuador*
- *Ghana*
- *India*
- *Mexico*
- *Morocco*
- *Nepal*
- *Panama*
- *Peru*
- *Philippines*
- *South Africa*
- *Thailand*

As a volunteer you would be matched to a "high-impact project" in your area of interest, including:

- **Construction:** build a school, a cleaner burning stove, an animal shelter; help locals construct more sustainable buildings.
- **Community Development:** support community centers and fair-trade initiatives; preserve history and encourage sustainable development through local team projects.
- **Education:** teach local children, women's groups, community English courses; assist at primary schools and nurseries.
- **Environment:** clean hiking trails; monitor invasive species; plant organic seeds; help local farmers thrive in the global economy.
- **Health:** work in local and rural clinics, helping to immunize, diagnose and treat patients; combat HIV/AIDS through public health education programs.
- **Women's Development:** nurture microfinance and entrepreneurial initiatives for women; support fair trade of women's crafts.

Another major agency matching volunteers with environmental programs abroad is *United Planet* (*www.UnitedPlanet.org/*), committed to a variety of environmental awareness projects around the world. Volunteer-abroad opportunities available through this agency are called "United Planet Quests," and include short-term and long-term, professional and non-professional assignments where "volunteers make a critical difference worldwide."

Short-term Quests (1–12 weeks), in countries like Costa Rica, Italy, Ghana, Nepal, Romania, Ecuador and Peru, involve a range of projects that support essential community development, such as orphanage care, teaching English, environmental work, or healthcare.

Volunteers are 100% immersed in the local culture through cultural activities, excursions, and host-family stays. They are asked to provide their own airfare, and also to pay a modest fee to cover preparation and training before departure, food and lodging in the host country, in-country transportation, emergency medical insurance, on-going support and supervision, as well as language lessons, cultural activities and excursions. For example, an 8-week "Quest" in Italy costs $2,885; a 6-week Quest in Tanzania, $3,875; a 4-week Quest in Peru, $2,915; a 3-week Quest in Nepal, $2,975; a 2-week quest in Costa Rica, $2,645; a 1-week Quest in Ecuador, $1,985.

If you are a Giver (NF)...

Your *Giver* temperament makes it essential that your work be meaningful and that it contributes to your own personal growth. You thrive by focusing on human potential and bringing out the best in others, providing services, products or solutions that...

Change the World, One Relationship at a Time

Child mentoring programs enlist volunteers to create a positive, supportive, one-on-one relationship with a child, by participating in everyday activities together such as playing basketball or going to the beach, and otherwise by contributing to the child's achievement of personal, social and educational growth.

Time commitments start at a few hours per week and span a full school year. Mentors meet with "their" child for one or more hours a week for the duration of the school year, playing games or helping with homework. Some mentors are assigned to children in foster care, with the goal of providing consistent adult role models to help the child handle the challenges of their foster care environment.

A search on *Volunteer Match* (*www.VolunteerMatch.org/*), yielded 126 virtual volunteer opportunities for mentors, including projects to spread free anti-drug, anti-violence curricula or to test out a new course on hydroponics and vertical farms created to bridge the Innovation Gap, the Opportunity Gap and the Gender Gap in STEM (Science, Technology, Engineering and Math) education.

Another large mentoring organization in the United States is *Big Brothers/Big Sisters www.BBBS.org,* matching at-risk youths with caring, adult role models in communities across the country. A nationwide study showed that children in the *Little Brothers and Little Sisters Program*, as compared to those not in the program, were:

- 46% less likely to begin using illegal drugs;

- 17% less likely to start using alcohol;

- 33% less likely to hit someone;
- 52% less likely to skip school;
- 94% more confident they will achieve their goals;
- better able to get along with their families.

Volunteering as a Big Brother or Big Sister is an opportunity to help shape a child's future for the better by empowering him or her to achieve. The mentoring provided by Big Brothers and Big Sisters has a long-lasting, positive effect on a child's confidence, grades, social skills, and life. According to an impact survey, 81% of former "Littles" reveal that their "Big" gave them hope and changed their perspective of what they thought possible.

Big Brother/Little Brother and Big Sister/Little Sister teams keep a consistent schedule of outings, meeting together on a regular basis for a few hours several times a month. They decide together what they want to do and obtain parental approval. Activities and outings vary—playing sports together, going on a hike, reading books, attending cultural events. By keeping a consistent presence in the life of their assigned child, "Bigs" have natural opportunities to provide guidance, advice and inspiration, and otherwise to have a life-changing impact, one child at a time.

Currently there are more than 21,000 boys and 10,500 girls ready and waiting to be matched with Big Sisters and Big Brothers across the country—twice the number of boys than girls.

If you are a Thinker (NT)...

With your drive to learn, achieve, and continuously improve, your best volunteer options are those where you will be adequately challenged, possibly by being the one to take on the design and leadership role of initiating suitable volunteer opportunities yourself. Your ability to see possibilities, understand complexities and design solutions can best be engaged when you...

Take Volunteerism One Step Further

The volunteer project where you could best contribute may not exist...yet. In fact, your efforts may serve a greater good, and your particular gifts be more fully engaged, if you establish and operate a volunteer program or change initiative of your own. Although other potential volunteers may be "actors in search of a play," you could be better suited to be the play's author.

Possibly you already have identified a viable organization in your community that could use the services of a vibrant, dedicated corps of volunteers, with you in the lead. Or you may have become aware of a problem that needs to be solved...a situation or place or group or opportunity that could and should be better, broader, more accessible, or otherwise restored, improved, rescued, or preserved.

If you have the time, the energy, and the leadership skills, what organization would not welcome you into their sphere of influence? And if the organization within which your efforts would fit does not exist—yet—who better than you to invent it yourself?

Go for it! Use your Google and amazon.com skills to find the many resources you can use to get the help you need. Also, you will find that sites such as *www.VolunteerHub.com* will provide you support and guidance for the process of developing, implementing and managing a successful volunteer program. You might also choose to use as a model a volunteer initiative from elsewhere in the country and take the lead to apply the same concept in your own locale.

For example, the *"Parks by You"* effort in Houston, Texas has set out to connect the city of Houston through a series of linear parks along the bayous and to improve existing neighborhood parks throughout the city. The vision is to engage local volunteers and neighborhoods to create a "park by you," so that the majority of the citizens of Houston will live within 1.5 miles of a park or green space. You could set in motion a similar vision in your community.

SNAPSHOT: Dr. Wesley Walton

Wesley was eager to volunteer his services after he retired, but only if he could do it HIS way, in support of something that he was passionate about. One of his prime causes was both personal and environmental. His retirement dream home in Bellaire Beach, Florida, on a narrow barrier island, was vulnerable, as were those of his neighbors, due to the severe beach erosion that had removed the beach completely. There was no beach. At high tide the Gulf of Mexico lapped against the sea wall, and during heavy storms, the entire island disappeared underwater.

Wesley tackled this problem from every direction, beginning by approaching the Town Council, meeting with town leaders and seeking out other associations, including condo HOAs, whose members had personal and financial interests in the problem.

He quickly discovered that all efforts to restore the beach, and thereby to protect the island and its inhabitants, had been brought to a firm halt. The obstruction was a small contingent of Gulf-front home owners who selfishly, and unwisely, had exerted pressure to keep the ocean views in front of their multi-million-dollar homes exclusive to themselves, even if this meant putting the entire island in jeopardy.

With this discovery, Wesley's "volunteer" efforts kicked into high gear. Soon he was authoring a weekly environmental science column for the local paper, "teaching" the community the how's and why's of environmental conditions and beach erosion. He created a "Photo Montage" that vividly showed the devastating impact of one heavy storm that covered the island in water, then nudged and prodded for permission to display his montage on the walls of City Hall—in the conference room where the City Council met regularly.

Wes came was seen as a visionary and leader by some, and a major nuisance by others. He attended every City Council meeting, where he was outspoken, and sometimes even volatile, about beach erosion and the undeniable necessity for beach renourishment. Using his career-long experience writing formal proposals for funding, complete with budgets, timelines, and detailed plans, he led efforts to seek and obtain federal funding for a beach renourishment project to replace the beach.

The outcome of all of this... The beach was saved. The sand was restored. The island was preserved. His legacy... Both now and for generations to come, a full diversity of people is once again able to enjoy the beauty, and the protection, of what is now a broad expanse of white, sandy beach.

But Where Do I Start?

Although you may have friends and family who have made volunteering a permanent, meaningful, important part of their lives... And although you suspect that a serious, long-term commitment to some type of volunteer service could produce a positive lasting effect in your life ahead... You still may be at a loss as to where to begin.

Begin by considering your SELF. What in your own view is the worthiest cause for you to support? What project, activity or cause would most engage your authentic commitment and enthusiasm?

Once you have some ideas in mind, write them down. Then follow through by taking the following eight actions to propel you in the direction of your own best volunteer engagement.

Action #1: Explore Online

We already have talked about several websites where you can begin your quest. Look back in this chapter to locate them and add them to your URL notebook as websites to explore fully and to consult frequently.

Some additional sites to visit include:

VolunteerMatch.org (*www.VolunteerMatch.org*)
This site offers you the opportunity to explore volunteer options by geographic location and/or by keyword topic search. The site reports having 13.4 million volunteers connected, and 3.7 million more volunteers needed.
Volunteers of America (*www.VOA.org*)
With offices throughout the US, the *Volunteers of America* site is searchable by zip code. Links for veterans are included.
Idealist (*www.Idealist.org*)
The premier clearinghouse for information on full-time internship and volunteer positions within the non-profit sector. You can identify target organizations by their mission and specific types of opportunities within various niches. Registered users

can also search for contacts in fields or organizations of interest and message them for networking purposes.
Experience Corps (*AARP.org/Experience-Corps*) This site, sponsored by AARP, emphasizes working with children in schools on literacy, reading, and tutoring.
National Park Service (*www.NPS.gov*) Check the "Get Involved" section.
Points of Light (*www.PointsofLight.org*) Search by location and type of work.
International Volunteer Programs Association (IVPA) *VolunteerInternational.org* Dedicated to promoting awareness and access to quality volunteer abroad programs.

Action #2: Research Your Options

Spend time learning about the causes or issues that are important to you. Look for a group that deals with topics about which you feel strongly. Start reading magazines, articles, and other publications related to the type of organizations for which you are interested in becoming a volunteer. The more you know, the more meaningful your decision will be. The first and most important thing about volunteering is to become involved with an organization that correlates with your values. If you choose a cause that you strongly believe in, you will find the time to commit, and, as a result, you will derive a sense of fulfillment, while making a significant contribution.

Action #3: Find That Life-Style Fit

At the outset, before you finalize any commitments, do a "lifestyle check" of how you want to structure your retirement.

- Are you planning to do a serious amount of travelling? Do you want to protect your flexibility? If so, you probably will not want to volunteer for tasks or projects that require a daily or weekly commitment.

- Are you a morning person or a night hawk? There are still many volunteer opportunities for those of us who like to live on an "off-beat" schedule.

- Are you a "gregarious Gregory," or do you prefer working on your own or one-on-one?

- How do you react to older people? Young people? Sick people? Problem people? Or do you just prefer animals?!

Action #4: Think Outside the Box

Many community groups that are looking for volunteers, such as neighborhood watch programs, prisons, disaster relief organizations, youth organizations, intergenerational programs, and park services, may not have occurred to you, but could just be the perfect fit. Schools, hospitals, and nursing homes have countless opportunities and critical needs for quality volunteers. Don't forget your local church organization, food pantries, and homeless shelters, as well as your local drama or theater group, and community music, library, museum, parks and recreational organizations.

Action #5: Make That Call

Sometimes the hardest step is the first one. Pick up that phone and punch in that number! Making that first point of contact will impel you to continue your new journey. Your phone conversation will probably result in an initial introductory meeting that you should approach just as you would a job interview. Be ready to describe your interests, qualifications, and background. Use this opportunity to learn as much as you can about the organization, how it operates, what benefits it offers volunteers, and how you will (or will not) fit within its structure.

Action #6: Show Up

Once you have found your perfect fit, establish yourself by providing a regular reliable presence at the organization or activity. This will indicate that you are truly committed to your chosen cause, and that you can be counted on to make a positive, consistent, substantive contribution. The quality of reliability cannot be underestimated or over emphasized. Others are counting on you for your presence on a regular basis. Don't disappoint them.

Action #7: Use Your Skills to Take on a Project

Don't wait to be asked. Offer to provide a specific, tangible service, to lead an activity, to participate in a program. You could initiate a fund-raiser, plan a basket raffle, chaperone a field trip, do accounting, develop a newsletter, update a web site. Once you achieve success on any one of many projects, you can be sure your services will be appreciated and called upon repeatedly.

Action #8: Have Fun

Volunteer work may be called "work," but it also should be fun—something you enjoy doing—something that adds a spring to your step, recharges your energy battery, and gives balance, meaning and perspective to your life. It should provide you with an outlet to do and to try things that you may have never had the time to experience before—even things that you never thought you could do or accomplish!

And it should make you feel engaged. Along with your time, you optimally will be donating your spirit as well. If the work feels like drudgery, you will not have much to offer. So, call a halt and look elsewhere. But if the work does engage and excite you…if it provides you with a sense of purpose and connection…you will put your heart into it as well as your hands. And that will make all the difference.

And So…

Throughout this book, we have explored our unique selves, determining who we are psychologically, and where we have been professionally. We know what unique strengths and personal passions we bring to bear on the types of causes we want to support.

As this chapter shows, whatever your temperament, your age, your background, there is need and opportunity galore for you to volunteer your services, according to your personality, interests, talents and time availability. Organizations near and far, serving every type of need, seek competent, reliable, volunteer talent to supplement and complement their paid employees. There never seem to be enough hands and heads to fill society's ever-increasing needs and demands for social services.

Did you want to become a veterinarian, but not have the financial resources to pursue the extensive demands of this profession? Now you can volunteer at your local animal rescue facility, or within a vet's office. Was your dream to enter a branch of the armed services, but a slight physical disability prohibited you from doing so? Now you have unlimited opportunities to work with veterans of all ages, as well as their families, assisting them with those physical and mental disabilities and limitations that resulted from their military service.

Were you a member of the medical profession, working in an enclosed antiseptic, environment, but longing for the great outdoors? Your timing couldn't be more opportune, with society's new awareness about the fragility of our planet. So many organizations promoting ecological environmental causes would welcome your participation and enthusiasm to work outdoors, close to nature's flora and fauna.

Did you lack the maturity and perspective in your youth to realize that you had a gift of relating to children, yet throughout your working life in the business world, often wish you could work directly with kids? Now is your chance. This chapter cites numerous venues for doing just that.

Perhaps it's an appropriate and fitting reward that, for our life's last passage, we find ourselves positioned to do exactly what we want to do, when and where we want to do it. In fact, even if during our prime working lives we were not able to pursue our lifelong career goal, now is the time we can do exactly that.

CHAPTER 13:
Step #5: Make Your Match & Move

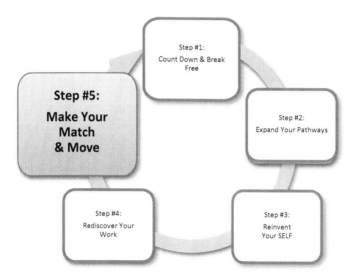

As delightful as it has been to think about potential pathways for your retirement, and then to reinvent your SELF and your WORK, and explore the five broad categories of potential work, the time eventually does come to take action. Many things are possible. With various barriers now removed, the questions are "What do you want to do now?" and "Who needs what you have to offer?" That will be time to make your match and move.

To quote Pogo, you are "surrounded by insurmountable opportunity." And from this mound of possibilities, it will be your task to choose a direction, then announce it to the world, and set off into your new life work—or into a new form of your old one. So, which of the many things you *could* do, do you *want* to do next?

Action #1: Define Your *Terms of Engagement*

The first action step is to define what future work *would* or *would not* engage and excite you. Think in general terms. I *would* like to create and learn. I *would* like my work to be intellectually stimulating and to have variety. I *would not* like my work to be repetitive or routine.

You already have uncovered the major clues you need to arrive at your own *Terms of Engagement* by developing your *SELF Statement* in Chapter 6. Would you want to work with people? If so, what people? The public? Children? Seniors? Or NOT? Would your work be with animals—or plants—or some aspect of science? Would you want to do creative work? Investigative work? Organizational work? Would you aspire to be in charge of people? Would you prefer to work independently?

As we have discussed, there is no need to limit your "woulds" to what you have done so far, or even to what you already are good at doing. Now it is time to focus on what you are most *enthusiastic* about doing, given your type and temperament, your interests and values, and your favorite skills and traits. Consider the *expanded* version of your SELF—including what you would like to learn as well as what you already know. Last, but certainly not least, base your choices on what you *value*, as well as on what you have to offer.

SNAPSHOT: Ted

After retiring from a lifelong career in education, Ted fulfilled a long-standing dream of buying a house in the mountains. Initially he went there to write, but soon made it a habit to take an afternoon break every day in the little mountain town, frequenting its galleries, shops and restaurants. He became involved in this small, creative community, and soon learned that, as with many such communities, their economy flourished during spring and summer months, but languished when winter set in.

He volunteered to work with local business leaders and the Chamber of Commerce, in a "position" of his own design. With his highly developed technology and communication skills, and 40 years' experience as an instruction design professor, Ted made three offers to the business leaders, all of which he would find stimulating and fulfilling.

First, he would design and present training to the local business leaders and owners, focusing on economic development of their town. Second, he would work with business owners to increase their web presence and thereby reach a broader base of customers to sustain

> *them through the lean months between their thriving summer seasons. Third, he would lead efforts to seek economic development funding that would enable the town to support small projects that held promise and would increase the economic vitality of their community.*
>
> *Through these offers, Ted donated considerable time and effort, as well as his particular expertise and enthusiasm, while doing work that he found to be highly engaging and satisfying.*

What do you see clearly now about what you *would* and what you *would not* want to do next?

I WOULD...	I WOULD NOT...

Action #2: Identify, Then EXPAND, Your *I Coulds*

With your *I woulds* and *I would not's* firmly in mind, shift your focus to what specifically you *could* do next. One or two thoughts may immediately come to mind. But why stop there? As part of shifting gears to your retirement work, make it a point to expand your horizons to include new skills and abilities, or to reengage skills you set aside in the past, for one reason or another. Then repackage yourself in this "new and improved" version.

Use action verbs when you speak about yourself, not categorical nouns. For example, say, "I *could* write," not "I am a writer." I *could* build garden benches," not "I am a woodworker." The point is to focus on *actions* in which you could engage, not on the "box" into which you might tend to squeeze yourself. "I *could* care for shut-ins." "I *could* create stained glass. "I *could* pilot a water taxi." "I *could* lead culinary tours through France."

Learn the Job Titles for What You *Could* Do

In the past, when you accepted each of your jobs, you knew what the *name* of the job was—the job title. You also had a job description that delineated what you would actually be *doing* on a daily, weekly and monthly basis. You were directed by the "wizard" behind the curtain. Now that you are in self-defining mode, you ARE the wizard. YOU are the one who will create your own job titles. Later you will be the one to write your own job/work descriptions for these job titles.

Seems daunting? Or does it sound intriguing? Either way, these tasks certainly will involve some challenges, given the combination of major changes in your personal and professional life, as well as in the work and the workplace. But the time you do devote to exploring the job titles for the work you *could* do will be time well spent. To consider a future doing a particular type of work, you will need to know what these jobs are actually called.

For example, *could* you be a Photogrammetrist? And if you were one, what would you actually *do*? Would this be a type of work that would engage and excite you? Before you can answer these questions, you first need to know what a "Photogrammetrist" is.

Good News—You Have the Resources to Find Out

Thanks to the Internet, you have the resources you need to research any and all job title questions quickly. "Google knows!" Treat this process like a treasure hunt and expect to find gold.

As a start, learn to use *The Occupational Outlook Handbook* (OOH) website at *www.BLS.gov/OOH*, published by the U.S. Department of Labor's *Bureau of Labor Statistics*, and described as "the Nation's premier source for career information." This site lists over *5000* job titles, indexed A to Z, each with a link to a webpage that provides detailed information for each job title, including:

- the purpose of the work;
- what you would do;
- what the work environment would be like;
- how you would prepare to do this work;
- what the work pays;
- the 2010-2020 employment outlook for this work.

Bookmark the *BLS.gov* website now so that you can return to it repeatedly throughout your search. This is where all of your efforts so far will begin to pay off. Working backwards from your SELF Statement, begin to consider sample job titles, whether you *could* do the work each job entails, and how congruent this work would be with the essential YOU. Here are some examples...

Are you excellent at gathering information and data, then providing accurate written answers to questions? You may be a natural as a...

Correspondence clerk

As a correspondence clerk you would review and respond to inquiries from the public, other businesses, or other departments in order to give accurate answers to questions and requests. You would gather information and data, then write letters or emails in reply to requests for merchandise, damage claims, credit and other information, delinquent accounts, incorrect billings, or unsatisfactory services.

Are you patient, positive, and proficient in reading, writing, and spoken English? You may find fulfillment as an...

ABE teacher (Adult Basic Education)

As an ABE teacher you would:

- Evaluate students' strengths and weaknesses and work individually with each student to overcome weaknesses;
- Plan and teach lessons to help students master spoken and written English or earn a GED;
- Monitor students' progress toward their goals;
- Emphasize skills that will help students find jobs;
- Help students develop effective study skills.

Do you know how to do something others may want to learn for fun or self-improvement... music, foreign languages, sketching, wood carving, Web searching, public speaking? You may enjoy working as a...

Self-enrichment teacher

Instruct in a variety of subjects that students take for fun or self-improvement, such as music, cooking, art and foreign languages. Some self-enrichment teachers offer instruction in computer programming, software use, public speaking, that help workers gain marketable skills to make themselves more attractive to prospective employers.

Employment for self-enrichment teachers is expected to grow by 21% from 2010 to 2020. This growth rate is faster than the average growth for education, training, and library occupations (15%), and also more than the projected total growth for all occupations (14%). Growth in demand is expected to continue as increasing numbers of adults and children seek new hobbies, pastimes, and skills.

Do you love working with shrubs and trees and are you artful at shaping them and improving their appearance and health? Maybe you have a future as an...

Arborist

Arborists, cut away dead or excess branches from trees or shrubs to clear roads, sidewalks and pathways, striving to improve the appearance and health of trees and plants. Some arborists specialize in diagnosing and treating tree diseases. Others specialize in pruning, trimming, and shaping ornamental trees and shrubs.

Think Beyond What You Can Do Already

As you explore the treasure trove of job titles on the *bls.gov* website, give yourself permission to be curious, daring, and maybe even a bit impractical. Be open to surprises. Think beyond what you already can do. Remember, you are not limited to skills that you currently possess. With so many readily available resources, online and at local colleges, you are within reach of learning whatever you need to be able to do, starting now.

Shift your thinking from "I don't know how to do that," to "I don't know how to do that YET." If there is something you need to learn to do, add it to your list of courses or lessons or workshops or programs or certifications you plan to pursue as you update yourself and prepare for what comes next. Augmenting your arsenal of skills and talents is a necessary part of the redefining process. And accomplishing this self-expansion will be exhilarating—even fun.

Could you be any of the following? Check all that may be worth looking into and take the time to learn more about what people in these professions actually do.

- ☐ Aesthetician
- ☐ Animal Care Worker
- ☐ Recreation Worker
- ☐ Greens Keeper
- ☐ Arson Investigator
- ☐ Asset Property Manager
- ☐ Association Planner
- ☐ Audio-Visual Production Specialist
- ☐ Autism Tutor
- ☐ Meeting, Convention and Event Planner
- ☐ Archivist
- ☐ Museum Technician
- ☐ Forester
- ☐ Hydrologist

To return to an earlier question, what skills would you need to add to your current arsenal to become a Photogrammetrist?

Photogrammetrist

As a Photogrammetrist you would use aerial photographs, satellite images, and light-imaging detection and ranging technology (LIDAR) to build 3-D models of the Earth's surface and features for purposes of creating maps. Also, you would collect and analyze spatial data such as latitude, longitude, elevation, and distance, and develop base maps.

Now What About You?

Take time now to complete your own personal *Expanded List of Job/Work Titles*. Have fun with this activity. Engage your curiosity. Resist the temptation to be limited by any engrained ideas you may have.

Expanded List of 10 Job/Work Titles

INSTRUCTIONS: Use the *Bureau of Labor Statistics* website at _www.BLS.gov/OOH_ to discover your choice of 10 job/work titles that sound interesting, and that you possibly *would* do and *could* do if you were determined to do so.

Include on your list even those job titles for which you would need to do some additional preparation. Do not be overly concerned at this point about practicalities. Later you will have a chance to winnow down your list.

For each of these 10 job titles, scan the information, including:
- job purpose and duties,
- potential earnings,
- 10-year employment outlook.

1.		2.	
3.		4.	
5.		6.	
7.		8.	
9.		10.	

Action #3: Write Your Own Job/Work Description

Your next task is to write job/work descriptions for *three* of the job/work titles on your list. If you are heading towards a part-time, or an online, or a volunteer version of the job, or even a business or partnership, carve out just the part you would want to do yourself, and define what others would interface with you to accomplish the remaining aspects of the work.

As a model, here is a brief job/work description for the job title: *Fitness Trainer*. The details for this came from the *Bureau of Labor Statistics* website: (_BLS.gov_). Locate and bookmark this site. We will be using it throughout this and future chapters.

Model job/work description: Fitness Trainer

PURPOSE: Fitness trainers are passionate about health, wellness, and exercise, and use their skills to help motivate others to reach their fitness and weight goals. The purpose of this job is to work with people from many different backgrounds and skill levels, from professional athletes to elderly people, helping them to improve their health through exercise and nutrition.

MAJOR DUTIES AND RESPONSIBILITIES:
- Demonstrate various exercises and routines.
- Watch clients complete exercises and demonstrate correct techniques to minimize injury and improve fitness.
- Design alternative exercises during workouts or classes for different levels of fitness and skill.
- Monitor clients' progress and adapt programs as needed.
- Explain and enforce safety rules and regulations on sports, recreational activities, and the use of exercise equipment.
- Give clients information or resources about nutrition, weight control, and lifestyle issues.

QUALIFICATIONS:
- *Certifications*: CPR Certification required. Also recommended is ACE Certification (from the *American Council on Exercise*: _www.AceFitness.org_).
- *Customer-Service & Motivational Skills:* Known ability to motivate and encourage clients while remaining friendly.
- *Listening Skills:* Ability to listen carefully to clients to determine their fitness levels and desired fitness goals.
- *Personal Physical Fitness:* Ability to serve as role model by being physically fit personally, as well as able to participate in classes and demonstrate exercises to clients.
- *Problem-solving Skills:* Ability to evaluate each client's level of fitness and create an appropriate fitness plan to meet his or her individual needs, while maintaining safety.
- *Speaking and Communication Skills:* Ability to explain exercises to clients, as well as to motivate them verbally.

To supplement the material you gather on the BLS site, do Google searches using each job title, along with other search terms such as "job description," "duties" and "requirements." For example, for example given, Google search for: *"Fitness Trainer Job Description,"* *"Fitness Trainer duties"* and *"Fitness Trainer requirements."*

Action #4: Build Your *"Break-free" Résumé*

The next action in the process of matching up your "re-invented" self is to repurpose your *Break-free Résumé* as part of a major paradigm shift in terms of how and where you present yourself. "Build it and they will come."

Since you already have a résumé—one that you have used successfully and repeatedly over the course of many years—developing an *all new* résumé may sound difficult. Résumés have a tendency to become "cast in stone." Yes, I know that your standard résumé looks so nice—formatted and perfected, even impressive. And that you have extra copies of it, beautifully printed on ivory parchment paper. And that it represents your highest levels of experience—the domains of your greatest victories and accomplishments—the level of authority and responsibility you achieved through your many years of effort and diligence.

All true. But there's just one problem. The résumé you already HAVE is no longer the résumé that you NEED. Where it once was a vehicle carrying you forward, it now is an obstacle, blocking your way. By all means, keep a copy of your former résumé for old times' sake. Then get to work developing your *Break-free Résumé.*

This all new résumé has a different purpose. It will be the guide and the measure that ensures that you have a clear concept of who you are going to "be" and what you are going to "do" moving forward. Who is this "new you" you will describe at that next cocktail party or alumni gathering or neighborhood picnic?

Write Three "Fantasy" Break-free Résumés

Your task goes beyond writing a single résumé. While you are at it, write *three*—one for each of the three job/work descriptions you developed for Action #3. Since these are "fantasy" résumés, and so will be refined and moderated later, include future skills and experiences you intend to add, along with past ones. Customize each résumé to one of the three job/work descriptions, noting what skills, strengths and experiences (current and future) would make you an excellent choice for that particular type of work. Locate model résumés for each of the three job/work descriptions. Google the job title followed by "*résumé*." For the example, Google "*Fitness Trainer Résumé*."

To develop these three résumés quickly and effectively, start out with one of the *Functional Résumé* templates available for free as part of MS WORD. With these templates to provide the format, all you will need to do is to add the words. For an excellent selection of résumé templates to download for free, go to:

Templates.Office.com

Now, using the model résumés as guides, and making sure that you use the appropriate lingo, "translate" between your own skills, experiences, capabilities and talents (past, present and future), and the tasks and requirements for each of these job/work titles. This translation process will require some thought.

Have you sold insurance or real estate or shoes? If so, then you know how to "describe, differentiate and market products," and you are skilled at "anticipating, hearing and responding to customer needs." With a few added skills, you could even "manage and update an online store that promotes and sells products to a niche market." Have you made presentations at conferences, or taught in a class-room, or written training materials, instructions, or reports? If so, you clearly could translate your skills into developing "webinars" or training videos or even interactive online training.

Throughout this translation process, enlist your ability to think di-vergently. You are by no means limited here by what you *were*. Em-brace the *expanded* version of your SELF, with all those skills and abilities you have renourished, and even those that you have added or plan to add.

Focus on *Function,* Not History

Focus your *Break-free Résumé* on *functions* you are able to perform, not just on the chronology of your past work. The *Functional* format is a better choice for you now than the *Chronological* format because it concentrates on what you have done and can do, rather than on the sequence and duties of your past jobs. It spotlights *you*, not your past employers and job descriptions.

Even more importantly, using this résumé format, you will be able to highlight your relevant skills, such as problem solving, communication, or motivating people, that translate to the job/work titles and descriptions you may hope to pursue next.

To create a *Functional Résumé*, take a sheet of paper and brainstorm everything relevant you have ever proven yourself able to do, at work or elsewhere. Include work you have done for yourself or for your family or friends, for school or during a training class or tutorial, and as a volunteer. Think of everything. What have you done? Who have you helped? What have you studied or read about in depth? If you wish, have a friend or partner help you with this process.

Once you have brainstormed and noted everything you can think of, then think again, this time more divergently. Have you done online research? Have you pulled that research together into a clear written format? Or used it to create an action plan or budget? Or to produce a PowerPoint presentation? Have you provided customer service and worked through "client" problems with either external or internal clients, family or friends? Have you engaged in finding solutions or resolutions to ensure repeat business? Have you offered counseling or advice? Or planned a new project with new clients or colleagues? Or with fellow members of the PTA? Have you answered questions, or provided guidance about how to perform a task...or how to perform it better?

What uses have you made of technology? Have you tracked and managed expenses using Excel? Posted communications using social media? Created, cropped, edited and uploaded photos or videos to Facebook? Have you maintained an active e-mail correspondence? Planned and scheduled a project or event? Researched and set up a trip using online resources?

Don't be shy. Own your capabilities—all of them!

Generate Bullets, Lots of Them

When you have generated a page filled with your brainstorm of everything you have proven yourself able to do, your next task is to turn these capabilities and accomplishments into bullet points. Focus on the activities and skills that directly address the essence of the particular job or work description for which each of your new résumés will be used. Choose *action* words for each bullet point.

Since these are your "fantasy" résumés, allow yourself to go wild. For now, the task is to invent—to craft—to think beyond your life and work so far. Later you will have a chance to make them more realistic, if necessary, before you actually put them to use.

Sample Bullet Points for "Fitness Trainer" Résumé

- Provided one-on-one guidance to clients, helping them to achieve their fitness goals.

- Measured and assessed blood pressures, heart recovery rates, and body fat ratios.

- Designed and advised on dietary programs.

- Provided personal training sessions to private clients in their home or work settings.

- Explained to clients the results they could expect from particular exercise regimes.

Think broadly. If you have not actually performed some of these functions YET as part of your past work, have you performed other functions that are related? Or have you carried out these types of tasks outside of work, for your family or friends? Or for yourself?

After you have noted and acknowledged everything you have already done, look back at your models from the résumé site to identify the types of skills and tasks that are not on your bullet list *yet*. Considering these missing but essential items, are there any that you could accomplish now? Could you study or do research to fill any gaps, or otherwise develop these needed additional skills? What outside resources could you call upon to become qualified? How soon could you do this? Brainstorm how you could develop these skills "immediately or sooner." Then add them to your bullet list as though you have already done them and get to work immediately to make these claims true!

For example, as a future *Fitness Trainer*, you may wish you had more expertise about nutrition and weight management, or about how to incorporate results-oriented exercise techniques, or how, specifically, to work with older adults. You can achieve all these learning goals by taking advantage of relevant continuing education classes such as those offered by *The American Council on Exercise* (*www.AceFitness.org*). You could start adding to your knowledge and skill base today.

Your goal here is to list as many *powerful* bullets as you can, including skills you plan to develop. Emphasize those accomplishments that are most relevant to the current position. Then generate a critical learning list so you can get started immediately filling any gaps.

Sort Your Bullet Points into Categories

Next sort and organize these bullet points into broad categories, using two or three subsection headings, such as: Organization. Supervision. Writing. Customer Relations. Design. Troubleshooting. Management. Quality Control.

As you create categories, this may stimulate you to recall additional bullet points. Make sure to include at least one category that pertains to the work you want to do next. Then generate bullet points to display what you have done in that category.

Now Add Your Work History & Education

Once you have generated your bullets, and sorted them into subsections, add to your résumé a list of your past jobs, in reverse chronological order. Then add your education background, training, and credentials, again in reverse order. But keep this section brief. Have mercy on potential employers. They will not want to read more than two pages, at most. Better yet, limit your résumé to one page.

Be Your Own Matchmaker as You Write

As you write your *Break-free Résumé*, think like a matchmaker. Your résumé is NOT all about *you*. For this résumé to be effective, the focus needs to be more about THEM—those employers or clients who will benefit from your efforts. Present yourself in the very best light to attract a good job/work "match." Make this new résumé as vital and communicative as if you were applying to *The Dating Game*.

Put yourself into the mindset of those people who *need* you to work for them—to assist them—to guide them—to create for them. Your résumé needs to answer for them the question: "How well would this person align with what I need to have done?"

Creating an excellent résumé is hard work. You may be tempted to rush through it to get it *over with.* DON'T! Think of it this way: your *Break-free Résumé* will, hopefully, make you money, now and far into the future. The time you spend on it will be time well spent.

WOW FACTOR

If you spend three hours to develop a 400-word *Break-free Résumé* that gains you $40,000 a year in work, over the course of 10 years this will add up to $400,000. That is the equivalent to being paid over $133,000 an hour, or $1000 per word! You will NEVER earn more per hour or per word than you will writing an excellent résumé.

After you complete the first of your *Break-free Résumés,* keep your momentum going and develop your other two, each targeted to a specific job/work description. As a "career changer," it is essential that you have more than one résumé to use, as needed—one for each area you may engage in next. There will be commonalities among your three résumés, so the second and third will likely come together much more quickly than the first.

Completing your three résumés is an accomplishment, but also an ongoing process. Every time you add additional work experience, or study and learn something new, update your résumés with additional bullet points, or even insert a whole new category of bullets. Your résumés are as much dynamic "works in progress" as you are!

It's Fine to Seek and Enlist Help

If you find the task of writing your own résumé to be overly stressful, consider enlisting your partner or a friend to help. An added, unexpected perk to soliciting input—he/she may reveal to you surprising strengths, skills and talents you took for granted, underestimated, or about which you were completely unaware. And it will probably be only a matter of time before you find yourself returning the favor.

Another option is to engage a résumé service, preferably one that is Boomer-friendly, with experience creating functional résumés for career changers.

Final Versions of Your *Break Free Résumés*

With your three "fantasy" résumés in hand, now it is time to refine, print, and distribute them. Even now, try to retain some of the sense of freedom you felt when developing your fantasy résumés. Your new résumés hopefully will be VERY different from the one that brought you (and kept you) where you are today.

Action #5: Create Your New Promotional Materials

Next, create your new business card. Then create your choice of additional promotional materials—brochures, postcard notifications, flyers, websites, video segments. The idea here is to get prepared to announce yourself when you embark on your retirement career.

Creating a card can be one of the fun parts of this entire process. Use VistaPrint (*www.Vistaprint.com*) to speed this along. Under the "Business Cards" category, select either "Premium" or "Personal," then pick out a template. You will be able to design your own unique and professional looking product, quickly and painlessly. Be sure to double check to make sure that ALL grammar and spelling are 100% perfect. What you DO NOT need is 1000 copies of a business card with spelling errors!

If you design a postcard announcement, VistaPrint even will mail out your postcards for you to a targeted mailing list according to the demographics, household make-up, income, and location you have selected as your market. You will receive a copy of this customized mailing list for reuse later.

Also, explore Google Adwords and Facebook ads as options for helping you connect with potential clients who are looking for you and your services. This form of advertising can be controlled by assigning a budget, limiting the geography where your ads will be shown, and otherwise tailoring your ad campaigns to suit your needs.

Action #6: Announce Your New SELF and Job Title

Have business cards, will travel... So, who needs to know about your new career and what you have to offer? And where will you go to find these potential clients? Start with three major frontiers:

1. Your current and expanded *Virtual Network*

2. Your current and expanded *Physical Network*

3. Your new and emerging *Invited Network*

New Worlds: Your *Virtual Network*

For starters, if you have not already done so, it is time for you to become a member of *LinkedIn*. LinkedIn is the place to network professionally with those you know, as well as with "those they know," enabling you to find jobs through your extended network. Additionally, you can join groups, participate in conversations, and follow companies you find interesting and relevant to your job search.

Go to *https://www.LinkedIn.com/* and register. Post your professional profile, including a current résumé, and begin to connect with old and new colleagues. This site is the "Facebook for Professionals."

And speaking of Facebook... Remember to "Update your Status" on Facebook as you venture out into your new retirement career. Also revise your profile. And if you create a website to promote your new enterprise, send a note to your Facebook friends asking them to visit your site and "Like it."

Old Worlds: Your *Physical Network*

What other networking options can provide you with powerful, effective ways to market your new creative abilities and skills? Do not underestimate the many traditional opportunities available to "get the news out" about your new career path.

Join as many local, civic, and social groups as your time and energy allow. Advertise in free brochures and community newsletters. Post your business card, descriptive brochure, or flyer on public bulletin boards in markets, colleges, and other business establishments. Offer to teach a community or adult education course. Sign up to be a guest presenter or speaker on your local cable channel or for the many clubs and civic organizations within your community.

And don't be shy about notifying members of your immediate and extended family about your new career direction. Undoubtedly, they will "know somebody who knows somebody" who can help you launch your new career path energetically and effectively.

Your Invited Network

Next, think of the network of professional colleagues and other associates you acquired along the way, but with whom you since may have lost touch. Reflect on every job or position you have ever held. You will easily be able to construct a significant scaffolding of people connections. Some will be worth the effort to relocate and reestablish as colleagues and associates.

And, thanks to current technologies (Facebook, LinkedIn, Plaxo, Twitter, Blogs, Google search, YouTube) it is easier than ever to reconnect with this network and even see what they have been up to!

Now What About You?

Compile your "A List" of connections, including those from your deeper past. These are the people with whom you will plan to stay connected or to reconnect—your "Intentional Network." Add to your list as you start moving ahead into your engaging and fulfilling "new" retirement.

Reflect back on your employment, but also think beyond employment to all those others with whom you have associated—classmates with whom you collaborated on significant projects, fellow community or school or church or organization members with whom you shared creative, organizational or leadership tasks. Consider which of your past contacts may continue to hold positive promise for you. Remember any projects you worked on with them, especially those areas where you enjoyed working together and where you both seemed to complement each other well.

Break these contacts out of their "boxes"! Think beyond the confines of the actual work, school, or organization in which you knew them. They represent more than what you knew them to be "back then." They are more multidimensional, more multi-talented, and certainly more connected now. Imagine the multifaceted web of experiences and contacts they, too, have woven over the past 25+ years.

If some members of your network are fellow Boomers, they probably are now engaged in a "reinvention" process like your own. You may find ways to mutually benefit each other.

Using current technologies like Google, Facebook, and LinkedIn, begin now to track down and reconnect with former contacts with whom you have lost touch over the years. When you relocate this, your network of choice, learn where they are now, what they are doing, what they would like to be doing, and even what they may consider doing in partnership with you. Which of these could become potential contacts, partners, mentors, collaborators, or even clients? Take the time now to consider, cull, reconnect with and reengage your own *Intentional Network*.

Make Your Own Match!

So, what will it be? What out of all the possibilities will you pursue next? Look back at what you have discovered so far and select your first match—*one that fits you, engages you, excites you, and makes full use of your value.*

Your retirement can, and probably will, be a work in progress. The direction you choose now may take you directly into a happy and engaging retirement life. Or you may find that you need to return later to the process, and shift directions once again.

If you need additional help to move ahead with your ideal retirement life and work plan, seek out a *Certified Retirement Coach* for one-on-one assistance or group sessions. To locate a coach near you, visit the *Retirement Coaches Association*, and click on "Find a Coach."

Online seminars and workshops presented by *Certified Retirement Coaches* can provide you the opportunity to talk through your ideas and issues, and to interact with others, who, like you, are in the process of designing their own happy retirement lives. One outstanding online option is "Retire & Be Happy," offered by Marianne Oehser: *RetireandBeHappyWorkshop.com*.

And So...

Yes, let's reiterate all the clichés... "Now is where the rubber meets the road" ... "It's time to walk the talk" ... "Put your money where your mouth is" ...

The bottom line—now is the time for you to act. But note the internal and external tools and resources you now have at your disposal to accomplish your tasks. And think about the sense of satisfaction and accomplishment you'll experience when you print out those three living-proof résumés of the newly invented you.

Your new adventure is just beginning. There is great fun in store as you re-discover all those virtual and physical network members, some of whom are destined to become members of your intentional and invited network.

Whether you realize it or not, you are on the cusp of weaving a fascinating web of past contacts, discovering where former colleagues are, how they arrived at that place, what they are doing now, their current "mojo." Reconnecting with these past professional and personal "significant others"—this endeavor alone will provide you with a plethora of surprises and realizations you could never have anticipated.

But first, there's work to be done! The résumés, the business cards, the marketing materials and strategies, the lists of networks! Let the work begin!

CHAPTER 14:
Current & Emerging Technologies That Impact Life & Work After Retirement

How does what's happening in the cyber world inform, serve, and impact the exploding population over 65? The phenomenon of current and emerging technology is changing the way we interact with each other. This new world of technology is available to current and soon-to-be retirees in many exciting formats.

Are retirees interested? Yes, we certainly are. Don't assume even for a minute that seniors are averse to embrace these marvelous new tools and systems, many of which are adapting themselves to the specific needs of older citizens. What role will these new technological phenomena play in our lives? How will these technology developments transform your retirement realities, fundamentally altering what will and will not be within your reach for the next 30 or so years of our lives. Barriers are falling away through five key areas of *Current and Emerging Technologies*:

1. Professional Technology Tools
2. Personal Technology Tools
3. Social Technology Tools
4. Independence Enhancing Technologies
5. Experience Enhancing Technologies

What are each of these, and how will they impact your retirement life and work in positive ways?

Professional Technology Tools

We already have discussed many of the technology tools that have transformed our professional lives, now and into the future. Thanks to the web, our work lives are no longer limited to our neighborhood, city, state, or even country. And we are no longer limited by our current knowledge level or native language.

Five groupings of professional technology tools include:

1. **Professional Networking** tools such as LinkedIn... We can connect professionally to support and be supported by past and current colleagues, all from our home computers.

2. **Online Learning Providers.** We have access to learn virtually any subject, to any level or depth, with or without obtaining credentials as an outcome of our efforts.

3. **Translation Tools**. We can communicate with, work for and collaborate with anyone, anywhere, unimpeded by language barriers.

4. **Ubiquitous Connections**. We can connect with and work virtually "any time, any place, any person, any pace."

5. **Assistive Technologies**. Online accessibility has been ensured for all. Hearing impairments, visual impairments, physical impairments need not exclude anyone from being able to participate, work, engage and contribute.

One organization deserves mention— www.aarp.org—whose sole focus is to improve quality of life for those 55 and over. Checking this site on a regular basis, provides seniors with a robust variety of information covering every aspect of professional development, whether it be career networking with others, professional learning, or job seeking strategies and sources.

Personal Technology Tools

Technology tools also have altered our personal lives profoundly and will continue to do so. Throughout our retirement lives, we will have the means to manage for ourselves our personal financial affairs, possessions, travel and hobbies, efficiently and expertly, without leaving home. Two such tools are *Microsoft Office* and *Smartphones*.

Microsoft Office. Most of us are familiar with the ubiquitous standard program, Microsoft Office. But one of its most useful features, yet best kept secrets, and underutilized tools, is the ready-made library of templates available to users—all at your disposal to manage your personal affairs and to uncomplicate your life.

For example, MS Excel provides templates to inventory your home possessions for insurance purposes, set up a family budget, and experiment with loan amortization hypotheses. If you're a job seeker, MS Word offers several attractive ready-made forms to make it easy to create your résumé and cover letter; a catchy flier announcing that baby shower, craft fair, or block party; a trifold newsletter or brochure highlighting your organization's activities and news events.

You'll receive kudos from all directions when you assume the role of chief multimedia producer at your next holiday party, wedding, birthday, or anniversary celebration. MS PowerPoint is the perfect vehicle for organizing, producing, and projecting a polished, crowd-pleasing multimedia presentation, including video, photography, audio tracks and text. And learning to use it is "intuitive."

Smartphones. Now let's consider that popular personal technology tool—the smartphone. Seniors are more digitally connected now than ever before. Four in ten seniors now own smartphones, almost twice the share in 2013 (23%). Almost six in ten seniors (59%) in the 65 to 69 age group are smartphone users. Ownership numbers are even higher among seniors who are more educated and/or more affluent. Two thirds (65%) of those with at a least bachelor's degree own one; 81% of those who live in households earning $75,000 or more a year use one (Pew Research Center: Internet & Technology. May 2017. *"Technology Use Among Seniors"*).

These high shares of seniors using smartphones are paralleled by the percentage who subscribe to home high-speed internet services. Two thirds of seniors (67%) now say they go online; over half (51%) have high-speed internet at home.

Our smartphones just keep getting smarter and smarter, and we're finding that they can make us smarter, too! With an almost infinite number of apps to accommodate every aspect of and interest in our lives—banking, travel, shopping, news media, music, hobbies, games, dining options, learning opportunities, domestic needs, job sources— our smartphones, because of their convenience, portability, power, versatility, and ubiquity, are rapidly lowering the bar for entry into internet use and connectedness. Where once a traditional computer workstation or laptop was necessary to connect, increasingly a smartphone will suffice.

How else can I carry with me my photo album, my music, my list of contacts, my ability to instantly communicate with others face-to-face, including internationally, my interactive GPS? No wonder our smartphones have become extensions of our hands!

Smartphone texting is the communication mode of choice for all generations, generating almost immediate response, even from our children and grandchildren, who have, in many cases, almost stopped answering phone calls unless they are prearranged. It is a powerhouse of practical operations and organization. Plan a trip to New Orleans for your book club... Orchestrate Thanksgiving, Christmas, and Easter family gatherings... Collaborate with your coauthor on a book project... Find a new tenant for your rental property... Speak Italian with the locals while you visit Rome... Find faucets and light fixtures for your rehab project... Explore healthcare costs and benefits in Costa Rica... Start a chess club... or a book club... or a Ping Pong club. Find answers to your every question...

And so ... as America is graying, retiring seniors are moving towards more digitally connected lives.

Social Technology Tools

We already have spoken at length about connectivity. Here we focus on tools that support *social* connections. And, yes, you can, (and perhaps you should!) consider adopting one or more of the current popular social technology tools, such as Facebook, Pinterest, Reddit, Snapchat, Instagram, and Twitter. Why? Primarily because these programs provide a powerful, fun way to connect with family and friends, both near and far.

However, in the interest of time invested and mental sanity, it might be wise to first start with your grandchildren! Yes, you heard right! Let them show you the pluses, minuses, and limitations of each of these tools before you jump in feet first!

For those of you who have not yet embraced one or more of these social networks, we provide a brief overview of each, meant to help you decide which, and whether, one or more of these most suit your lifestyle and social inclinations.

Facebook is a social networking site that makes it easy to connect and share with family and friends online. Users create a personal profile and then can post comments, send messages, share photographs and links to news or other interesting content on the Web, play games, chat live, and even stream live video. Anyone over the age of 13 with a valid email address can join Facebook, the world's largest social network, with more than 1 billion users worldwide. What makes Facebook unique is its ability to connect and share with multiple others at the same time.

Pinterest is like an online pin board, mostly for collecting visual pieces of multimedia and favorite images. Users can create and organize "boards," each focused on a particular interest or hobby. For example, if you like pictures of zoo animals, you can create a board labeled "Animals." If you also like collecting recipes, you can create another board named "Recipes." Chihuly glass? Places you would love to visit when you travel? Create as many boards as you like. Pinterest users interact with each other through liking, commenting, and "repinning" each other's stuff.

Reddit is an American social news aggregation, web-content-rating, and discussion website. By subscribing and unsubscribing to various subreddits, users can create their own "front page." Registered members submit content to the site such as links, text posts, and images that then are commented upon and voted up or down by other members. In other words, Reddit is a social news website and forum where stories are curated and promoted by users.

Snapchat is a free program that exists only as a mobile app to download to your iPhone or Android smartphone. Users can "chat" with their friends by sending them photos, short videos, text, and drawings up to 10 seconds long. One of the principle aspects of Snapchat is that pictures and messages are only available for a short time (between 1 and 10 seconds). Snapchat is particularly popular with young people.

Instagram is a social networking app made for sharing photos and videos from a smartphone. Like Facebook or Twitter, everyone who creates an Instagram account has a profile and a newsfeed. When you post a photo or video on Instagram, it will be displayed on your profile. *Instagram Direct* is its private messaging feature that allows users to share photos, videos or just plain text messages with just one specific user or multiple users as part of a group.

Twitter and "tweeting" is about broadcasting daily short-burst messages to the world, with the hope that your messages are useful and interesting to someone. Twitter is also about discovering interesting people online and following their burst messages. Registered users can post tweets, but those who are unregistered can only read them. Twitter is used to share information in real-time. When major events take place, Twitter lights up with "tweets."

A few questions you might want answered for each

As you explore using these programs and technologies yourself, here are some questions you may ask before you decide:

1. How steep is the learning curve? How long is it going to take to master this gentle giant before I can comfortably use it with confidence and ease? At this stage in our lives, we may choose that all learning experiences, while challenging, be enjoyable, not dreaded ordeals!

2. Do I need any additional exotic technology equipment or software? Can my current smartphone or laptop and network accommodate whatever specs the program requires?

3. What's the projected lifespan of this program? Is it already being pre-empted by the next bright idea? (In the interest of full disclosure here, your grandchildren are probably not an authoritative source to respond to this concern! They are too invested in whatever is the "hot app of the hour!")

4. What are the app's limitations? What can, and can't it do compared with other social applications?

Independence-Enhancing Tools

Some of the most significant and impactful technology tools now emerging or on the horizon are those that dramatically alter our ability to remain independent, now and into the future. Whereas our concerns once may have been about how we would manage our lives after we became less able to travel about, drive, walk and stand, see and hear, these worries can increasingly be put to rest as technologies flood the market to handle many of these life demands for us. Some of the most life-changing of these include:

1. Immediate remote access to goods, including meals

2. Barrier-free access to transportation

3. Assistance from Artificial Intelligence (AI) devices

4. Remote healthcare

5. Memory backup

6. Robotics

Immediate remote access to goods, including meals

Technology developments are increasingly eliminating the necessity to leave home to meet our shopping needs, or even to provide meals for ourselves and our families. Whether you wish to avoid going out to shop just because you would rather not, or because you are no longer able to do so independently, the choice to shop from home is yours to make. Two key technology players include:

- Amazon Prime

- Amazon Now

Amazon Prime provides immediate two-day shipping on over 50 million items. Four out of every $10 spent online in the U.S. is with Amazon (43%). Eighty percent of online growth comes from Amazon sales. Currently, there are approximately 80 million Amazon Prime members—that's an astounding 64% of households in the U.S.

The Amazon search engine is extremely powerful, and specific. Enter the part number for your printer ink cartridges... a description of the bangle your Secret Santa recipient requested... where and when you want to go deep-sea fishing... the model number of the faucet you need to replace... your bra size... Immediately you will have screens filled with exactly what you need, ready for purchase.

And for each item, you generally will find postings from other users who have purchased and evaluated this item themselves. So, you will be able to ensure the quality you want as well as to obtain the precise item you need, all without wandering lost and forlorn from store to store and possibly coming home empty-handed.

Amazon uses Artificial Intelligence (AI) to personalize your shopping experience and tailor offerings to you. This transforms your shopping experience and saves your precious time and energy. And no form of incapacity, now or in the future, will ever limit your ability to obtain what you need, when you need it, and have it delivered promptly to your door.

A bonus of Amazon Prime is that it is a rich source of entertainment—books, movies, TV series. So, it will forever be available to provide you with endless and interesting pursuits to enjoy in your leisure time.

Amazon Prime *Now*. To make a significant difference in meeting your meal needs, delivery services had to become more immediate. And now they have. Amazon Prime has expanded its offerings to include Prime *Now*—same-day as well as one-day shipping. This makes it possible to order what you need from Whole Foods and have your purchases delivered in time to cook tonight's dinner.

Many Whole Foods products (including meat, eggs and alcohol), are now available via the Prime Now 2-hour delivery service offered to Prime members in select cities. These offerings will expand into less populated regions. And, again, each item is accompanied by reviews that will improve the outcome of your shopping and your meals by drawing important feedback from other diners' experiences.

Home delivery services are also available from a wide list of restaurants through Prime Now. Make your meal selection at Gamin's

Deli in San Francisco, enter your delivery address, set a delivery time and check out. Your chicken breast plate, small green salad and large bottled water will be on its way for a modest delivery fee of $2.99. If you opt to purchase more than one meal at a time, and increase your order to over $40, delivery will be free.

Barrier-free access to transportation

So too with transportation. Here again technology developments have eliminated dependency; driving ability is decreasingly a potential limitation to independence. Whereas, in an earlier age, visual impairments or physical limitations could and would have been game changers, leaving you trapped in the house, unable to meet your own needs without depending on family or friends to drive you, now these incapacitating barriers have been lifted permanently.

Two prime technologies that have merged to solve the transportation dilemma, and make it possible for you to live in your own home independently and indefinitely, even after you have turned over your car keys, include:

- Uber (or Lyft)
- Self-driving cars (coming soon)

Uber is a global on-demand taxi and food delivery technology company, founded in 2009, headquartered in San Francisco, and operating in 633 cities worldwide. Uber drivers use their own cars and clock in using the Uber app whenever they are available as drivers. Here ends the need for "Driving Miss Daisy."

The Uber company has been a pioneer in the "sharing economy," so much so that the profound changes it has produced in its industry, now being replicated in other industries, have been referred to as "Uberisation." In 2015 Uber completed its 1 billionth ride, with 40 million riders using the service in the month of October 2016 alone.

Uber drivers undergo a background check. When you are matched with a driver, the app immediately shows you their name, license plate number, photo and rating. Their vehicles must pass annual safety inspections and display an Uber emblem in the passenger window. Passengers also are vetted and prechecked in advance by registering for an account, providing their name and phone number and credit card information for payment, all before they are allowed to request a ride.

In most cities, Uber offers upfront "dynamic pricing"; the rider is quoted the estimated fare based on the level of demand *before* they request the ride or the delivery. At the end of the ride, payment is made based on the rider's pre-selected preferences, which could be a credit card on file, cash, or other methods such as Google Wallet.

Other Uber services include:

- **UberEats.** Allows users to have meals delivered by Uber drivers from participating restaurants.
- **UberRush.** A courier package delivery service available in New Your City, San Francisco and Chicago.
- **UberBOAT.** Available as a water-taxi service, especially during special events.
- **UberAIR.** A program that debuts in 2020 in LA, Dallas-Fort Worth and Dubai using vertical takeoff and landing aircraft, commonly known as "flying cars."

Ratings of Uber drivers, as well as users, on a 1 to 5-star scale determine whether a driver remains active or whether a user has service available. If a driver rates a rider at three stars or below, the rider will never be paired with that driver again.

The Uber company has been conducting self-driving car research since 2015. They announced in November 2017 plans to purchase up to 24,000 Volvo cars designed to accept autonomous technology between 2019 and 2021. Uber also has been looking into urban transportation with flying vehicles—UberCHOPPER— to be used in cities with extreme traffic congestion or for special events in locations with limited access such as the Cannes Film Festival.

Self-Driving Cars

As recently as two years ago, self-driving cars were considered figments of the sci-fi imagination, the stuff that dreams are made of!

Retirees and seniors might have dismissed this technology as a phenomenon that we in the over-65 group would never need to deal with.

Oops! Take another look! Think again! The December 18, 2017 issue of TIME magazine featured a one-page spread entitled, "The Year in Smart Auto," chronicling "milestones from the world of self-driving and electric cars." Google, Ford, Tesla, Mercedes-Benz, GM, The US House of Representatives, Uber, VW, California, Las Vegas, Phoenix, France, Germany, UK, China, Taiwan. Have we name-dropped enough "early adapters" of this technology to convince you that this technology is imminent?

Whoa! Before you don your "resistance hat," think of the pros! No more exorbitant auto insurance bills! And why will you need a traditional "driver's license?" Granted, you will need to know how to program a type of GPS, but most of us are already best friends with this technology. These autos are guided with radar, global positioning systems (GPS), and on-board cameras.

So, just sit back, listen to your music, play "Words with Friends," watch a Netflix movie, or treat yourself to something on Amazon Prime! Eureka! Self-driving technology adds new meaning, and lends a new dimension, to multi-tasking and autonomy. The best part—research attests that 90+% of auto accidents are caused by driver error! My, my! Car travel may once again become a pleasurable experience!

Assistance from Artificial intelligence (AI) Devices

Artificial intelligence technology gives us the ability to use computers to perform tasks that usually require human intelligence. One aspect of artificial intelligence, according to *SeniorCareCorner.com,* is referred to as "cognitive computing." Cognitive computing uses a computer system or application to mimic our thought processes. This technology promises tremendous benefits for aging, health and safety, allowing seniors and family caregivers to solve problems without the delay or costs of needing a person present.

In an article entitled, "5 Ways Artificial Intelligence May Help Us Live at Home Longer" (*www.NextAvenue.org,* May 2017), author

Randi Rieland talks about how our aging population can most benefit from embracing the innovations of AI:

- Personal Assistant Devices
- Smart homes
- Remote Healthcare
- Memory Backup

Your Own Personal Assistant. Talking devices are interacting with humans in more engaging ways. Siri, Cortana, Google Home, and Echo-enabled Alexa are examples of artificial intelligence using voice recognition technology that adapts to one individual voice and language. These computerized personal assistants can help answer questions and do specific tasks—no typing required! Now, the next generation of home assistants is being developed, designed to connect more with people, and not simply respond to requests.

Smart Homes Are Getting Smarter. The next phase purports to enable smart homes to become more proactive by taking actions based on what has been learned about your preferences and behavior. For example, an AI device in your home could turn on the coffee machine based on what it knows about your morning schedule or adjust lighting or music in response to what it recognizes in your body language.

Access to Remote Healthcare. Artificial intelligence will increasingly give us the ability to receive healthcare from home. Analysis of data gathered by sensors can help predict problems. Scientists are also finding they can learn quite a bit about the behaviors of older adults through sensors installed in their homes. And, they say, using AI algorithms to evaluate patterns of activity from the data those sensors collect can help make predictions about what behavior changes might mean.

Machines are learning to diagnose diseases. Recently Google announced that its research teams have developed algorithms enabling machines to diagnose an eye disease related to diabetes that can lead to blindness and to detect breast cancer. Researchers at Stanford University followed a similar process in helping a machine diagnose skin cancer. Another Stanford study looked at whether artificial intelligence could be effective at predicting heart attacks.

Backup Your Memory. One day you could be able to back up your own memory. One of the great challenges of getting older is fading memory. Not being able to remember names, places or events can make taking care of yourself that much harder. But what if your own memory could be as good as computer memory? Scientists are convinced that using machines to dramatically enhance our memories is inevitable.

Already computers and phones gather data constantly about our day-to-day lives, including photos of friends and family, the news we read and the music we listen to. It's only a matter of time before all of this is stored in a more systematic way to allow for easy memory retrieval. Just think of the enormous potential a backup memory system has, particularly for people with conditions like dementia or Alzheimer's.

Robotics

Digital companion robots, such as ElliQ or BUDDY can prove to be excellent companions for senior citizens. They can ensure the well-being of senior citizens at home by providing social interaction and assistance, encouraging an active and engaged lifestyle, reminding them about upcoming events, appointments, and deliveries.

In addition, these types of companion robots can monitor the homes of seniors who choose to live alone. They may even be able to detect falls and unusual activity and provide medication reminders. Additionally, robots can ease seniors' loneliness, providing them access to communication technology, like Skype and Facetime, with much more simplicity.

Yes, robots have the potential to not only help care for our elders, but to increase their independence and to reduce their social isolation. And while some tasks may always remain out of reach of robotic technology, mechanical caregivers can offer at least one clear advantage over human counterparts. Machines, unlike people, are available 24/7, at no extra cost!

Experience-Enhancing Technologies

Still on the leading edge, or even the "bleeding edge" of technology advances are the *Experience-Enhancing Technologies*. These offer continued access to experiences throughout retirement. Two key technologies that provide digital versions of reality are:

- **Virtual Reality** (VR). Imaginary experiences that are made to seem real.

- **Augmented Reality** (AR) Real experiences, enhanced with additional pertinent information.

Virtual Reality (VR)

Wikipedia describes *virtual reality* as "a computer technology that uses virtual reality headsets or multi-projected environments, sometimes in combination with physical environments or props, to generate realistic images, sounds and other sensations that simulate a user's physical presence in a virtual or imaginary environment." A person using virtual reality equipment can "look around" the artificial world, and with high quality VR, move around in it and interact with virtual features or items. The effect is commonly created by VR headsets consisting of a head-mounted display with a small screen in front of the eyes, but can also be created through specially designed rooms with multiple large screens.

By now, you are probably shaking your head in disbelief, thinking "TMI" (too much information)! But this is not as space-age as you may think. Yes, as you are probably aware, this technology was initially embraced mostly by those members of younger generations who are immersed in interactive video games and sci-fi pursuits. But since 2010 the "serious game" industry has become increasingly robust, enlisting VR technologies for defense training, education, scientific exploration, health care, emergency management, city planning, and engineering. For those who are learning to run nuclear plants, VR versions of the plant and all its controls are their training ground—much better to make errors in a VR environment than with the real thing.

In your future may be VR travel experiences... Pretend adventures... Hands-on learning... You may still have a chance to accomplish your bucket-list item of climbing Machu Picchu without ending up short of breath.

And don't be surprised if your grandchildren list such a system on their holiday must-have list, convince you that your linear world is obsolete, and insist that you must view the world via this exciting, multi-dimensional, multi-sensory experience. Our advice—just grin and bear it! You might be justifiably impressed!

Augmented Reality (AR)

According to Wikipedia, *Augmented Reality* is a "live direct or indirect view of a physical, real-world environment whose elements are "augmented" by computer-generated or computer-extracted real-world sensory input such as sound, video, and graphics, altering and enhancing one's view of reality." In other words, whatever it is you are standing in front of, AR will provide you more pertinent information. Scoreboards during a football game... Historic information at a well-known site... Illuminating information about the masterpiece you are viewing in an art museum...

In contrast to *Virtual Reality*, that *replaces* the real world with a simulated, artificial one, *Augmented Reality* enhances and enriches an experienced environment by superimposing a layer of digital information on top of the user's environment in real time.

Originally, *Immersive Augmented Reality* experiences were used in entertainment and game businesses, but now other business industries are also getting interested about augmented reality's possibilities, such as knowledge-sharing, training, managing the information flood and organizing distant meetings.

And So...

As these technology developments transform how professional work and networking is accomplished, how personal connections are developed and maintained, how social interactions are stimulated and enriched, how independence is supported throughout life and even how reality is experienced through imaginary or the actual world, so too will your retirement life be fundamentally altered and advanced.

What will and will not be within your reach for the next 30 or so years of your life will be dramatically different than it would have been before, as barriers fall away and more of life is but a mouse-click or a voice-command away.

CHAPTER 15:
Parting Words

We hope you have experienced your own unique "happening" as you have journeyed through the chapters of this book. Wasn't it awesome, and even daunting, to remind ourselves of who we are as a generation in terms of what we have accomplished... advancing the fields of technology, business, medicine, and education... transforming the political, social, economic, intellectual, and technical landscape of the second half of the 20th century... And, in the process, becoming the most educated, affluent, healthy generation in US history.

This is the legacy that we now find ourselves in a position to leverage as we "shift gears" into a new life phase. But even more daunting is the conviction and determination that we are not finished—yet! We have saved the best for last!

The realizations and the inspirations you have experienced through your reading hopefully have generated your "new birth," the re-invented, re-energized you who knows that this is just the beginning of what will be, no doubt, the final and penultimate chapter of your biography. Determine to make this next phase your best. Your happiest. Your most gratifying. And, yes, even your most productive.

Armed with the tools, strategies, and connections (both tangible and virtual) that you now have at your disposal, you can and will accomplish what you set out to do—next.

You know where you've been—your past accomplishments. You know who and where you are—your current self-awareness and self-assessment. And you know where you are going next—your new life paradigm, with career options galore. Hopefully, you also now know how to get there, or at least where to start. So, what are the operative concepts that should prevail in this glorious next period of your life? We leave you with these six treasures.

Savor the Richness in Full

Whether we remember or acknowledge it or not, we have spent too much time in the past "short-cutting" so many of those small, but important, "minute vacations" and stops to smell the roses.

Now is the time to retire the "I'd like to, but I don't have the time" mantra in favor of "Yes, I can indulge—in that second glass of wine, that lengthy, somewhat frivolous phone call, that "chick flick" or "action movie" matinee, that extra round of golf, that beer or coffee and cake break with my friend, that no-buy (or buy-buy!) shopping spree.

Whenever you start to by-pass a "carpe diem" moment, ask yourself: "If not now, when?" Then tell yourself: "I deserve it now!"

Frivolity is a Luxury You *Can* Afford

Who said you are too old to ride that Zip Line across the Costa Rican rain forest? Where is it written that you are beyond the "adolescent phase" of taking an impulsive skinny dip in that mountain lake, or getting that tattoo of a phoenix rising from the ashes? And, no, it is not too late to buy that Harley that you have secretly coveted, along with the black leather jacket, to complement the tattoo!

Maybe, just maybe, blending into the crowd, acting with proper decorum, and always dressing, speaking, and acting "appropriately" are conventional wisdoms that are outworn and overrated.

As Boomers, haven't we earned the right to "loosen up and live a little closer to the edge"? So...go put on those Nikes or buy that mountain bike or take up line dancing. Just do it!

Live in the Moment.

My very dear friend, who happens to be a Quaker, once shared with me a basic precept of this gentle sect: "Be where you are." I can't tell you how many times I have applied this wisdom in my own personal life—in mundane as well as complex situations.

When I was frazzled and frantic in an endless, seemingly unmoving line at the supermarket checkout, in five o'clock rush hour traffic, or on overload with job projects... When I was in the middle of house-work or cooking—both chores that I abhor... Or stuck in an airport after missing my flight, and facing a night attempting to sleep upright on a plastic seat... After my mental and emotional hysteria subsided, "be where you are" always came to the rescue, providing me with a sense of calm, sanity and perspective. "Be where you are" has become for me the psychological equivalent of "take a deep breath."

As Boomers, we have seen our share of tragedies and triumphs. We have learned the sobering life lesson that often waiting is the hard part of any experience and waiting for clarity is the hardest. Whether in good times or bad, we also have come to know the meaning of "this, too, shall pass"—whatever the "it" has been. And in time it did pass.

Living in the moment has been one of the most ignored habits we haven't mastered. Now is the time to become experts at it. Because, in reality, the moment is all we are assured.

Be True to Yourself

However accustomed you have become to doing, doing, doing for others—caring for them, working for them, raising them, being their spouse or their friend—the time is now to break free and learn to be true to yourself. Shakespeare had it right when he wrote, "This above all, to thine own self be true. And it must follow, as the night the day. Thou canst not then be false to any man."

Give yourself permission, immediately, to take charge of your own life and to speak up for yourself. After a lifetime of effort to avoid be-ing "selfish," or otherwise putting your own self first, this is the time that you have been waiting for. Now it is your turn.

Move forward, firmly, with no regrets from the past, into the fu-ture. Find your own way—your own work—your own legacy. Surpris-ingly, you will be of more value to the others in your life when you are acting as your own true self than you ever were when you were at-tempting to put your own self—your wants, enthusiasms, passions, and purpose—on hold in favor of accommodating others, or other-wise setting yourself aside.

Revise the Revisions: Serial Retirement

As a Boomer, you remember Arlo Guthrie's mishap while singing *Alice's Restaurant,* when he got into a tangle and missed some of the words. But he just kept playing, saying "That's all right. It'll come back 'round again..." And when it did come back 'round again, he picked up where he'd left off and sang the rest of the song.

So, too, will your *Next Phase* life "come back 'round again." If you find that your first set of plans and directions do not suit you after all, just come at it again from another direction.

Considering how dramatic and deep your life changes may be at this point, and how eager you may have been to choose your next direction, any direction, and end the suspense... you may find yourself heading off, energetically and with great speed, down the wrong path. If so, the faster you go—the harder you push down on that pedal—the further afield you will find yourself before you finally do call a halt, put on the brakes, and turn around.

You may find that you have made too many compromises, possibly in your attempt to align your *Next Phase* goals and plans with those of your spouse...or a close friend...or your children and their children. *Perhaps you have allowed your next life to choose you instead of you choosing it.* As with most things, "not to decide is to decide."

A sign that may indicate you have "veered off" in a direction that is not optimum for you, is the sense that you are waking up into someone else's life. If this has happened to you, the heart of the matter, most likely, is that your concept and sense of your true self, in all its uniqueness, has somehow been sidetracked. Your most essential self may be telling you that you are not there yet.

Your shift to your life and work after retirement may end up taking the form of a 3-phase process. In *Phase I: Vacation Mode,* you may need time to recover from work exhaustion by taking a long, well-deserved break. During this phase, your paramount goal may be to relish all those activities that were out of reach for you during your career—sleeping until 9:00, reading whole books, traveling the world, spending time with family and friends. This phase will pass eventually, as soon as you have had your fill. After you have read 257 books... Or played golf for 100 days in a row... Or gone fishing so often your freezer, as well as the freezers of all your family and friends, is overstuffed with your catch... Or taken a 3-week trip to France... The day will come when you will say "enough of this" and look around for what you want to do with the rest of your life.

This will bring you to *Phase II: High Intensity Retirement Life & Work*. This is when you will need most to go through the 5-step process of designing your retirement life and work, as outlined in this book. If, during your first read-through of the book, you were still in Phase I, you may not have been ready yet to complete the intensive self-examination and exploration outlined here. So, you may do well to start again on *Page 1,* and, like Arlo, let it "come back 'round again."

What you devise during *Phase II* may itself undergo another revision, arriving at *Phase III: Moderation & New Balance*. After some time of settling in with your retirement life and work, you may find that you've taken on too much and are working harder than you ever did during your earlier work life. There is such a thing as "too much wonderful." Marie ended up with three demanding, time-consuming jobs before she finally settled down to "just" one. Carolee embarked on a retirement career of writing and publishing that involved traveling the world and creating six series of "Your Great Trip" travel books, on a planned publishing schedule of five books a year. In Phase III, she regrouped to a more modest publishing schedule in order to have more time left over for life.

If you find that you need to let your retirement life "come back 'round again," grant yourself the liberty to revise, and then to revise the revisions, *until* you are on the right course for you. And you know you are on the right course. And you know that you know.

Now Pass It On: Your Legacy as a Role Model

You already may have embarked on your new life's adventure before you connected with this book. If so, your reading may have enhanced, enriched, and given added impetus to your new career, providing you with new connections, perspectives, and strategies.

Or you may be embracing this book at the very beginning of your "re-invention" stage. If so, we hope our words have proven to be an effective, inspiring, and empowering "yellow brick road" to help you expand your thinking, find your way, and reach your own intended destination.

In either case, now we ask that you "pay it forward." Share your own *Senior Snapshot*—your new adventure—with your fellow Boomer colleagues who may still be in search of their own next lives. And, when possible, help them through the process of clarifying their own journeys—but *their* way.

After all, the greatest legacy we can leave each other is the camaraderie and confidence we share by showing fellow Boomers "how we did it," and cheering them on to do the same, as we reinvent retirement for ourselves and as models for the generations to come.

May the wind be at your back.

TABLE OF URLS

Although we have done our best to assure that our list of websites is up-to-date and accurate, be aware that sites change frequently, both in title, content and in web location.

Site	URL
16 Personalities	https://www.16personalities.com/
AARP Worksearch	https://www.aarp.org/work
AB Global Translations	http://abglobal.net
ABC Go--Shark Tank	https://abc.go.com/shows/shark-tank
AccounTemps	https://www.AccounTemps.com
Ace Fitness	https://www.acefitness.org
Amazon	https://www.amazon.com
American Heart Assoc.	https://www.ahajournals.org
Ameriglide	https://www.ameriglide.com
Assist U	https://assistu.com
B & V Staffing	http://bvstaffing.com
Baby Boomer Magazine	https://babyboomer-magazine.com
Balance Your Books	http://BalanceYourBooks.com/
Big Brothers Big Sisters	https://www.bbbs.org
Biz Filings	https://www.bizfilings.com
Bureau of Labor Statistics	https://www.bls.gov
Business USA	https://www.busa.org/
Career Builder	https://www.careerbuilder.com
Career Zone	https://www.cacareerzone.org
Certified Professional Retirement Coach	https://certifiedretirementcoach.org
ChildStats.Gov	https://www.childstats.gov
Chord Buddy	https://www.chordbuddy.com
Click-N-Work	https//www.clicknwork.com
Coolworks	https://www.coolworks.com/
CraigsList	https://www.craigslist.org/about/sites
rystal Underground	https://www.crystalunderground.com/

Demographics Now	https://www.demographicsnow.com
Desktop Staff	https://www.linkedin.com/jobs/search/?key-words=desktop%20staff
Dice.com	https://www.dice.com/
Dreamstime	https://www.dreamstime.com/
eLance (now Upwork)	https://www.upwork.com/
Elder Gadget	http://www.Eldergadget.com
Employment 911	https://www.employment911.com
Entrepreneur	https://www.entrepreneur.com
Experience Corps	https://www.aarp.org/experience-corps/
EzineArticles	https://EzineArticles.com
Financial Industry Regulatory Authority	https://www.finra.org/investors/professional-designations/cprc
Flex Jobs	https://www.flexJobs.com
Freelancer	https://www.freelancer.com
Freelancer	https://www.freelancer.com/
Freelancers	https://www.freelancers.net
Genuine Jobs	https://genuinejobs.com
Glassdoor	https://www.glassdoor.com/index.htm
Global Staffing Solutions	http://www.global-staffingsolutions.com/
GoDaddy	https://www.godaddy.com/
Green Africa Foundation	http://www.greenafricafoundation.org
Guardian Ad Litem	https://guardianadlitem.org
Guru.Com	https://www.Guru.com
HireAbility	https://www.hireability.com
Home Job Stop	https://www.homejobstop.com
Home Job Stop	https://www.homejobstop.com
Homeworkers	http://www.homeworkers.org
Idealist	https://www.idealist.org
Indeed	https://www.indeed.com/q-Convention-Center-jobs.html
Indeed	https://www.indeed.com/
Indeed.com	https://www.indeed.com/
Insights Association	https://www.insightsassociation.org/
International Living	https://internationalliving.com

International Volunteer Programs Association	http://volunteerinternational.org/
Intuit	https://sbconnect.intuit.com/
IQ BackOffice	http://www.iqbackoffice.com/
Job Accept	https://www.jobaccept.com
Job.com	https://www.job.com/
JobBank USA	https://www.jobbankusa.com
Jobline International	http://jobline.net
Jobvertise	https://www.jobvertise.com/
JuJu	https://www.juju.com
Jumpstart	https://www.jstart.org/
Life Goes Strong	http://www.lifegoesstrong.com
Link Up	https://www.linkup.com/
LinkedIn	https://www.linkedin.com
Live Career	https://www.livecareer.com/
Market Watch	https://www.marketwatch.com/
Meet the Blanks	https://www.blanksstudios.com/
Money CNN	https://money.cnn.com
Money US News	https://money.usnews.com
Monster	https://www.monster.com/
Monster	https://www.monster.com
National & Community Service	https://www.nationalservice.gov/
National Assoc. of Baby Boomer Women	https://nabbw.com/
National Association of Home Builders	http://www.nbnnews.com
National Education Association	http://www.nea.org
National Geographic Expeditions	https://www.nationalgeographicexpeditions.com
National Park Service	https://www.nps.gov
National Substitute Teachers	https://www.nsta.org
Nature Conservatory	https://www.nature.org
Next Avenue	https://www.nextavenue.org/
Now What Jobs	http://www.nowwhatjobs.net
Occupational Outlook Handbook	https://www.bls.gov/ooh/

oDesk (now Upwork)	https://www.upwork.com/
Oodle Marketplace	https://jobs.oodle.com/careers
Outsource 2000	http://www.outsource2000.com
OutSource Your Books	http://www.osyb.com/
Pay Scale	https://www.payscale.com
Personality Pathways	https://www.personalitypathways.com
Pet Place	https://www.petplace.com
Points of Light	http://www.pointsoflight.org
Pro-World Volunteers	https://proworldvolunteers.org
QuickBooks	https://quickbooks.intuit.com
Readerest	https://www.readerest.com
Rent–A-Grandma	http://www.rentagrandma.com
Retire & Be Happy	https://retireandbehappyworkshop.com/
Retire & Consult	http://consultantjournal.com/blog/retire-and-consult
Retired Brains	https://www.retiredbrains.com/search-jobs.html
Retirement Jobs	http://www.retirementjobs.com
Retirement Options	https://www.retirementoptions.com/
Road Scholar	https://www.roadscholar.org
Scam.Com	https://www.scam.com
Senior Care Corner	http://seniorcarecorner.com/
Senior Job Bank	http://www.seniorjobbank.com
Shark Tank Success Blog-spot	https://sharktanksuccess.blogspot.com
Shopper Trak	https://www.shoppertrak.com/
Simply Hired	https://www.simplyhired.com/
Small Business Admin-istration	https://www.sba.gov
Smart Volunteer	http://smartvolunteer.org
SmarThinking	https://www.pearson.com/us/higher-educa-tion/products-services-institutions/smarthink-ing/for-tutors.html
SMG World	http://www.SMGWorld.com
Smithsonian Journeys	https://www.smithsonianjourneys.org
Startup Compete	https://www.jstart.org
Supportibles	https://supportibles.com/

Teacher.org	https://www.teacher.org/career/substitute-teacher
Templates for MS Office	https://templates.office.com/
The Ladders	https://www.theladders.com
The Recruiter Network	https://www.therecruiternetwork.com
Transcribe 1-2-3	https//www.youdictate.net
Transgenerational	http://transgenerational.org
Tutor	https://www.tutor.com
United Planet	https://www.unitedplanet.org
UpWork	https://www.upwork.com
US.Jobs	https://us.jobs/
USA Jobs	https://www.usajobs.gov/
USA.gov	https://www.usa.gov/start-business
Varsity	https://www.varsitybranding.com/
Vayable	https://www.vayable.com/jobs
VIA Character	https://www.viacharacter.org/www/Charac-ter-Strengths
VIP Desk	https://vipdeskconnect.com/current-open-ings/
Virtual Corp	https://www.virtual-corp.com
Virtual Office Temps	http://virtualassistantJobs.com
Virtual Staffing Partners	https://www.virtualstaffingpartners.com/
Virtual Staffing Source	http://www.vrtualstaffingsource.com
Virtual Vocations	https://www.virtualvocations.com/
Vista Print	https://www.vistaprint.com
Volunteer Hub	https://www.volunteerhub.com/blog/volun-teer-training-program/
Volunteer Match	https://www.volunteermatch.org
Volunteering & Civil Life in America	https://www.nationalservice.gov/vcla
Volunteers of America	https://www.voa.org/
What's Next?	https://www.whatsnext.com/life-values-self-assessment-test
Work Search	https://www.aarp.org/aarp-foundation/
World Force 50	https://www.workforce50.com
Zip Recruiter	https://www.ziprecruiter.com/

Sorted by Category

Category	Site	URL
AARP	AARP Worksearch	https://www.aarp.org/work
Boomer Magazines	Baby Boomer Magazine	https://babyboomer-magazine.com
Boomer Magazines	National Assoc. of Baby Boomer Women	https://nabbw.com/
Business Startup	Biz Filings	https://www.bizfilings.com
Business Startup	Business USA	https://www.busa.org/
Business Startup	Entrepreneur	https://www.entrepreneur.com
Business Startup	Small Business Administration	https://www.sba.gov
Business Startup	USA.gov	https://www.usa.gov/start-business
Career Opportunities	Bureau of Labor Statistics	https://www.bls.gov
Career Opportunities	Occupational Outlook Handbook	https://www.bls.gov/ooh/
Certified Retirement Coach	Certified Professional Retirement Coach	https://certifiedretirementcoach.org
Certified Retirement Coach	Financial Industry Regulatory Authority	https://www.finra.org/investors/professional-designations/cprc
Entrepreneur Models	Crystal Underground	https://www.crystalunderground.com/
Entrepreneur Models	Readerest	https://www.readerest.com
Entrepreneur Models	Rent–A–Grandma	http://www.rentagrandma.com
Entrepreneur Models	Shark Tank Success Blogspot	https://sharktanksuccess.blogspot.com
Entrepreneur Models	Pet Place	https://www.petplace.com

Entrepreneur Resources	Dreamstime	https://www.dreamstime.com/
Entrepreneur Resources	Intuit	https://sbconnect.intuit.com/
Entrepreneur Resources	QuickBooks	https://quickbooks.intuit.com
Entrepreneurial	ABC Go--Shark Tank	https://abc.go.com/shows/shark-tank
Entrepreneurial	Money US News	https://money.usnews.com
Entrepreneurial	Vayable	https://www.vayable.com/jobs
Entretrueneur Options	Shopper Trak	https://www.shoppertrak.com/
Event Management Jobs	Indeed	https://www.indeed.com/q-Convention-Center-jobs.html
Event Management Jobs	SMG World	http://www.SMGWorld.com
Freelance Networks	Freelancer	https://www.freelancer.com
Freelance Networks	Freelancer	https://www.freelancer.com/
Freelance Networks	Freelancers	https://www.freelancers.net
Freelance Networks	UpWork	https://www.upwork.com
General Research	Amazon	https://www.amazon.com
Health	American Heart Assoc.	https://www.ahajournals.org
Health	Next Avenue	https://www.nextavenue.org/
Health Care Advances	Senior Care Corner	http://seniorcarecorner.com/
Health Careers	Ace Fitness	https://www.acefitness.org
Job Newsletters/ Newsgroups	Home Job Stop	https://www.homejobstop.com

Job Newsletters/ Newsgroups	Indeed.com	https://www.indeed.com/
Job Newsletters/ Newsgroups	Monster	https://www.monster.com/
Job Sites for Seniors	Now What Jobs	http://www.nowwhatjobs.net
Job Sites for Seniors	Retire & Consult	http://consultantjournal.com/blog/retire-and-consult
Job Sites for Seniors	Retired Brains	https://www.retiredbrains.com/search-jobs.html
Job Sites for Seniors	Retirement Jobs	http://www.retirementjobs.com
Job Sites for Seniors	Senior Job Bank	http://www.seniorjobbank.com
Job Sites for Seniors	USA Jobs	https://www.usajobs.gov/
Job Sites for Seniors	Work Search	https://www.aarp.org/aarp-foundation/
Job Sites for Seniors	World Force 50	https://www.workforce50.com
Living & Working Abroad	International Living	https://internationalliving.com
Market & Survey Research Jobs	Insights Association	https://www.insightsassociation.org/
Market Research	Market Watch	https://www.marketwatch.com/
Marketing to Boomers	Varsity	https://www.varsitybranding.com/
Models for Entrepreneurs	Chord Buddy	https://www.chordbuddy.com
Models for Entrepreneurs	Meet the Blanks	https://www.blanksstudios.com/
Networking	LinkedIn	https://www.linkedin.com
Online Classified Ads	CraigsList	https://www.craigslist.org/about/sites
Online Classified Ads	CraigsList	https://www.craigslist.org/about/sites

Online Classified Ads	Jobvertise	https://www.jobvertise.com/
Online Classified Ads	Oodle Marketplace	https://jobs.oodle.com/careers
Online Employment Agencies	Assist U	https://assistu.com
Online Employment Agencies	Desktop Staff	https://www.linkedin.com/jobs/search/?keywords=desktop%20staff
Online Employment Agencies	HireAbility	https://www.hireability.com
Online Employment Agencies	The Recruiter Network	https://www.therecruiternetwork.com
Online Employment Agencies	Transcribe 1-2-3	https//www.youdictate.net
Online Employment Agencies	Virtual Vocations	https://www.virtualvocations.com/
Online Job Boards	Career Builder	https://www.careerbuilder.com
Online Job Boards	Genuine Jobs	https://genuinejobs.com
Online Job Boards	Guru.Com	https://www.Guru.com
Online Job Boards	Home Job Stop	https://www.homejobstop.com
Online Job Boards	Homeworkers	http://www.homeworkers.org
Online Job Boards	Job Accept	https://www.jobaccept.com
Online Job Boards	Jobline International	http://jobline.net
Online Job Boards	JuJu	https://www.juju.com
Online Job Boards	Live Career	https://www.livecareer.com/
Online Job Search Sites	Coolworks	https://www.coolworks.com/
Online Job Search Sites	Dice.com	https://www.dice.com/
Online Job Search Sites	Employment 911	https://www.employment911.com

Online Job Search Sites	Flex Jobs	https://www.flexJobs.com
Online Job Search Sites	Glassdoor	https://www.glassdoor.com/index.htm
Online Job Search Sites	Indeed	https://www.indeed.com/
Online Job Search Sites	Job.com	https://www.job.com/
Online Job Search Sites	Link Up	https://www.linkup.com/
Online Job Search Sites	Monster	https://www.monster.com
Online Job Search Sites	Outsource 2000	http://www.outsource2000.com
Online Job Search Sites	Simply Hired	https://www.simplyhired.com/
Online Job Search Sites	The Ladders	https://www.theladders.com
Online Job Search Sites	US Jobs	https://us.jobs/
Online Job Search Sites	Zip Recruiter	https://www.ziprecruiter.com/
Online Out-sourcing	AB Global Translations	http://abglobal.net
Online Out-sourcing	AccounTemps	https://www.AccounTemps.com
Online Out-sourcing	Balance Your Books	http://BalanceYourBooks.com/
Online Out-sourcing	Click-N-Work	https//www.clicknwork.com
Online Out-sourcing	eLance (now Upwork)	https://www.upwork.com/
Online Out-sourcing	IQ BackOffice	http://www.iqbackoffice.com/
Online Out-sourcing	oDesk (now Upwork)	https://www.upwork.com/
Online Out-sourcing	OutSource Your Books	http://www.osyb.com/
Online Out-sourcing	VIP Desk	https://vipdeskconnect.com/current-open-ings/
Online Staff-ing Services	B & V Staffing	http://bvstaffing.com
Online Staff-ing Services	Global Staffing Solutions	http://www.global-staffingsolutions.com/

Online Staffing Services	Supportibles	https://supportibles.com/
Online Staffing Services	Virtual Corp	https://www.virtual-corp.com
Online Staffing Services	Virtual Office Temps	http://virtualassistantJobs.com
Online Staffing Services	Virtual Staffing Partners	https://www.virtualstaffingpartners.com/
Online Staffing Services	Virtual Staffing Source	http://www.vrtualstaffingsource.com
Pay Rates	Pay Scale	https://www.payscale.com
Public Education Jobs	National Education Association	http://www.nea.org
Public Education Jobs	National Substitute Teachers	https://www.nsta.org
Public Education Jobs	Teacher.org	https://www.teacher.org/career/substitute-teacher
Resources for Entrepreneurs	GoDaddy	https://www.godaddy.com/
Resources for Entrepreneurs	Vista Print	https://www.vistaprint.com
Résumé Services	JobBank USA	https://www.jobbankusa.com
Retirement Coach	Retire & Be Happy	https://retireandbehappyworkshop.com/
Retirement Options	Retirement Options	https://www.retirementoptions.com/
Security Services	Scam.Com	https://www.scam.com
Self-Discovery	16 Personalities	https://www.16personalities.com/
Self-Discovery	Career Zone	https://www.cacareerzone.org
Self-Discovery	Personality Pathways	https://www.personalitypathways.com
Self-Discovery	VIA Character	https://www.viacharacter.org/www/Character-Strengths

Self-Discovery	What's Next?	https://www.whatsnext.com/life-values-self-assessment-test
Senior Fitness	Life Goes Strong	http://www.lifegoesstrong.com
Statistics	ChildStats.Gov	https://www.childstats.gov
Statistics	Demographics Now	https://www.demographicsnow.com
Statistics	Money CNN	https://money.cnn.com
Technology Use	Elder Gadget	http://www.Eldergadget.com
Technology Use	National Association of Home Builders	http://www.nbnnews.com
Tools	Templates for MS Office	https://templates.office.com/
Transgenerational Design	Ameriglide	https://www.ameriglide.com
Transgenerational Design	Transgenerational	http://transgenerational.org
Travel	National Geographic Expeditions	https://www.nationalgeographicexpeditions.com
Travel	Road Scholar	https://www.roadscholar.org
Travel	Smithsonian Journeys	https://www.smithsonianjourneys.org
Tutoring/Test Prep Jobs	SmarThinking	https://www.pearson.com/us/higher-education/products-services-institutions/smarthinking/for-tutors.html
Tutoring/Test Prep Jobs	Tutor	https://www.tutor.com
Volunteering	Big Brothers Big Sisters	https://www.bbbs.org
Volunteering	Experience Corps	https://www.aarp.org/experience-corps/
Volunteering	Green Africa Foundation	http://www.greenafricafoundation.org

Volunteering	Guardian Ad Litem	https://guardianadlitem.org
Volunteering	Idealist	https://www.idealist.org
Volunteering	International Volunteer Programs Association (IVPA)	http://volunteerinternational.org/
Volunteering	Jumpstart	https://www.jstart.org/
Volunteering	National & Community Service	https://www.nationalservice.gov/
Volunteering	National Park Service	https://www.nps.gov
Volunteering	Nature Conservatory	https://www.nature.org
Volunteering	Points of Light	http://www.pointsoflight.org
Volunteering	Pro-World Volunteers	https://proworldvolunteers.org
Volunteering	Smart Volunteer	http://smartvolunteer.org
Volunteering	Startup Compete	https://www.jstart.org
Volunteering	United Planet	https://www.unitedplanet.org
Volunteering	Volunteer Hub	https://www.volunteerhub.com/blog/volunteer-training-program/
Volunteering	Volunteer Match	https://www.volunteermatch.org
Volunteering	Volunteering & Civil Life in America	https://www.nationalservice.gov/vcla
Volunteering	Volunteers of America	https://www.voa.org/
Writing	EzineArticles	https://EzineArticles.com

REFERENCES

Florida, R. (2004). *The Rise of the Creative Class: And How It's Transforming Work, Leisure, Community and Everyday Life*. Basic Books.

Harris, D. J. (1983). Psychological Aspects of Retirement. *Canadian Family Physician. 29,* 527-530.

Holtzman, E. (2002). Emotional Aspects of Retirement. *Amherst College Faculty and Staff Assistance Program.*

Johnson, R. J. (2012). *The shifting retiree migration.* Urban Wire. *www.urban.org.*

Jones, L. Y. (2008). *Great Expectations: America and the Baby Boom Generation.* New York: Ballantine Books.

Kauffman, E. M. (2013). *Retiring Outside the United States: A Special Report: How Grown-ups Run Away from Home. Kansas City, Mo: Ewing Marion Kauffman Foundation.*

Kubler-Ross, E. & Kessler, D. (2013). *The 5 Stages of Loss and Grief.*

Limelight Networks (2016). *The State of the User Experience Annual Survey.*

Merrill Lynch (2012). *Affluent Insights Survey: National Fact Sheet.* Bank of America Corporation.

MetLife Mature Marketing Institute (2003-13). *Retirement.* New York: Metropolitan Life Insurance Company.

Miller, Mark (2012). *Retirees move, but not very far.* Reuters. www.reuters.com.

Moeller, P. (2013). The Best Life: Success and Happiness In Older Age. *U.S. News and World Report.*

Peddicord, K. (2010). "On Retirement: How To Retire At Any Age." *U.S. News And World Report.*

Pew Research Center (2006). *Working after Retirement: The Gap between Expectations and Reality*.

Satter, M. Y. (2017). *More Americans retiring overseas, report says.*Benefits Pro Magazine.

Smith, C. (1990). "The Long Weekend: Transition and Growth in Retirement." *NIU Annuitants' Association*.

Smith, J. W. & Clurman. A. (2007). *Generation Ageless: How Baby Boomers Are Changing the Way We Live Today . . . And They're Just Getting Started*. New York: HarperCollins Publishers.

T

V

W

Y

Made in the USA
Las Vegas, NV
02 August 2021

27438905R00188